THE
LIFE
OF
JESUS

THE LIFE OF JESUS

with an Introduction and Commentary by
POPE FRANCIS

ANDREA TORNIELLI

Translated from the Italian by Bernadette Mary Reis, FSP

LOYOLAPRESS.
A JESUIT MINISTRY
Chicago

LOYOLA PRESS.
A JESUIT MINISTRY

www.loyolapress.com

The Life of Jesus
by Andrea Tornielli
© 2023 Mondadori Libri S.p.A.
Originally published in Italy as
Vita di Gesù.
by Andrea Tornielli
© 2022 Mondadori Libri S.p.A.
Published by Mondadori under the imprint of Piemme

English translation copyright © 2023 by Andrea Tornielli.

ISBN: 978-0-8294-5794-0
Library of Congress Control Number: 2023942608

Printed in the United States of America.
23 24 25 26 27 28 29 30 31 32 LSC 10 9 8 7 6 5 4 3 2 1

Christianity abides essentially in Christ, less in his teaching than in his Person. Therefore, its texts cannot be detached from Him without immediately losing their meaning and life. All the perspicacity of its scholars, all of their patience, all of their integrity, have been able to render, and have effectively rendered eminent service in the material study of the books in which the primitive Church synthesized what she believes: Without faith, however, they have not been able to initiate them into the interior life of the texts, make them understand the continuity therein, the movement, and the mystery in the splendor of the Presence that is their soul.

—Maurice Zundel
(Le Poème de la Sainte Liturgie)

To little Joseph, with every wish that he might meet the Protagonist of this book, and that he might be granted the grace of being attracted by Him.

Contents

The Gospel Every Day to Encounter Jesus

Introduction by Pope Francis

For some time, I have been continually advising everyone to be in direct and daily contact with the Gospels. Why? Because if we do not have daily contact with a person we love, it is difficult to love that person.

Love cannot be lived via mail; it cannot be cultivated from long-distance. Sometimes this can happen, certainly, but they are the exceptions. Love needs continual contact, continuous dialogue. It means listening to the other, accepting the other, looking at the other. It is the sharing of life. If we do not experience the living Christ, the person with whom the Gospels put us in contact, we risk grasping solely onto ideas, or worse yet, onto ideologies, about the Gospels. We would not be in contact with Jesus, the Living One, but with some opinions and thoughts about him—some of them true, others not.

But we have not been saved by ideas, but by a person, Jesus Christ. So carrying a pocket-size Gospel, and opening it up even a few times during the day to read something, is like carrying a daily "snack" with us. It is fundamental that we "nourish ourselves" with Jesus, nourish ourselves on Jesus.

As the Council taught us, there are two tables: the Eucharist and the Word. Opening the Gospel—a small pocket-size Gospel, the large Bible we have at home, the Readings of the Day that we can access on our smartphones—is a way to see Jesus concretely, to be in contact with him. This is a way we can welcome him that is different than how he is presented to us by theologians or exegetes, which is precious, but is something else. Salvation is, in fact, something, Someone concrete. Therefore, it takes place in the concreteness of a personal encounter. For centuries, God communicated the tidings of salvation through the voice of the prophets. But at a certain point, that time ended and he himself took on flesh, he became man, and came to dwell in our midst. To have the Gospel handy to read a few times a day—a small amount of time is enough—means welcoming the Word who became flesh, it means understanding that what we believe is not just a list of articles of faith, but is a living person, Jesus. Our faith is Jesus. We can know all the dogmas, we can be enlightened Catholics, but without constant contact with the Gospels we will be Christians in our heads only and the faith will not penetrate our hearts, it will not inhabit our lives. In order to be Christians, it is necessary that the word, that is the Word of God in Scripture, descend upon us and come to dwell in us.

≈

The Gospel is not only a story that took place in the past or an edifying narrative with good moral teachings. The purpose of the Word of God is not so much to speak to our minds. It is meant to be *an encounter*. The Word of God is the gift for an encounter—the Lord came to us with his Son—who is his Word—to *encounter us*. Without an encounter, the Gospel remains a story that I read, that talks to me about a Teacher who offers some teachings for life. Instead, when I have an encounter with the Lord in his word, a sense of *amazement* is born and reborn, something that is difficult to feel if we read the Gospels only intellectually like a historical account. Amazement is the *perfume* God leaves as he passes by at that moment.

It often happens that we read and then reread a passage from the Gospel and nothing happens. Then one day, listening to or reading that same passage again touches our heart, and we understand the profundity of what we read or heard. The Holy Spirit does this. He makes Christ alive and real in us; he reveals Christ's presence to us in the Gospels. If I listen to the good news about God solely with my intellect or out of curiosity, it will be difficult for me to involve myself and mature. But when I feel amazed—which is a grace from the Holy Spirit, a gift of his grace—I will then feel that the Lord is present there, that he touches my heart with his tenderness.

Let us pick up the Gospels with simplicity and love. God himself will gift us with amazement and allow us to encounter him. In the Gospels, we will encounter, *sine glossa*, the style of God—his nearness. And within this nearness are true compassion and tenderness. These are the three signs of God's style. The incarnation of the Word, the descent of the Word, entailed the humiliation of God that the Greeks call *synkatabasis*, that is, the condescension of the Almighty. The Creator of all things made himself little, he became a baby. The nearness of the Lord is understood only by entering into that lowering of himself, into that humbling of himself, allowing him to envelop us in his compassion and his tenderness. This is God's style, and this is why Jesus adopted

God's very own style when he worked healings. For myself, for example, my heart is touched when I reread the part of the Gospel in which Jesus restores life to the daughter of Jairus. He takes her by the hand and compassionately and tenderly gives her back to her parents, asking them to give her something to eat. With the boy, the son of the widow of Nain, he does the same thing—Jesus gives him to his mother. This is God's nearness.

~

A significant aspect that always strikes me when reading the Gospel is the importance of the looks that are exchanged, a detail on which this *Life of Christ* will also dwell often. Some glances cross each other—let's think of Zacchaeus, who climbed up the tree somewhat clumsily. He wants to see Jesus without being seen, but instead the Lord looks at him and tells him he wants to go to his house. Let's take the blind man of Jericho—he could not see but was seeking God's gaze. He wanted to be looked at by Jesus and would not stop screaming, asking, begging, till he found that gaze resting on him. There are looks on every page of the Gospel. This is how people encountered Jesus. There are also the looks of the doctors of the law, of those who were seeking to put him to the test, and even the amazed looks of those who did not understand. The way they looked at each other is important; the looks the people involved exchanged are important.

It is not enough only to read or listen. It is beautiful to enter personally into the Gospel episodes, reproducing Jesus's look in my mind and heart, to imagine, for example, among the many other people who were there, his eyes resting on a poor widow who offers a few small coins in the temple. Jesus's eyes had been observing the teachers of the law walking in the temple so as to be noticed and to show themselves off as perfect. Then his eyes were attracted to that widow who was offering two coins, two cents—more than everyone else because it was all she had. That look is the canonization of her generosity.

Let's think again about Jairus, who goes to ask for help for his seriously ill daughter, and, while he stands before the Teacher, is told that in the meantime she has died. He looks at Jesus, and Jesus looks at him and reassures him. Jesus has the unique ability of looking into others' eyes. And while Jairus is telling Jesus that it is useless to go to his house, Jesus continues on and brings his daughter back to life. But everything began with a look.

Even the widow of Nain certainly looked at the Lord when he approached her with his disciples. What could that afflicted woman, bowed down with sorrow, have been asking with her eyes? Certainly not the life of her son, for it was certain that he was dead and no one could bring him back to life. And yet, she was asking something with her eyes. Looking at her and her sorrow, Jesus was profoundly moved. He drew near the funeral procession and raised her dead son, giving him back to his mother.

Other times we find ourselves before the looks of those who at first are not capable of seeing the Lord. Let's think of the disciples of Emmaus. It was as if their eyes were veiled. Let's think of Mary Magdalene when she went to the tomb and mistook the risen Jesus for the gardener. And then the Lord manifested himself.

The same thing happens to us when we take the Gospel in our hands, when we read something, and at a certain moment the Lord reveals himself before our eyes, manifests himself, and we live the unique spiritual experience of amazement through which we encounter Jesus.

~

I repeat—there is no faith without an encounter, because faith is a personal encounter with Jesus. Faith is that "I believe, Lord, help me so that my faith might increase; help me because I am weak." One of the things that helps us when we have the Gospels before our eyes is to imagine those encounters with Jesus—re-create them, look at him ourselves, meet him ourselves. In the Gospels, *to look* and *to see* are two very important verbs.

So let us approach the episodes in the life of Jesus with eyes filled with contemplation. It is true that faith begins with hearing, but the encounter begins with *seeing*. This is why it is important to listen to and see Jesus in the Gospels. Memory is connected more easily with seeing. This makes the Christian life grow. It is, as Saint John teaches, but which is also found in more general terms throughout all of sacred Scripture, the memory of those things that we have *seen and heard.*

This book was written using the words of the Gospels. This book, *The Life of Jesus,* can help us enter into contact with him so that he does not remain only a great figure—a historical protagonist, a religious leader, or a teacher of morals—but that he might become each person's Lord each day—the Lord of life. I hope that those who read it might *see* Jesus, *encounter* Jesus, and receive the grace—which is a gift of the Holy Spirit—of allowing themselves to be attracted by him.

Franciscus

Note to the Reader

This book originated due to a phone call from a priest friend, Father Primo Soldi. One morning during the lockdown of 2020, he called me and bluntly said, "Why don't you write a life of Jesus with comments by Pope Francis?" This happened during the tense days of the first phase of the pandemic when the Bishop of Rome was accompanying millions of people all over the world through Mass in the Santa Marta Chapel being broadcast live via radio, television, and the Internet.

I told Father Primo I would think about it, even if the challenge seemed almost insurmountable to me. How could I presume to write a life of Jesus? Above all, how could I presume to do so without having an adequate theological, biblical, or philological background?

True, the fact that throughout the narrative the Pope's thought would be present as a commentary was reassuring, since I would use his texts, homilies, documents, and off-the-cuff discourses.

I have always been impressed by the insistence with which Pope Francis continues to ask the faithful to take a small Gospel in their pockets whenever they leave their homes so as not to lose daily contact with Christ's encounters with people, and his words. Today, the more "techy" generations can even do without the printed text, receiving the Gospel of the Day from a priest friend, perhaps accompanied by a few words of commentary. In his homilies, especially his off-the-cuff ones, I have also been very struck by the insistence with which Pope Francis invites us to "go there," to enter into the Gospel scene, to stop and take a look at the characters being described. This meditative practice of "entering into" the Gospel, reliving it, and making it real, belongs in a particular way to the Jesuit tradition.

What Father Primo proposed to me during that telephone call was a compelling challenge. Initially, however, I did not seriously consider the idea, even though I began every now and then to save texts, passages from homilies, notes I thought could be useful should I eventually decide to attempt it.

In 2004 and 2005, I had ventured out with two short informative books entitled *Inchiesta su Gesù Bambino* (*Inquiry into the Infant Jesus*) and *Inchiesta sulla Resurrezione* (*Inquiry into the Resurrection*) in which I tried to apply the rules of journalist inquiry to the events that begin and end the evangelical narrative. However, this time was different. First of all, there was, in fact, no need to utilize some specific professional skill, synthesizing the theses and exegesis of the best scholars. Instead, it meant putting myself into play. It meant getting in touch with myself—with all of my obvious limitations—with the Christian story recounted in the Gospels. It meant trying to identify with, to enter into those scenes written almost two thousand years ago by passionate eyewitnesses of Jesus, people who believed in him and, precisely because of this, had carefully and scrupulously transmitted what they had seen, heard, experienced, collected, lived, regarding him. It meant trying to be there and to allow myself to be struck, surprised, amazed, moved by the look and words of the Nazarene—to encounter him, his Person, which is the authentic heart of Christian faith.

It is precisely in order to emphasize this, with the awareness of being a dwarf making strides on the shoulders of giants, that I wanted to preface the book with a quotation from the French mystic and priest Maurice Zundel. It is a phrase I "stole" from another and much more profound and authoritative *Life of Jesus*, written in 1936 by the French journalist, playwright, and Nobel Prize for Literature laureate François Mauriac. Mauriac had prefaced his highly successful best seller with these words of Zundel: "Christianity abides essentially in Christ, less in his teaching than in his Person. Therefore, its texts cannot be detached from Him without immediately losing their meaning and life."

Emphasizing this in this prologue does not mean to in any way detract from the precious work of philologists, exegetes, and theologians who have examined every Gospel verse under the magnifying glass an infinite number of times, providing commentary and explanations. Rather, it means recognizing that encountering Jesus today, just as it was two thousand years ago, is a matter of the heart, of crossing gazes, of emotions that sink into the gut—that it is more about his Person than his teaching, which would become doctrine.

To avoid any misunderstanding, I state at the outset that I am well aware of how much this modest attempt of mine is naïve and incomplete, as far as the final result is concerned, first of all due to my little faith.

I have tried to narrate the story of Jesus's earthly life from beginning to end, composing one ongoing narrative from the texts of the four Gospels, using my imagination to reconstruct it, even trying to identify everything the evangelists did not write. I have made choices regarding the placing and dating of the scenes to frame them within a context, always trying to prefer the hypotheses considered the most plausible and accepted by scholars. *Life of Christ* by Fr. Giuseppe Ricciotti, first published in 1941 and reprinted many times since then, served as a compass on my journey.

⁓

Thanks to the wonderful work of scholars (particularly of the historians and archeologists, as well as passionate journalists such as Vittorio Messori, whom I thank for the goodness and patience he has always shown me), the possibility of retracing clues regarding the historical Jesus within the evangelical texts has always been a source of comfort for my faith. These clues are small signs that help anchor the narrative to history.

A little while ago, while I was listening to the reading of a Gospel passage from Luke during morning Mass in the Vatican Radio Chapel, I was astounded on hearing again the list of the twelve apostles that repeats three names twice: among those who followed Jesus, who lived every moment of his public life with him, were two men called Simon, two called James, and two called Judas. I had heard that passage many times. But only then did I think: *What novelist, what playwright, what author who was free to "invent" and adapt the data in his possession for catechetical purposes would have introduced that effectively confusing element into the names of the protagonists of his story—a confusion that would always force him to specify, to use a nickname or the name of the person's father, to distinguish which of the two Simons, of the two Jameses, of the two Judases he was speaking of at that moment?*

Being neither an exegete, nor having any knowledge of textual criticism, it seemed to me that this was yet another tiny indication of the fact that those men—mostly fishermen or tax collectors, and therefore extremely concrete men—had been eyewitnesses to everything they had recounted, described, handed on. Yes, their eyes were the eyes of Easter faith, but their faith was founded on their lived experience with Jesus, lived together with Jesus and with the other apostles and disciples. There must be a reason why even to this day there has never been a reliable discovery capable of disproving even one of the Gospel verses.

Rivers of ink have been written on these topics and even I, as a journalist and writer, have often written about them in articles, interviews, book reviews, essays. It is as if now, after a "catechumenate" of interest and curiosity lasting almost half a century, and over thirty years of professional activity, I am being challenged to take another step—to no longer write focusing on the details, on the discussions regarding the historicity of the Gospels, of the many reasons for believing, but rather to "enter into" the Gospel, so as to meet its Protagonist, "to live him," "to see him," to speak, to be moved, to communicate his merciful gaze and his redemptive and liberating word.

Thanks to the testimony of his friends, the Gospel, the story of Jesus's life, takes on its full meaning only from the awareness and experience that he, the Nazarene, is alive today and that without him we can do nothing, and that it is possible to encounter him today in exactly the same way people encountered him two thousand years ago along the banks of the Sea of Galilee, by encountering his face, his gestures, his words, his signs, and the faces and accounts of his friends who were fascinated by him.

We need to encounter Jesus alive today. We need to see him in the faces of those who are distant, in those who suffer. We need to find him by looking for the "Gospel facts" (© by Luigi Accattoli, my friend and teacher), those "Gospel facts" present all around us. We need to encounter him alive today in the faces of those who live for him and who witness to us what it means to love, to welcome, to embrace, to be merciful and free like Jesus teaches us, which happens every time that, instead of chasing after power, structures, doctrine and rules, we make room for him and allow him to come to encounter us, to say to us, "Come and see."

a.t.

Note from the Author

The text in roman letters is my narrative, and therefore, the fruit of my own imagination.

In italics, single verses of the Gospels of Matthew, Mark, Luke, and John are inserted here and there within my text, and, at other times, longer citations. In the last chapter, a citation from the Acts of the Apostles also appears. So as not to interrupt the flow of the narrative, the Gospel texts are not accompanied by citations. References can be found in the Permissions section at the end of the book indicating which Gospel chapter and verses were used to develop the narrative.

The commentary in italics, within quotation marks, inserted in the narrative and accompanied by a footnote, are from Pope Francis. Among the many possibilities, I tried to choose those that have helped me most in these years to identify with the details of Jesus's life.

Last, regarding the dating of the events, I chose to go by the dates deemed most credible by scholars, who hold that the birth of Jesus should actually be placed in the year 5 BC, and therefore, about six years prior to the traditional date from which the Christian era is calculated.

That Breeze in the House of Nazareth

Year 6 BC

The Annunciation to Mary. Joseph's Decision. The Journey to Elizabeth.

The sand-colored curtain separating the small room from the rest of the house began to flutter in waves. Mary was sitting down on a low stool next to the bedding made of mats. At first, she did not notice the mysterious light breeze. A ray of light, the last remnant of the setting sun, shone through the tiny window, tracing a strange squiggle on the dirt floor.

Nazareth was nothing more than a handful of brick huts chiseled into the rock on a hill in front of the plain of Esdraelon in Galilee, the extreme outskirts of a province on the periphery of the Roman Empire. There was nothing noteworthy about Nazareth even to receive marginal mention in the chronicles of the time. The grand radar of that historical epoch of peace under the Emperor Octavian Augustus picks up nothing newsworthy about it.

An instant before everything happened, Mary was absorbed, as if enraptured by that play of light. For a few moments she stopped spinning the flax she had in her hands. Her large dark black eyes stood out in her fifteen-year-old face.

In the sixth month the angel Gabriel was sent from God to a city of Galilee named Nazareth, to a virgin betrothed to a man whose name was Joseph, of the house of David. And the virgin's name was Mary.

Then the curtain swayed faster, and the girl caught sight of someone walking through it. A wave of fear, then peace. The unidentifiable and indefinable figure was translucent and luminous at the same time. Mary knew immediately she could trust the being. Even so, her heart began beating wildly. The young creature knelt before Mary, who felt as if she were enveloped by that breeze whose origins she knew not. Time seemed to halt.

And he came to her and said, "Greetings, O favored one, the Lord is with you!" But she was greatly troubled at the saying, and tried to discern what sort of greeting this might be. And the angel said to her, "Do not be afraid, Mary, for you have found favor with God. And behold, you will conceive in your womb and bear a son, and you shall call his name Jesus. He will be great and will be called the Son of the Most High. And the Lord God will give to him the throne of his father David, and he will reign over the house of Jacob forever, and of his kingdom there will be no end."

Her first instinct was not to retreat but to seek understanding. How would all of this happen? "I do not know man." Sure, there was Joseph, the carpenter, her betrothed spouse. But they were still not living under the same roof.

Smiling, Gabriel responded, *"The Holy Spirit will come upon you, and the power of the Most High will overshadow you; therefore the child to be born will be called holy—the Son of God."*

"Son of God." Those words would have shocked anyone. Not her! She simply responded yes. Abandoning herself.

And Mary said, "Behold, I am the servant of the Lord; let it be to me according to your word." And the angel departed from her.

That mysterious messenger returned from whence it had come. And she, after that yes, remained alone in the small room, now wrapped in the semi-darkness of dusk. Alone with her secret. Alone with her questions. The most important joint-venture in the history of humanity had just begun—the Almighty had made his plan contingent on the free consent of a young girl of the people of Israel. And she, in the blink of an eye, had accepted.

Now, however, an instant after the light and wind had vanished, and the reassuring voice of that strange, heavenly creature was no more to be heard, she gradually became aware of what had happened to her. She had said yes, but now she was feeling afraid. She had responded yes, but her heart continued pounding in the silence that now reigned over that little room. She felt small, inadequate. . . . Since her childhood, she had received the gift of a faith so profound that it struck anyone who knew her, and it was that faith that allowed her yes to burst forth. She tried to remember every single word the angel had said. The angel had said that nothing is impossible to God and that even her elderly relative Elizabeth was pregnant. But Elizabeth, whom everyone said was barren, was married to someone just as elderly. For her, for Mary, everything was completely different.

"Mary's is a complete, total 'yes,' for her entire life, without conditions. And just as the original 'no' had closed the passage of man to God, so Mary's 'yes' opened the path to God among us. It is the most important 'yes' in history, the humble 'yes' that overturns the proud original 'no,' the faithful 'yes' that heals disobedience, the willing 'yes' that overturns the selfishness of sin."[1]

Time began ticking again as the infinite took on flesh in the girl's womb in the little house of Nazareth constructed partly of brick and partly chiseled into the rock. Mary kept the secret in her heart. How would she explain it to her promised spouse? How would she face the indiscreet looks and prejudice of the people in her village?

Her first response had been a free and unconditional yes, while the first initiative she took after that extraterrestrial annunciation was to put herself immediately at someone else's service. She left Nazareth to go to assist Elizabeth in Ein Karem, an ancient village at the gates of Jerusalem. She left in a hurry.

"True freedom is always given to her by the Lord. . . . The freedom to give herself and to do so joyfully, like the Virgin of Nazareth who is free from herself. She does not get caught up in her own situation—and she had good reason to do so!—but thinks of someone who at that moment was in greater need. She is free in the freedom of God, which is fulfilled in love. And this is the freedom that God has given us, and we must not lose it."[2]

Just on the brink of becoming the mother of John the Baptist, Mary's elderly relative, filled with amazement and joy at the unexpected visit, saw her coming from afar. When they embraced each other, with her baby leaping within her, Elizabeth was inspired to greet her in this way:

"Blessed are you among women, and blessed is the fruit of your womb!"

Elizabeth knew. . . .

Mary responded,

> *"My soul magnifies the Lord,*
> *and my spirit rejoices in God my Savior*
> *for he has looked on the humble estate of his servant."*

Mary remained with Elizabeth, helping her with the household chores.

---

1. Pope Francis, Angelus, December 8, 2016.

2. Pope Francis, Homily, Old Romagnoli Stadium, Campobasso, July 5, 2014.

A pregnancy causes so many transformations in a woman's body and her daily life. But for a woman in her ripe old age, everything was more difficult, despite the joy of this completely unexpected gift. Then, after having stayed in Elizabeth's house for about three months to assist her, Mary returned to Nazareth.

Now it was her own pregnancy that was progressing to the point of being visibly noticeable. Now it was her turn to need assistance. It was by now impossible to hide what had happened to her—that baby growing in her womb, taking form in her belly, was the tangible sign of the miracle the angel had foretold. Now Mary could no longer hide from the man with whom she had decided to share her life what had happened to her. She told him she was pregnant, trying to find the right words to share this unexpected and unheard-of annunciation she had received. *Her husband Joseph, being a just man and unwilling to put her to shame, resolved to divorce her quietly.*

How many thoughts, how many questions, how many hours pierced by anguish. Why was this happening to him? What a tangle of conflicting feelings filled the heart of this sturdy man with calloused hands and curly, very black hair that framed his face and blended in with his beard. Called to be a father without being the father, serving in silence. Mary, his Mary, was expecting a son. And the son was not even his. He had listened to her, had seen the glimmer of truth in her transparent and penetrating gaze. But could he completely believe her? And yet, the true and sincere love he felt for this girl prevailed over the law and its established traditions.

No. The carpenter, accustomed to the grueling work with stone and wood, used to mounting doorposts and doors, would not publicly accuse her, would not repudiate her. He would never reject her, leaving her alone with a child to face the villagers' gossip. He would never annul their union so as to be free to take another girl as his wife. He would divorce her, yes, but only secretly, between the walls of their house in Nazareth—that house he had so skillfully and passionately fixed up for his new family. The others, all the others, no one must know. He would welcome and raise this son as though he were his own. . . .

They were not easy days for Joseph the practical man, accustomed to observing a lot and speaking little . . . a man with a huge heart. *But as he considered these things, behold, an angel of the Lord appeared to him in a dream, saying, "Joseph, son of David, do not fear to take Mary as your wife, for that which is conceived in her is from the Holy Spirit. She will bear a son, and you shall call his name Jesus, for he will save his people from their sins."*

What had been revealed to Mary by the angel enveloped by the mysterious breeze was revealed to Joseph in a dream while he was resting at his work site, heartbroken, on a sunny summer afternoon. He was working in Sepphoris, a large city that was under construction only about four miles from Nazareth. Would that dream, from which he awoke shaken and bathed in sweat, be enough to convince him? It was a herculean task—to protect his wife who had become the mother of the Messiah, and to watch over the first steps of the Son of God.

Joseph knew the Scriptures and was humble like his spouse. He decided to trust by abandoning himself. His response was also a free one. After Mary's free yes came that of her husband. Their freedom intersected with God's freedom that casts down the mighty from their thrones and lifts up the lowly. That annunciation had come from heaven. A young married couple, alone with an unimaginable secret, were offering their hearts and their bodies so that the most radical and decisive transformation in the history of humanity could take place. Joseph would obey, naming his son *Yeshua*, Jesus, just as the angel had asked him in the dream.

"Humility is the golden rule. For Christians, making progress means lowering themselves. . . . At the moment of the annunciation, Mary humbles herself. She does not understand well, but she is free. She grasps only the essential, and says 'yes.' . . . She surrenders her soul to God's will. And Joseph her fiancé—they were not yet married—also lowers himself and takes this tremendously great responsibility upon himself. Mary and Joseph's own style shows how God, in order to reach us with all of his love, takes the path of humility. The humble God wanted to walk with his people."[3]

"In her canticle, Mary does not say that she is happy because God looked on her virginity, her goodness, her gentleness, the many virtues she possessed. Rather, she exults because God has regarded the humility of his servant, her littleness."[4]

~

Alone, but no longer alone, Mary and Joseph lived those last months of her pregnancy. He took care of her, and she took care of him. Then the emperor's edict, like an echo in the grand scheme of things destined to intersect with a marginal and apparently insignificant story, reached them. Thus they were forced to set out on a journey.

---

3. *The Golden Rule of Humility*, Homily, Santa Marta Chapel, April 8, 2013.
4. Homily, Santa Marta Chapel, March 24, 2014.

2

During the Night in Bethlehem

Year 6 BC

On the Journey for the Census. Birth in Bethlehem.
Adoration of the Shepherds. The Presentation of Jesus in the Temple.

"When will we get there?" She tried to ask him with a smile on her lips so as not to add in any way to the stress and suffering weighing on him because of the trip. The blinding light of the blazing sun mingled with gusts of dry wind, and the dust in the air dried their skin and seemed to penetrate their bones. As night fell, the temperature dropped sharply, and the sudden chill rekindled their nostalgia for home. No, it was not a comfortable journey. "We'll be there soon," he assured her, caressing her forehead.

On its back, the donkey carried clean clothing, a bit of cheese, flour to make bread, and a large leather canteen. When Mary could no longer follow on foot, Joseph would put her on the beast of burden, who accepted it well enough, without ever rebelling against the additional weight. The girl could not tell what was more fatiguing—walking on her aching legs over the rocky, sandy path, or putting up with the continuous bouncing on the back of the donkey, to which the little creature she carried in her womb would "respond" every now and then with a kick in his mother's belly.

The end of her pregnancy had indeed come—her grey tunic and large white linen veil that sheltered her from the sun and wind could no longer hide the fact that she was about to become a mother. Both of them would have liked that the baby be born in the peace of Nazareth, sheltered in the discreet walls of their home. This would have provided protection to the son that had been given to them in such an unexpected and unheard-of way.

The nine months after the angel's annunciation had gone by tranquilly. But questions sometimes surfaced in their minds, becoming obvious on their faces and insinuating themselves in their eyes, especially in quiet moments, in the evening, after they had eaten dinner together. Singing psalms helped them.

Reading the Scriptures sustained them. How many prophecies, what a sense of expectation emerged from those pages! What they were guarding together heartened them. Was everything truly being fulfilled there, in that place, at that moment? Was it God who was taking on human form inside the body of that girl from Nazareth? Was it God who had begun to dwell in that family? Did he need them to fulfill his mysterious plan?

Mary and Joseph remained human beings and, as such, were weak by nature. Joseph especially felt the burning responsibility. True, the will of the Almighty was at work, but the arms that would have to protect mother and child were his. Was he capable of doing that? Whenever these thoughts assailed him, this husband gratefully contemplated the candor of his young wife, her pure gaze, always able to see good everywhere. She was incapable of conceiving the slightest bad thought, or saying anything bad. He was deeply in love with her, of the grace that accompanied every one of her words and actions.

～

Throwing their plans into upheaval once more was an irruption in world history that would intersect with their own small story, robbing that family of even the little security they had up until that moment.

In those days a decree went out from Caesar Augustus that all the world should be registered. This was the first registration when Quirinius was governor of Syria. And all went to be registered, each to his own town. And Joseph also went up from Galilee, from the town of Nazareth, to Judea, to the city of David, which is called Bethlehem, because he was of the house and lineage of David, to be registered with Mary, his betrothed, who was with child.

Caesar Octavian Augustus, the Roman Emperor who had imposed peace over the then-known world, was redefining the statistical and financial structure of his vast and diverse kingdom. For this first universal census, which was not reserved only for Roman citizens, he had ordered that everyone who, in one way or another, fell within the orbit of Rome, had to be registered. In a society that maintained a very deep sense of family and tribal bonds, like that of the people of Israel, it was natural that this should take place on the basis of paternal lineage. Later as an adult, after being shown a coin with the image of the emperor, Jesus, with his invitation to "render to Caesar the things that are Caesar's, and to God the things that are God's," was really only sanctioning what his earthly father had done on the eve of his own birth—obey an edict of the established authority.

Bethlehem was about ninety-three miles from Nazareth. The journey took a minimum of three entire days, more likely four, or even five, in their case. At night they accommodated themselves in public stops like other travelers and pilgrims, lying down on the ground on mats, warmed by a small fire. Men, women, children, donkeys, camels . . . everyone together. Everyone traveling toward a destination.

They never spoke about it during those difficult days, but both Mary and Joseph were ardently hoping that their child would not be born on the journey.

Finally, they arrived. They were exhausted, but they were there. Because of the census, the city of David, little more than a small village, was swarming with people those days.

And while they were there, the time came for her to give birth.

The moment they had so long been waiting for had arrived. The caravan camp, where travelers who had no place to go sought lodging for the night, was packed. Was it possible that a young mother about to give birth might not be able to find a free corner? *There was no place for them in the inn.*

Every inch of space was packed with people under the porch. Too many people were already crammed there.

"Their hearts were full of hope and expectation because of the child about to be born. Instead, their steps were weighed down by the uncertainties and dangers that attend those who have to leave their home behind. Then they found themselves having to face perhaps the most difficult thing of all. They arrived in Bethlehem and discovered that it was a land that was not expecting them, a land where there was no place for them."[5]

Joseph continued looking for a secluded place where Mary might give birth, far away from prying eyes. A place "for them." They would have to be content with a small cave used as a stable, out of the way and safe, that had been hewn near a house at the far eastern end of the village. An elderly woman, with skin wrinkled like bark, had directed them to it and made it available to them.

The husband bustled about, coming and going to make it a welcoming emergency refuge. First, he procured dry, clean hay. Then he lit a fire between two stone blocks that had already been set up, and stacked up wood to last the entire night. He fiddled with a beam so as to construct a makeshift curtain to shield the most secluded corner from the rest of the ravine. It was a stable.

---

5. Homily, Christmas Midnight Mass, December 24, 2017.

But in Mary's eyes, who was watching while he worked, it began to assume the form and warmth of home. From the entrance freed from brambles, they could now glimpse the starry sky.

Then silence descended. Absolute, almost surreal silence descended that night over Bethlehem, teaming with travelers and pilgrims. It was as if the entire city of David were holding its breath for an event that no one knew about except God and this young couple who had taken refuge in a stable—an event unknown to everyone, and yet awaited by generations of prophets. Time stood still that night.

And she gave birth to her firstborn son and wrapped him in swaddling cloths and laid him in a manger.

His mother's eyes, bathed with tears and filled with amazement, gazed on her son with jet-black hair like her own who, after his first wails, had fallen asleep in her arms. Wet with tears, Joseph's eyes watched Mary and the baby. They were tears of joy. In the secret of that very clear and cold December night, the carpenter took the baby in his arms so Mary could rest. She succumbed to a deep sleep. From that moment, as Joseph tenderly cradled the baby with his rough and calloused hands to his chest, that baby became "his" son.

God, the infinitely great, the almighty Sabaoth, the God of hosts and of angelic ranks, the God of the covenant with Israel, had become a helpless baby, completely dependent on the care of a mother and a father, like every man and woman on earth. God was a newborn, in need of protection, nourishment, warmth, security.

"What a surprise to see God acting exactly like we do: he sleeps, drinks milk from his mother, cries and plays like every other child! As always, God baffles us. He is unpredictable, constantly doing what we least expect."[6]

A manger was the first crib of the King of kings, predestined to become food for the salvation of many. Bethlehem, *Bet-lehem*, means "House of bread." And he would be offered as the "bread of life."

The intimacy of these moments was not destined to last long. The angels who had kept silent watch over the couple after the annunciation to Mary, began to manifest themselves again.

And in the same region there were shepherds out in the field, keeping watch over their flock by night. And an angel of the Lord appeared to them, and the glory of the Lord shone around them.

---

6. Apostolic Letter, *Admirabile signum*, 8.

The shepherds, covered from head to toe with the odor of their sheep, nomads for twelve months of the year, their faces blanched by the sun and the wind, half asleep, sitting beside the last embers over which they had roasted a bit of food for their dinner, were shaken by those tidings. The dazzling yet harmonious light, streaming from the strange creature who had come to brighten their darkness, had stunned them. What was it, and what did it want from them?

They were filled with great fear. And the angel said to them, "Fear not, for behold, I bring you good news of great joy that will be for all the people. For unto you is born this day in the city of David a Savior, who is Christ the Lord. And this will be a sign for you: you will find a baby wrapped in swaddling cloths and lying in a manger." And suddenly there was with the angel a multitude of the heavenly host praising God and saying,

> *"Glory to God in the highest,*
> *and on earth peace among those with whom he is pleased!"*

When the angels went away from them into heaven, the shepherds said to one another, "Let us go over to Bethlehem and see this thing that has happened, which the Lord has made known to us."

The shepherds were simple, concrete people. Their only "treasures" were the few animals they looked after day and night from which they earned what was necessary to live.

"On that night, the One who had no place to be born is announced to those who had no place at the tables or on the streets of the city. The shepherds are the first to hear this Good News. Because of their work, they were men and women who were forced to live on the margins of society. The conditions in which they lived, and the places where they had to stay, prevented them from observing all the ritual prescriptions of religious purification. As a result, they were considered unclean. Their skin, their clothing, their smell, their way of speaking, their origin, betrayed them. Everything about them generated mistrust. They were men and women from whom it was necessary to keep a distance, to be fearful of. They were considered pagans among the believers, sinners among the just, foreigners among the citizens."[7]

They, the "impure" and castaways, were the first to hear the tidings, the first to see the child.

---

7. Homily, Christmas Midnight Mass, December 24, 2017.

They went with haste and found Mary and Joseph, and the baby lying in a manger. And when they saw it, they made known the saying that had been told them concerning this child.

First, they had been shocked on hearing the angelic tidings that had awakened them from their slumber. Now, after having run to the stable of Bethlehem, they were filled with amazement. They had found what the heavenly creature had indicated to them. Now their eyes were filled with gratitude, for they had found the child, the Savior. Sheepskins, a bowl of milk, and pieces of cheese were now lying at the entrance to the stable—poor gifts to share with the Messiah in swaddling cloths, that king who was so different from what they had imagined and expected him to be.

The shepherds' gifts heartened Mary and Joseph. Finally, a little bit of warmth and welcoming after those cutting, icy glances that the two young newlyweds had pretended not to see from the people at the caravan stop with "no vacancy." *He came to his own, and his own people did not receive him.*

"Unlike so many other people, intent on doing a thousand other things, the shepherds become the first to witness what is essential, that is, salvation given as a gift. The humblest and poorest are the ones who know how to welcome the event of the Incarnation. The shepherds respond to God, who comes to meet us in the Infant Jesus, by setting out on a journey toward him, for an encounter of love and grateful awe."[8]

These shepherds, with their rough and smelly clothes, returned just as they had arrived, disappearing along with their sheep, like shadows in the night. But they did not remain silent along the way. What they had witnessed was too wonderful. A young couple with a newborn child huddled together in the recesses of a cave. If the heavens had bothered to proclaim to them, "Unto you is born a Savior," then something grandiose was happening in the city of David at that very moment.

All who heard it wondered at what the shepherds told them. But Mary treasured up all these things, pondering them in her heart. And the shepherds returned, glorifying and praising God for all they had heard and seen, as it had been told them.

"And there . . . amid the gloom of a city that had no room or place for the stranger come from afar . . . it was precisely there that the revolutionary spark of God's tenderness was kindled. In Bethlehem, a small crack opens for those who have

---

8. Apostolic Letter, *Admirabile signum*, 5.

lost their land, their country, their dreams, even for those who have succumbed to
the asphyxia produced by a life of captivity."[9]

∽

Waking up at the crack of dawn that first day of a new era was not easy. The
chill had become even more bitter. That hole in the rock had provided protection from the world for the first hours of the Savior's earthly life. But now they
needed to find a home. After making sure that Mary and the little Jesus were
well, Joseph went back to the elderly woman who had directed them to the
stable the previous evening. She had a small house in which she had welcomed
many of her relatives who had come to Bethlehem for the census. "They will
leave tomorrow," she told the carpenter from Nazareth, who had offered to
work for her in exchange for hospitality for a little while. They would not be
able to face the return trip home with a newborn baby.

Joseph fulfilled his duty, registering himself in the city of David. Then he
set about preparing the home of the elderly woman who had welcomed them.
Now he, Mary, and the baby had a small room where they could take refuge.
It was a cramped space, but finally, it was home.

And at the end of eight days, when he was circumcised, he was called Jesus, the
name given by the angel before he was conceived in the womb.

When the days of their spiritual purification were up, they brought the
newborn to Jerusalem to present him to the Lord. No one paid attention to
them or to the small offerings they brought with them to the temple. Only
two elderly people passing through the grand portico sensed it, moved by the
Spirit. An old man, who had reached the end of his life, had prayed for a long
time that he would be able to see the Messiah before closing his eyes definitively. All of a sudden, he greeted the tiny baby Jesus wrapped in swaddling
cloths as "the salvation" prepared by the Lord "before of all the peoples."

And his father and his mother marveled at what was said about him. And
Simeon blessed them and said to Mary his mother, "Behold, this child is appointed
for the fall and rising of many in Israel, and for a sign that is opposed (and a sword
will pierce through your own soul also), so that thoughts from many hearts may be
revealed."

---

9. Homily, Christmas Midnight Mass, December 24, 2017.

Anna, an elderly prophetess and the daughter of Phanuel, was also there. Having been widowed at a young age, she never left the temple, serving God with fasting and prayer. She, too, recognized the redemption of Jerusalem in the baby.

The pure and simple eyes of these two elderly dreamers had perceived what the rest of the crowd did not see. For the others, for everyone else, this young couple and their baby were only one of the many observant couples who had come that morning to fulfill what the Mosaic law prescribed.

On the road back to Bethlehem, as Mary watched her son, she thought about Simeon's words regarding the sword that would pierce her soul.

3

The Magi, the Flight, and Innocent Blood

Year 5 BC

The Magi's Visit. Herod's Jealousy. The Massacre of the Innocents.
A Family Flees to Egypt.

The caravan with its huge entourage moved slowly along. Each of the Magi had brought two servants along, and a good number of pack animals that took turns. They had already been traveling a good number of weeks after departing from the Persian city of Saba. Balthasar was the oldest and most pensive in the group. He had been scrutinizing the stars and the teachings of Zoroaster for years, working out complicated hypotheses and calculating stellar coincidences. He never moved one step without having studied every possibility, dissecting every possible interpretation.

"Had it been up to you," Gaspar and Melchior teased him, "we would never have left home. . . ." They had convinced him to depart, daring him to go beyond the obstacles his heart feared. This time they had no certainty whatsoever, only a deep and inexplicable yearning that had convinced them to leave their families and their peaceful lives. More than by the brilliant stars in the heavenly vault, they were moved by an interior intuition—one bright "star" only they could see.

Gaspar knew the languages of the most ancient texts. He could decipher every sign, every hieroglyph, no matter how obscure and incomprehensible. He was greatly esteemed in the palaces of the powerful, by kings and priests. When they had doubts, they would consult him amid great secrecy, compensating him very well. In his sumptuous home in Saba, the rooms in his library, filled with papyri, parchments, and inscriptions, received the greatest care. His own children were allowed to enter it only in the company of their father. He dedicated all his time and passion to the "treasure" of knowledge. And if it were not for his wife, a practical but especially indulgent woman, he would not even have known how to dress himself, so immersed was he in his own world.

Melchior was the youngest and most enterprising of the trio. The others called him "the young adept," even though he was already in his forties. When it came to philosophical and scientific knowledge, he was already capable of giving lessons to the other two, who were his first and only teachers. Of the three, he was the one who had moved about the most since Balthasar and Gaspar would often send him to distant lands to make contact with other wise men and scientists, with other nostalgic sky gazers. Thus, he had contacts among the Essenes of Qumran, the astronomers in Babylonia, the Nabateans, and the Arabs in the desert. Thanks to his youthful appearance (his beard was still completely black), and to his jovial personality (so distant from the stereotypical scholar separated from the common people and jealous of his knowledge), he was a proactive man. With his ability to forge relationships and friendships, he never returned home empty-handed, providing the other two with precious material to work with and to compare with their own dis-coveries. Such was the case one time when, after four months of wandering in distant lands, he triumphantly presented himself, radiant, with a wooden chest that contained an astrolabe. When the three magi discussed things together, bent over maps of the stars, codices, and ancient prophecies, time seemed to stand still. Sometimes they even forgot to eat and drink, so absorbed were they in their deliberations.

But this time it was different. This time their hearts, and that mysterious interior enlightenment, prevailed over their calculations. It was as if all their knowledge, their studies, their theories, had all of a sudden proved to be insuf-ficient in satisfying that infinite hunger that drove them. True, they were def-initely scientists and philosophers, but they were still able to be filled with awe before the stars they studied without ever presuming to possess them with their erudite learning. Their desire for the infinite, and their decision to set out without delay, made them so similar to the shepherds of Bethlehem, even though they were light-years away from them in terms of how they lived.

They had uncovered a prophecy in the Zoroastrian writings about the birth of a king among the Hebrew people who would bring peace to the world. That year, the triple conjunction of Jupiter and Saturn in the constel-lation Pisces appeared in the celestial vault. For the peoples of the Middle East, Jupiter was the symbol of kingship and power. Saturn symbolized justice. The constellation Pisces, the sign of water, was associated with Moses and the Hebrew people. Therefore, the astrological significance of this conjunction was as follows: a great king, the bearer of justice to the world, was about to be born in the land of Moses.

A rare astronomical event without any spectacular consequences went unnoticed by the vast majority of people, but not by the Magi. And yet, not even that would have been enough, had not something moved within them. An inspiration? A revelation? It was as if a fragment of a star, that is, of the infinite, had penetrated their hearts.

"These men saw a star that made them set out. The discovery of something unusual in the heavens sparked a numberless series of events. The star did not shine exclusively for them, nor did they have special DNA to discover it. . . . The Magi did not set out because they had seen the star, but they saw the star because they had already set out. . . . Their hearts were open to the horizon, and they could see what the heavens were showing them because they were driven by a desire in them. They were open to something new. . . . In this way, the Magi personify those who believe, those who long for God." [10]

Balthasar, Gaspar, and Melchior headed toward the holy city of the people of Israel. Ahead of them shone the conjunction of the two planets. It was so bright that it seemed to weaken the light of the other stars. They were seeking a king about to be born, or a newborn king. So they headed where they imagined they would find him, the palace of the king.

Now after Jesus was born in Bethlehem of Judea in the days of Herod the king, behold, wise men from the east came to Jerusalem, saying, "Where is he who has been born king of the Jews? For we saw his star when it rose and have come to worship him." When Herod the king heard this, he was troubled, and all Jerusalem with him; and assembling all the chief priests and scribes of the people, he inquired of them where the Christ was to be born. They told him, "In Bethlehem of Judea, for so it is written by the prophet:

> *'And you, O Bethlehem, in the land of Judah,*
>   *are by no means least among the rulers of Judah;*
> *For from you shall come a ruler*
>   *who will shepherd my people Israel.'"*

Then Herod summoned the wise men secretly and ascertained from them what time the star had appeared. And he sent them to Bethlehem, saying, "Go and search diligently for the child, and when you have found him, bring me word, that I too may come and worship him."

~

---

10. Homily of Epiphany Mass, January 6, 2017.

The strange party of the Magi with their exotic clothing had certainly not gone unnoticed in Jerusalem. Herod's spies had gathered testimonies about their story and referred it immediately to the king. The bloodthirsty, power-hungry king, who governed with an iron fist, cared little for religion and prophecy unless he could use them for his own designs. But this rumor about the new king of the Jews worried him greatly, especially because of the consequences it could have on the population, triggering revolts and riots.

Already nearing the end of his life, and succumbing increasingly to the delirium of power, Herod was a pudgy, bearded man, in love with himself. His fingers were adorned with rings of pure gold, and he wore clothing studded with precious stones. He was a cruel man, deprived of any sense of moderation, quick to anger, heedless of justice, the son of a prime minister of the corrupt Hasmonean dynasty, half Idumean and half Nabatean. He had reconstructed Solomon's temple, the city of Caesarea Maritima, and the fortress of Masada, and he had already prepared a colossal mausoleum, the Herodium. Money, and power in particular, came before family bonds. He had killed his wife Mariamne, the couple's two children, Alexander and Aristobulus, his wife's brother, and his mother-in-law. And he would also kill Antipater, his other son by his first wife, before his death.

So what was this story about a prophecy regarding the king of Israel? He asked for information from the priests and the leaders of the people whom the people hated, but who were always ready to run off to court. He made them explain the words of the prophet Micah in the Scriptures, which specifically indicated that Bethlehem was the place where this mysterious king would be born. Then he made them call the Magi, but secretly. He did not want anyone to know, but wanted them to be his privileged informants, his unsuspecting spies.

Balthasar, Gaspar, and Melchior, having entered through a side entrance, felt uncomfortable in the presence of the irascible king, even though they were accustomed to frequenting the palaces of the powerful as sought-after researchers, counselors whose advice was heeded. Melchior above all, the most expert in sizing up the human qualities of whomever he found himself before, felt a strange presentiment. They played Herod's game, promising him they would return with information. They left secretly, the same way they had been admitted into the king's presence.

After listening to the king, they went on their way. And behold, the star that they had seen when it rose went before them until it came to rest over the place where the child was. When they saw the star, they rejoiced exceedingly with great joy.

The journey from Jerusalem to Bethlehem took just a few hours, even given the slowness of the caravan with the provisions and supplies in tow, which had been enriched at each stop with a few additional things the Magi had discovered and acquired that would be valuable for their research. The final leg of their very long journey was accompanied by a singular atmosphere. Herod's megalomaniacal ambitions and his tremendous fear of losing the power he had acquired through great bloodshed were now a far-distant echo. The Magis' longing for the infinite had definitively gained the upper hand; their hearts were beating ever more strongly; their eyes were fixed ahead as they scrutinized the horizon and the first white huts of the city of Judah, where an unsuspecting married couple, hidden to the world, were raising a child who had been born in a cave a few months before.

"Nostalgia for God has its roots in the past yet does not remain there but goes in search of the future. The 'nostalgic' believer, driven by faith, goes in search of God like the Magi did, to the least-known corners of history, for they know that the Lord is awaiting them there. To encounter their Lord, they go to the peripheries, to the frontiers, to places not yet evangelized. And they do not do this with an attitude of superiority, but rather as beggars who cannot ignore the eyes of those for whom the Good News is still unexplored territory. A short distance from Bethlehem, an entirely different attitude reigned in Herod's palace, where no one realized what was taking place. As the Magi journeyed on their way, Jerusalem was sleeping, sleeping in collusion with a Herod who, rather than seeking, was also sleeping. He was sleeping under the anesthesia of a cauterized conscience."[11]

If the Magi's party had not passed unnoticed in Jerusalem, their arrival in Bethlehem at nightfall was quite an event with their harnessed horses and the patter of hooves on the stones, the camels and dromedaries with their placid, rambling gait. Then those three strange characters, with their fancy but strange clothing, their eyes focused on something beyond them that they needed to reach. The noisy retinue of servants was intent on making sure none of the food fell from the backs of the beasts. Many people abandoned their meals on

---

11. *Ibid.*

the table that evening to go out and see the sight. Who were they? Where had they come from and why? What did they want?

The caravan camp that had closed its doors to Mary and Joseph almost a year before, welcomed the Magi with the highest honors. They settled in, awaiting the new day so they could finally explore the city, thus bringing to fulfillment that inner movement confirmed by the stars. None of the three could sleep that last night as they waited. They spent it contemplating the starry sky, not to look for new mysterious prophecies, but to find peace. That star was now fixed over them and within them. The time of expectation was coming to an end.

With the first lights of dawn, they had already eaten their first meal and were fully clothed. The servants had already harnessed their animals. The chests with the gifts for the King of the Jews were on hand, ready to be offered to the child. They started off in solemn procession, once again being greeted with the curious looks of the Bethlehemites, "escorted" by a throng of barefoot children goading the horses and camels, singing, and shouting.

Jesus, still in diapers, who had been revealed only to a small group of local shepherds, was about to receive the homage of the gentiles, of the wise, of those who turn their backs on so many reasonable objections, and who set out in search on a journey.

They arrived at the house where Jesus's family was living. Almost a year old, the tiny child was taking his first steps, calling out, "*Imma*," turning around and smiling at Mary, and calling out, "Abba" when calling for Joseph. Mary was informed by a traveler that those interesting people seemed to be coming precisely toward the house where she, her husband, and the baby continued to be hosted. Joseph was about to leave for work, but he held back and waited for them. "God be with you," Mary said, seeing them arrive.

And going into the house, they saw the child with Mary his mother, and they fell down and worshiped him. Then, opening their treasures, they offered him gifts, gold and frankincense and myrrh.

Instead of sitting down as they had been invited to do, the Magi knelt down, sitting back on their heels. Their servants did the same. At first, the couple was astonished, then they perceived everything. They willingly accepted the Magi's symbolic gifts, even though they were a bit embarrassed as little Jesus curiously moved freely from one to the other, attracted by the color of their exotic clothing.

That visit did not last long. The Magi did not want to disturb this family's life with their cumbersome presence. Their eyes and their hearts were now overflowing with gratitude and awe for what they had seen. What a contrast between this "king" and the other one, Herod. What a difference between this white hut with the stable attached to it, and the palace of power in Jerusalem.

"To discover that God wanted to be born where we least expected him, where we perhaps do not want him, or where we so often refuse him. To discover that in God's eyes there is room for the wounded, the weary, the mistreated, the abandoned, and that his strength and his power are called mercy. Jerusalem is so far from Bethlehem for some people! . . . Feeling nostalgia, the Magi no longer wanted what was usual. They were all too familiar with, accustomed to, and weary of the Herods of their day. But in Bethlehem, there was a promise of newness, a promise of gratuitousness. Something new was taking place there. The Magi were able to worship because they had the courage to set out on the journey, and by prostrating themselves before the little one, by prostrating themselves before the poor one, by prostrating themselves before the defenseless one, by prostrating themselves before the unusual and unknown Child of Bethlehem, they discovered the Glory of God." [12]

Balthasar, Gaspar, and Melchior returned to the caravan camp to rest and spend the afternoon there. That night, they finally fell into a deep sleep, a sleep interrupted by a revelation. *And being warned in a dream not to return to Herod, they departed to their own country by another way.*

The more intuitive Melchior was the first to awaken, startled. Everything around was still dark. It was a matter of moments before the other two woke as well, looking each other in the eyes. They had all been warned. Each of them had "seen" and knew what to do. Only a few barely whispered words were needed, an order muttered under their breath to the servants concentrated on preparing food for their breakfast, and the caravan that had come from the East set off again in a hurry before sunrise, leaving Bethlehem behind forever. They carefully avoided any of the crossroads leading to Jerusalem so as not to run the risk of stumbling upon Herod's guards.

Now when they had departed, behold, an angel of the Lord appeared to Joseph in a dream and said, "Rise, take the child and his mother, and flee to Egypt, and remain there until I tell you, for Herod is about to search for the child, to destroy him."

And he rose and took the child and his mother by night and departed to Egypt.

---

12. *Ibid.*

Not even a year had gone by when their adventurous journey that had brought them to Bethlehem had begun. Now they needed to quickly leave, not even having time to prepare their belongings. This time it was not on a difficult but planned journey because of the census. This time they had to escape. They had to run far away where Herod had no jurisdiction. The life of their child, God-made-man, was in danger. He needed Joseph to protect him, and he needed the traditional hospitality of a country where refugees had always found a place.

"Saint Joseph was the first to be called on to protect the joy of Salvation. Faced with the atrocious crimes that were taking place, Saint Joseph—the model of an obedient and loyal man—was capable of heeding God's voice and the mission the Father entrusted to him. Because he was able to listen to God's voice, and allowed himself to be guided by his will, Joseph became more sensitive to what was going on around him and was able to read these events realistically." [13]

And so, Mary and Joseph became displaced migrants, pursued by the wickedness of the king bent on annihilating anyone who threatened his power.

Their journey was marked by fear, at least the first few days. Jesus was still incapable of understanding. For him, that trip with his parents, seated on the back of the mule, became an occasion to play and have fun. Despite everything, Mary tried to keep smiling at him. Joseph was continuously looking over his shoulder, afraid that from one moment to another Herod's scoundrels might suddenly come out from behind a tree or from the top of one of the sandy hills to take the little one and kill him.

"Has the moment already come for the blade to pierce my heart?" Mary asked herself silently while trying to hold her curious child, who was getting distracted by everything they came across along the way.

～

Thanks to the angel's warning, this small family and the Magi had about a twenty-four-hour advantage. News of the departure of the three wise men from the caravan camp reached the palace at nightfall.

Then Herod, when he saw that he had been tricked by the wise men, became furious, and he sent and killed all the male children in Bethlehem and in all that region who were two years old or under, according to the time that he had ascertained from the wise men.

---

13. Letter to Bishops on the Feast of the Holy Innocents, December 28, 2016.

The inhuman order did not surprise the corrupt king's officers. They were accustomed to his cruelty and some of them were even happy to carry out his orders. What was in their hearts as they tore down the doors of those houses in search of baby boys, killing them on the spot, slitting their throats like sacrificial lambs? They did it because they no longer had hearts. The slaughter began the afternoon after the mob had made sure the gates of Bethlehem had been secured. About twenty little boys under two years of age were killed with swords amidst the heartrending cries of their mothers, fathers, brothers and sisters, and grandparents. Very few managed to escape.

Herod *"was bewildered. He was afraid. It is the bewilderment that, when faced with the newness that revolutionizes history, closes in on itself, on its own achievements, its own knowledge, its own successes. The bewilderment of someone who sits atop his wealth yet cannot see beyond it. A bewilderment lodged in the hearts of those who want to control everything and everyone. . . . Herod was afraid, and that fear led him to seek security in crime."* [14]

From his first steps, Jesus's life was colored with blood and was grafted onto the tragedy of the martyrdom of little innocents.

"Whether we like it or not, Christmas is also accompanied by tears. The Evangelists did not permit themselves to disguise reality to make it more credible or palatable. . . . On the contrary, they recount the birth of the Son of God as an event which is also fraught with tragedy and grief." [15]

While Bethlehem was still reeling from the invasion of the king's hired assassins, and almost every family was directly or indirectly caught up in mourning, Jesus, Mary, and Joseph managed to reach safety. Prudence had moved Joseph to avoid taking the most direct and shortest route along the sea normally used by the caravans that passed through Hebron and then through Gaza. That route was the most dangerous because of the checkpoints guarded by Herod's soldiers. He chose, instead, the same route of the ancient Hebrew exodus, going toward the East, toward the Jordan River and the Dead Sea. It passed through the desert, but there was less of a risk of unwanted encounters.

Finally, after almost three weeks on the road, they found refuge in the delta region along the Nile River, at Bubastis. They remained there for two months in an encampment of Jewish exiles who had also fled from Herod. Then, thanks to Joseph's work, they moved to a small house a short distance away, about fifty-six miles from Cairo.

---

14. Homily of Epiphany Mass, January 6, 2017.
15. Letter to Bishops on the Feast of the Holy Innocents, December 28, 2016.

4

Return to Nazareth—Jesus's Hidden Life

Years 4 BC and AD 7.

Traveling to Galilee. The Twelve-Year-Old Jesus with the Doctors in the Temple of Jerusalem. Jesus Works in Joseph's Workshop.

Two years. They waited two years for the news. Egypt was where they were living, but it was not their homeland. Mary and Joseph longed to go back to Nazareth where everything had begun and where both of them wanted to return. Joseph often thought about his workshop outside on the side of the house, where he used to do woodworking. He wondered if it was still standing. Their neighbors had not heard any news from the couple since they left suddenly for Bethlehem for the census. Mary's parents, Joachim and Anne, were no more. But the couple hoped that another young couple friend of theirs would have taken care to check every now and then on their empty home, which Joseph had prudently boarded up, not knowing how long their journey would last.

As soon as possible, Mary and Joseph so wanted their little Jesus to get to know the village of Nazareth, its modest but well-kept synagogue, their parents' friends, and their son's peers. They did not want their child to grow up as a refugee, an immigrant, continually hanging in uncertainty. Joseph wanted to introduce his son to the knowledge of sacred Scripture and hoped to do that where it had taken root. But until he received indications to the contrary (an angel had already appeared to him twice in a dream telling him what he needed to do), he had decided to teach his child his own craft of woodworking to create carts, doorposts, and doors. As soon as his age permitted it, he wanted to bring Jesus with him to the construction site in Sepphoris so Jesus could see with his own eyes how a house is constructed, from the foundation up.

Jesus did not seem to be at all aware of the situation his parents were living in as exiles in Egypt. At almost three years old, he was a vivacious and curious toddler, playing in the courtyard with other children. He would fall asleep in his mother's arms in the evening after hearing Joseph tell him stories from salvation history, about the covenant God had entered into with his people, the people of Israel.

The settlements surrounding the city of Bubastis swarmed with Jews fleeing for various reasons, but there were also refugees from other lands come in search of salvation and a future. Languages and cultures mingled together. As is always the case, the children were the freest. For them there were no Jews, Egyptians, Persians, or Greeks. There were only other friends with whom they all shared the same spaces with simplicity, united by the same dignified poverty.

Every evening after Jesus had fallen asleep, Mary and Joseph would look into each other's eyes for a few moments without saying anything. That was the moment they remembered Nazareth, a moment that always ended with a prayer to God that he might watch over their child and help them go back home.

Every now and then on some long and sunny afternoon, it would happen that Joseph would return home early from the work he was doing in the service of some of the nearby families. He would stop to watch Jesus from a distance as he ran around playing with the other children. As Joseph secretly watched Jesus, he would ask himself if the other children knew or had at least already picked up something about his origins and mission. No one would have guessed, seeing him happy, carefree, perfectly inserted into that happy group of children. This is what the carpenter thought to himself, this just man accustomed to speaking little and observing a lot. Then Jesus would notice him and, no matter what game he was playing at the moment, would run into his arms, calling him "Abba!"

How long would he maintain this carefreeness? When would he know who he really was and why he had come into the world? Joseph, like any father, dreamed of having him by his side, working with him. But he knew that his son had another mission. He was expected to protect him and bring him up. He had to become the King of the Jews . . . and yet, that kingship seemed so unprecedented and strange, at least the way it had unfolded up to that moment—a manger instead of a throne, a stable instead of a palace, poor stinky shepherds instead of perfumed servants in starched uniforms.

"Saint Joseph plays an important role in the life of Jesus and Mary. He is the guardian who tirelessly protects his family. . . . In his heart, Joseph carried the great mystery surrounding Jesus and Mary, his spouse. As a just man, he entrusted himself always to God's will, and put it into practice." [16]

~

After two years, the news finally arrived. King Herod the Great, the king who had reigned in Jerusalem pursuing his delusions of grandeur, had died. His thirst for power had not guaranteed even one extra day of life on this earth. Very few people mourned his death.

Then one night came a new order.

But when Herod died, behold, an angel of the Lord appeared in a dream to Joseph in Egypt, saying, "Rise, take the child and his mother and go to the land of Israel, for those who sought the child's life are dead." And he rose and took the child and his mother and went to the land of Israel.

Joseph obeyed as he had always done. He knew these nocturnal revelations that came to him in dreams came from God. Once more he prepared their belongings, putting them together with a few necessary items, prepared the mule, and waited for dawn. Then he left, along with Jesus and Mary, to return to their homeland. This time, too, the trip was long, but now Nazareth was in the sights and hearts of this family. They were filled with expectation and hope. There was no more fear.

When the sun had already begun to set, they entered the village they had left three years earlier. Almost nothing had changed. On the path leading to their home, they met two old women who recognized first Joseph, then Mary. They drew near to welcome them back.

The house had remained intact. Even the garden was still there, although it had been overtaken by weeds. Mary lit the fire immediately to prepare dinner, but that was not necessary. Neighbors began to knock on their door—one person brought fresh sheep's milk, another person brought freshly baked bread, someone else brought fresh fruit and dates. Their life as a family began again in the simplicity of Nazareth. It was not difficult for Joseph to find work again at the construction site. He was a precise, reliable craftsman. No one had forgotten him.

~

---

16. Apostolic Letter, *Admirabile signum*, 7.

Until the age of five, children were entrusted to the care of their mothers. Then they began their religious studies in the synagogue while simultaneously learning their father's trade. The life of the Son of God was no different from that of his peers in the village.

"We know little about the Child Jesus, but we can learn much about him if we watch the lives of children. It is a beautiful habit that parents and grandparents have of watching children, what they do. First of all, we discover, that children want our attention. They have to be at the center. Why? Because they need to feel protected. It is important that we too place Jesus at the center of our lives and know, even if it may seem paradoxical, that we have the responsibility to protect him. He wants to be in our arms, he wants to be looked after, and to be able to look into our eyes. Furthermore, we must make the Child Jesus smile, to show him our love and our joy because he is in our midst. His smile is a sign of the love that gives us the assurance of being loved. Lastly, children, love to play. Playing with children, however, means abandoning our logic to enter into theirs. If we want them to have fun, we need to understand what they like, and not be selfish and make them do the things we like. . . . Before Jesus we are called to abandon our pretense of autonomy . . . to accept instead the true form of freedom that consists in knowing who is in front of us, and serving him. He, this Child, is the Son of God who comes to save us." [17]

When Jesus reached the age of seven, Mary seemed to detect a different reflection in his eyes. She would sometimes see him raising his eyes toward heaven. Was he perhaps beginning to understand who he was? Was he beginning to be aware of his other divine nature, which had not imposed itself on him, overpowering his human nature, but was accompanying it side by side? They were only small, almost imperceptible signs that his mother noticed, only to quickly push away the thoughts about her child's future and his mission. "God will provide," she would whisper. Both she and Joseph imagined that sooner or later their son, who completely resembled his mother, would leave Nazareth.

And the child grew and became strong, filled with wisdom. And the favor of God was upon him.

～

---

17. General Audience, December 30, 2015.

At the age of twelve, the boys who were preparing for their religious initiation, their *bar mitzvah*, would go with their families to the temple of Jerusalem. There they would meet the doctors of the law and engage with them in discussion. This was the moment in which each boy would publicly read the *Torah* for the first time. They would read a passage from the biblical law revealed by God through Moses. *Bar mitzvah* meant "son of the commandment," and was a significant rite of passage to adulthood.

~

Traditionally, there were three pilgrimages to the Holy City each year. But poor families, especially those who lived farther away, would partake in only one, to celebrate Passover. Large groups would form on their way to Jerusalem. The city teamed with pilgrims who were camped out everywhere. Even Nazareth seemed to have completely emptied out into the areas around the temple.

This time, too, just like every other year, Mary with the twelve-year-old Jesus prepared the food rationed out for the journey. Joseph occupied himself with the beasts of burden. Every pilgrimage was a group event. Families did not always remain in separate units but would travel together in larger groups. Young children enjoyed a certain freedom to move about, coming and going, as long as they never lost contact with the caravan as it slowly advanced along the road.

Now his parents went to Jerusalem every year at the Feast of the Passover. And when he was twelve years old, they went up according to custom. And when the feast was ended, as they were returning, the boy Jesus stayed behind in Jerusalem. His parents did not know it.

Joseph and Mary trusted their son. He had eaten with them the previous evening after finding them in the camp, but they had not seen him the next morning when the caravan set out toward Nazareth. They thought he was traveling with some of his other friends from the village.

Supposing him to be in the group they went a day's journey, but then they began to search for him among their relatives and acquaintances.

By nightfall there was no trace of him. He had not looked for them, he had not come to ask for food or to spend the night with them. Instead of eating dinner, Mary and Joseph began to look for him. This was easier to do when everyone was camped in small groups around their fires. They asked their relatives, friends, acquaintances, and then strangers. In fact, no one from the village had seen him, no one remembered traveling a piece of the road with him that day, no one knew anything. The faces of the people they asked expressed their solidarity with those parents anguished over their son. No sooner had Mary and Joseph gone, than they, too, got up to look for their own children.

When they did not find him, they returned to Jerusalem, searching for him.

Mary and Joseph did not sleep that night, but retraced their steps, climbing back up against the tide of pilgrims leaving the Holy City. Despite their fatigue, they walked hastily, never taking their eyes off the groups they met along the way. They were hoping to spot his head with its jet-black hair, peeking from behind a cart, sitting on top of a donkey, or emerging from a group of noisy children. They were hoping to recognize his voice with its unmistakable Galilean Aramaic accent. Instead, nothing.

When they entered the gates of Jerusalem again, it was already broad daylight, and they were exhausted. They quickly got something to eat, then began looking for him again. This was not easy in this city still teaming with pilgrims. Many times, they thought they saw him, but it was not him. Joseph especially gave himself no peace. What had happened to him? Why couldn't they find him? They spent the entire day searching, to no avail. Then they slept a few hours, sheltered under the small roof of a dilapidated, abandoned house.

The following morning, they finally headed toward the place that attracted people the most. People were continuously going in and coming out. It was a striking sight perhaps for anyone who stopped to observe the scene; disconcerting for anyone in search of a lost child.

After three days they found him in the temple, sitting among the teachers, listening to them and asking them questions. And all who heard him were amazed at his understanding and his answers.

They stopped suddenly under the outer portico of the temple of Jerusalem in front of a group of elders who seemed to hang on the words of a young boy. It is true that the *bar mitzvah* included a dialogue between the boys and the doctors of the law, but here the roles seemed to be reversed. Jesus was listening and asking questions, but his questions were so appropriate and deep that they struck the minds of these men of learning. At times his questions were more surprising than his answers.

This is exactly what was happening at that moment among the doctors in the temple and other curious people who were witnessing the dialogue. There were not only the Pharisees with whom they were acquainted from their synagogue in Nazareth. Sadducees and Zealots were also in the temple. All of them were attracted by this boy's words. Jesus's questions were so deep that at a certain point, these wise men were the ones who asked him for explanations. It seemed he had already learned every nuance of the Mosaic law, but he presented the core of the teachings with a depth that even the doctors had not grasped. It was as if this boy from Nazareth knew Scripture "from the inside." It seemed as if Scripture were a part of every fiber of his being.

Even Mary and Joseph were enchanted while they watched him speak in a way they had never heard him speak before.

And when his parents saw him, they were astonished.

Then their feelings prevailed, and they spoke to him after taking him aside.

And his mother said to him, "Son, why have you treated us so? Behold, your father and I have been searching for you in great distress." And he said to them, "Why were you looking for me? Did you not know that I must be in my Father's house?" And they did not understand the saying that he spoke to them.

These words are not enough to understand that scene. For they were accompanied by looks, by faces, expressing the fatigue of three days and two nights spent with almost no rest, with the uncertainty and fear of having lost their son. As is always the case in these situations, it was his mother who spoke. Jesus's apparently harsh response was spoken with a smile on his lips, placing the harsh truth before the couple. His detachment from them had begun—that detachment that every mother and every father go through when their children take their own path, asserting their own autonomy. He had to occupy himself with his Father's affairs.

"Amazement never waned in the family of Nazareth, not even in such a dramatic moment as the losing of Jesus. It is the ability to be amazed before the gradual manifestation of the Son of God. It is the same amazement that strikes even the doctors in the Temple, 'amazed at his understanding and his answers.'. . . Being amazed and astonished is the opposite of taking everything for granted. It is the opposite of interpreting the reality that surrounds us and historical events according to our criteria alone. . . .

"The second element . . . is the anxiety that Mary and Joseph experienced when they could not find Jesus. This anxiety reveals Jesus's centrality in the Holy Family. The Virgin and her husband had welcomed that son, protected him, and watched him grow in age, wisdom and grace in their midst. But above all, he grew in their hearts, and, little by little, their affection for him and their understanding of him grew. This is why the family of Nazareth is holy, because it was centered on Jesus. All of Mary and Joseph's attention and concern was directed toward him.

The anxiety they experienced during the three days that Jesus was lost should also be our anxiety when we are far away from him, when we are distant from Jesus. "[18]

Mary and Joseph, tired but happy about having found their son safe and sound, did not understand the meaning of those words that would remain and settle for a long time in his mother's heart. They started out again on the road and returned home.

And he went down with them and came to Nazareth and was submissive to them. And his mother treasured up all these things in her heart. And Jesus increased in wisdom and in stature and in favor with God and man.

~

He grew in wisdom, age, and grace. He learned Joseph's trade and began going with him regularly to the construction sites. Later, Jesus would recall what he had learned from Joseph when he gave examples and told parables. Jesus would often remain up in the evening. By the dim light of the lamp, he would ease his father's burdens by finishing his work for him. Jesus had grown tall and strong. Even Mary could always count on him for whatever she needed.

Then all of a sudden, when their son was almost thirty, Joseph fell sick. He remained immobile in his bed for two weeks without the fever abating. Neither could he eat. Mary and Jesus never left him alone. One morning, Joseph felt that death was close at hand. He asked Jesus to take care of his mother, and asked Mary to be strong. Then Joseph died serenely, holding his wife's hand. As he closed his eyes, the last thing he saw on earth were those eyes, filled with love and gratitude, of the Son of God whom he had raised and protected as his own son. The first thing he saw when his reopened his eyes again in eternity's light was the equally loving and grateful gaze of God the Father.

From that moment on, Jesus had two fathers in heaven watching over him. His brief but intense public life was about to begin.

---

18. Angelus, December 30, 2018.

5

The Baptism, the Temptations, and the Wine That Ran Out

Year AD 28, January—March.

*Along the Jordan with John the Baptist. Confrontation with Satan.
Meeting John and Andrew. The Call of the Apostles.
Miracle of the Wedding at Cana.*

Several times now she had seen him pray with an intensity she had never seen before. It did not happen often that Mary witnessed these moments of dialogue between the Son and his Father because Jesus prayed alone in his little room in the house of Nazareth, where he had lived since he was a child and where he remained, after Joseph's death, alone with his mother.

He did not need to tell her; she understood. The moment had now arrived, and the sword that would pierce her heart, according to Simeon's prophecy, slowly began to move. They remained longer than usual at table that last evening before he left. Jesus had just finished building a sturdy wagon and was explaining to her that the person who commissioned it would be coming by the next morning to pick it up. Jesus intended to set out on foot while Nazareth was still shrouded in darkness.

When he got up that night, he found a sack of food and water prepared for him. Jesus took it in his hands, smiled and whispered, "Mamma. . . ." He left, thinking of her and Joseph, about the love that had surrounded him, and how they had taken care of him when he was a child. He was also thinking about what was awaiting him, of that journey that would change everything, about the beginning of his public life. In the darkness, he recognized the voices of some friends with whom he would be traveling. Their destination was Bethany along the Jordan, where there was a man whom many recognized as a prophet, and some were even saying was the Messiah. He was baptizing with water in the river and would shout, *"Repent, for the kingdom of heaven is at hand!"*

In the fifteenth year of the reign of Tiberius Caesar, Pontius Pilate being gover-
nor of Judea, and Herod being tetrarch of Galilee, and his brother Philip tetrarch
of the region of Ituraea and Trachonitis, and Lysanias tetrarch of Abilene, during
the high priesthood of Annas and Caiaphas, the word of God came to John the son
of Zechariah in the wilderness. And he went into all the region around the Jordan,
proclaiming a baptism of repentance for the forgiveness of sins.

John and Jesus had never met each other, even though they had been very
near each other when both were in the wombs of their respective mothers—John
had leaped in his mother's womb when Mary, who had been pregnant for a few
days, came near. John's parents, Zechariah and Elizabeth, had already been dead
for many years. John had left his home and his people early to live as a hermit,
praying and fasting. His clothing was made of camel hides, and he survived on
locusts in the desert. He had a magnetic gaze, a cutting voice, and a sturdy build,
notwithstanding his frequent fasts. Long hair and a thick beard framed his face.
You could tell his words came from God. Many went to seek him out in the cavern that had become his home. He would baptize them and then make them stay
for a period of prayer, fasting, and penance in the desert.

His invitation to conversion was a call to change direction in life. He
harshly criticized the formalism of those who belonged to the two opposing
religious factions, the Pharisees and the Sadducees. The public confession of
one's personal faults, and the washing of the body, were two rituals present in
Judaism that belonged to the tradition of the people. The novelty John introduced was his proclamation that the kingdom of God was near at hand. The
public recognition of sin and the purifying bath in the waters of the Jordan
thus became a preparation for that imminent event.

There was also another difference that distanced John from other messianic
preachers—he did not promise either dominion or supremacy to his people but
remained aloof from the frequent call to arms against the Roman invaders, as
well as from any political interest whatsoever. He did not perform prodigious
signs either. Precisely because of these differences, many Israelites began asking
themselves if he could be the One they had been waiting for so long.

John answered them all, saying, "I baptize you with water, but he who is
mightier than I is coming, the strap of whose sandals I am not worthy to untie. He
will baptize you with the Holy Spirit and fire."

He insistently repeated he was not the Messiah. *"I am the voice of one crying*
out in the wilderness, 'Make straight the way of the Lord.'" Then it happened that
he found the Messiah in front of him.

~

There were a lot of people that day along the banks of the river, common people, but also Pharisees with their ornate clothing. Some rich, well recognizable people were also there, along with many poor people. They, too, were easily recognizable. The sun was shining warmly, a light breeze made the walk less arduous. John appeared to be particularly inspired. He was standing on a rock that jutted out, preaching with his usual rough, cutting style. His voice imposed itself over the buzz of the people in whom he instilled both awe and respect.

Jesus, who had made a good part of the journey together with his other companions from Nazareth, had arrived alone, going downriver behind John. Even before seeing him, the baptist suddenly felt the presence of his cousin and turned around. Jesus approached him smiling. Tied to his belt with a cord cut to a precise length, the prophet dropped the gourd shell he was using to pour water on the heads of the people he was baptizing.

John's eyes filled with joy and surprise. He exclaimed, *"Behold, the Lamb of God, who takes away the sin of the world! This is he of whom I said, 'After me comes a man who ranks before me, because he was before me.' I myself did not know him, but for this purpose I came baptizing with water, that he might be revealed to Israel."*

Most of the people there did not hear what John had said. As much as his speech was vibrant and vehement when preaching, his voice became stammering and broken with emotion in Jesus's presence. The precursor was disappearing to make room for the true Messiah. The power of his prophetic words was vanishing in the presence of the Word of God become man. The nervous gesticulation of that unusual prophet in the desert gave way to the authoritative meekness of the Son of God who had arrived there, mingling in with everyone else. Jesus asked John to be baptized . . . baptized like everyone else.

John would have prevented him, saying, "I need to be baptized by you, and do you come to me?" But Jesus answered him, "Let it be so now, for thus it is fitting for us to fulfill all righteousness." Then he consented.

Jesus took off his mantle and tunic, and waded half-naked into the river water to the point where it was almost still and about three feet deep. Trembling, John did it, pouring the water that he scooped up with the dried gourd over the uncovered head of the Nazarene. At that very moment, the sun seemed to spin and come closer to them. A strange light split the sky in two and a small dove fluttered over their heads while a voice from above said, *"This is my beloved Son, with whom I am well pleased."*

Not everyone heard it; very few understood; some ended up attributing that sign to the baptist. Jesus came out of the water to get dressed and mingled once again among the crowd.

"*Jesus is in the midst of the people.* . . . *Before immersing himself in the water, Jesus 'immerses' himself in the crowd. He joins them, fully taking on our human condition, sharing everything, except sin.* . . . *By joining the people asking John for the baptism of conversion, Jesus also shares with them the deep desire for inner renewal. And the Holy Spirit who descends upon him* . . . *is a sign that a new world is being initiated with Jesus, a 'new creation' in which all those who welcome Jesus into their life participate.* . . . *This love of the Father that all of us received on the day of our Baptism is a flame that was lit in our heart, and needs to be nourished through prayer and charity.*"[19]

After being baptized, Jesus took the desert road to spend a period of time in prayer and fasting in solitude. He walked along the ground, parched and scorched by the sun. There were no green bushes, only brambles and dry grass, and rocks that destroyed his sandals. He climbed to a height of about sixteen hundred feet, to the top of the mountain where the last of the Maccabees had been killed. It was a place that overlooked the Jordan valley. He spotted a rocky overhang that created a type of natural roof under which he found a bit of shade. It was not rare in places like this to find hermits taking refuge in these caves. The only thing he had with him was the sack his mother had prepared in Nazareth, even if the food he had rationed so carefully was almost finished. Three stones worn smooth over time would serve as his bed. He began to pray, watching the hues of the sunset, and continued to keep vigil for the entire first night. Soon, a bitter, piercing cold suddenly replaced the dry heat of day.

He was God, but now he faced his Father as man, feeling the pangs of hunger, a burning in his throat because of lack of water, the immense and silent solitude of the desert. He spent many days and many nights this way. The more his strength abandoned him, the more his abandonment to the Father grew. He had been led there for a reason.

It was then, about three in the afternoon, the hottest hour, the moment in which he was physically exhausted, that Jesus saw a figure. When he saw him in the distance, he was not sure at first if it was real or an illusion caused by a play of light. Until that moment he had not come upon another living soul. He was slowly advancing toward Jesus, and was dressed in a dark-colored, light-weight mantel; a white cloth was wrapped around his head. He did not

---

19. Angelus, January 13, 2019.

seem to have been worn out by the desert crossing. Jesus was seated under the rock when that unsettling man, agile and slender, with penetrating eyes and thin lips, began to speak to Jesus as if they had always known each other.

"What are you doing here alone?" Satan asked him.

Jesus raised his eyes toward him for an instant but did not respond. He continued to pray.

"I'm speaking to you. . . . Are you lost? Come with me to the river. We'll find water and bread. . . ."

Once again, Jesus remained silent.

"I know you well. You know that, right? I recognize you. I know who you are and why you're here. But you need to trust me and follow me."

Once again, no response.

The devil came out into the open. "You pray to the almighty Eternal One. But you're here now, on the earth, in my kingdom, a man among men. It's better for you to trust in me. You are good . . . but it's useless for you to sacrifice yourself for men. They think only about money, food, satisfying their senses. Don't suffer for them. . . ."

Still no reaction from Jesus, although his forehead was beaded more and more with sweat, and hunger pangs were gripping his stomach.

The other changed his tone. "Poor thing, you must really be hungry. . . . I don't have any bread to offer you right now. . . . But if you want, you can change these rocks into sweet-smelling bread. You can change these brambles into perfumed dates and this sand into honey. . . . We could satiate our hunger together!"

In the end, he challenged Jesus. *"If you are the Son of God, command these stones to become loaves of bread."*

Jesus raised his eyes and said faintly, *"It is written,*

> *'Man shall not live by bread alone,*
> *but by every word that comes from the mouth of God.'"*

Satan immediately changed the subject. He said he wanted to bring Jesus to the pinnacle of the temple of Jerusalem to see from the highest point how the swarm of people seemed like ants. He told Jesus that even the priests were compromised men. He urged Jesus to manifest his divinity in all its power by throwing himself into thin air so that the angels would come to his aid to rescue him.

"If you are the Son of God, throw yourself down, for it is written,

'He will command his angels concerning you,' and
'On their hands they will bear you up,
    lest you strike your foot against a stone.'"

Jesus said to him, "Again it is written, 'You shall not put the Lord your God to the test.'"

The man with the white turban ground his teeth in dissatisfaction. Jesus was not dialoguing with him. Jesus was resisting him, repelling his assaults using the word of God as a shield.

He tried one last attack even though he knew he would not succeed even this time to make Jesus vacillate with his temptations. He made all the kingdoms of the earth and their beauty flash before the tired eyes of the Nazarene—luxurious cities, enormous monuments, powerful armies with innumerable soldiers armed to the teeth, treasures and riches, stupendous imperial palaces. And he said, *"All these I will give you, if you will fall down and worship me."*

He asked Jesus to worship him just for an instant. He begged Jesus to satisfy his longing to be recognized and venerated as lord of all the earth.

It was at that point that Jesus regained his strength. He stood up, and looking Satan in the eye this time, said with a firm, thundering voice, *"Be gone, Satan! For it is written,*

'You shall worship the Lord your God
    and him only shall you serve.'"

A piercing scream rent the desert's silence. The mysterious creature with the ambiguous human face became twisted like a wounded beast and seemed to melt into the nothingness from which it had come.

Jesus raised his eyes to heaven, thanking his Father for having given him the strength to resist. Then he collapsed sweaty on the stones to rest. It was then that, almost without him noticing, the angels made a soft breeze blow to give him some relief. Even his hunger subsided. He succumbed to deep sleep.

"The three temptations indicate three paths the world always proposes, promising great success, three paths to deceive us: the greed to possess, human vainglory, and the exploitation of God. These are three paths that will lead us to ruin. . . . These are the paths that are set before us, with the illusion that this is the way to obtain success and happiness. But in reality, they are completely extraneous to God's way of acting. Rather, they in fact distance us from God, because they are the work of Satan. Facing these tests personally, Jesus conquers temptation three times in order to fully adhere to the Father's plan. And he reveals the remedies to us: an interior life, faith in God, the certainty that God loves us, that he is a Father, and

that with this certainty we will conquer every temptation. . . . In responding to the tempter, Jesus does not enter into dialogue, but responds to the three challenges solely with the Word of God. This teaches us not to dialogue with the devil. You must not dialogue; you only respond to him with the Word of God." [20]

Jesus had spent forty days and forty nights in the desert, fasting and praying. Now he was ready to go back down to the valley, toward the Jordan, backtracking along the same road that would lead him back to the place where John was baptizing.

He arrived at the river about midday. There were still people coming and going who were asking to be baptized and were listening to John's preaching. A small group of followers had formed around the prophet precursor dressed in camel's hair. They were helping him, trying to organize the flow of people, and feeding the elderly and those who were sick.

The next day again John was standing with two of his disciples, and he looked at Jesus as he walked by and said, "Behold, the Lamb of God!"

Two of the disciples, Andrew and John, saw the baptist's eyes rest on a man who had mingled among the small crowd that was waiting. They heard his words. They were the only ones who were impressed. It was the same man who had been baptized a few weeks earlier, that day when the heavens seemed to "open themselves up" and the sun seemed to draw closer. Now that man appeared thinner, his skin darkened and dried from exposure to the desert wind. But it was the same man.

The two disciples heard him say this, and they followed Jesus.

They promptly followed in his footsteps, walking behind him at a short distance, curious because of John the Baptist's words and even more so by his look filled with veneration for that man. One of the two had the hardy physique of a fisherman used to hard work. The other was very young.

Jesus turned and saw them following and said to them, "What are you seeking?" And they said to him, "Rabbi" (which means Teacher), "where are you staying?" He said to them, "Come and you will see." So they came and saw where he was staying, and they stayed with him that day, for it was about the tenth hour.

Everything had finally begun. John the Baptist would soon end up in the clutches of Herod the Tetrarch, who would throw him into prison and would then kill him, beheading him on the whim of Herodias, his brother's wife. The two disciples of the "precursor," the ones whose souls were pure and open to the newness of God, had recognized Jesus and were captivated by him.

---

20. Angelus, March 10, 2019.

That meeting was destined to change their lives. Rather, their lives had already been changed to such an extent that the youngest of the two remembered the time when they reached the camp where Jesus was staying with the other Nazarenes—four o'clock in the afternoon. They had been walking for about an hour behind him, following him at a distance. Then they walked at his side for at least another hour, exchanging words with him.

Jesus spoke little along the way. He was not in a hurry to teach but felt the urgency to share his life with them. And they did not begin by asking him what the "program" was, even less what "religious" advice he might offer them, even though they were curious to know if he truly was the Lamb of God. They had immediately asked him where he was staying, and they had heard him respond, "Come and see." Who was this man really? Where did his gentle authoritativeness come from? How was he able to see inside them? They felt loved, called, welcomed, moved to their very core by something indescribable that their meeting along the banks of the Jordan had set in motion.

"For those two, it is the 'spark.' They leave their first teacher and begin to follow Jesus. On the way, he turns to them and asks the decisive question: 'What are you seeking?' In the Gospels, Jesus appears as an expert of the human heart. At that moment he had met two young men who were searching, with a healthy restlessness. Indeed, what youth is a satisfied youth, without any quest for meaning? Young people who seek nothing are not young people—they are in retirement, having grown old prematurely. . . . And throughout the entire Gospel, in all of the encounters that take place along the road, Jesus appears to be someone who 'sets hearts on fire.' This is where his question arises that tries to bring out the desire for life and happiness that every young person bears inside. . . . John and Andrew's vocation begins in this way—it is the beginning of such a strong friendship with Jesus that it imposes a commonality of life and of passions with him. The two disciples begin to stay with Jesus and are immediately transformed into missionaries, because when the encounter ends, they do not calmly return home. . . . It was such a touching, such a happy meeting that the disciples will forever remember that day that illuminated and oriented their youth." [21]

They did not keep what they had experienced to themselves.

One of the two who heard John speak and followed Jesus was Andrew, Simon Peter's brother. He first found his own brother Simon and said to him, "We have found the Messiah" (which means Christ). He brought him to Jesus.

---

21. General Audience, August 30, 2017.

For Simon, the first meeting with Jesus was Andrew's face that enthusiastically proclaimed to him, "We have found the Messiah." The second meeting was when he found himself in front of Jesus, who looked at him as no one else had ever looked at him in his life.

Simon was shorter than his brother, Andrew. He, too, was sturdily built. They had both been born in Bethsaida and worked together in a small fishing business along the coast leading to Capernaum, also along the banks of the Sea of Galilee, where they both lived with their respective families. Simon's character was generous and impetuous. He was a humble, observant Jew who regularly attended synagogue. He knew how to look after his family and took every opportunity that Capernaum, a crossroads for trade and commerce, had to offer. As a fisherman, he was considered one of the best. He knew how to read the clouds and, listening to the wind, was able to predict if a storm was brewing. He knew how to sell fish, and his boat was one of the largest in the area.

When his brother, Andrew, told him he had found the Messiah, Simon did not hesitate. He had never asked Andrew questions he could not answer. So he set out with Andrew back to the camp where Jesus was staying—to see him, to meet him. Andrew was neither a mystic nor a visionary, neither was he prone to give credit to itinerant preachers. If he had reacted this way, if he said he had found the Messiah, there had to be something true about it. Anyway, it was worth checking out his brother's story for himself, even if his first reaction deep down had been not to believe him, thinking that he was the victim of a blunder, perhaps caused by fasting, and by that strange atmosphere that surrounded John the Baptist and his preaching. But what had convinced him to go with Andrew was that light in his eyes. The reflection of that light. . . . After all, what did he have to lose to go in person to meet that man?

The Nazarene was waiting for the two brothers and saw them arriving in the distance. They were walking at a good pace and were close by in no time at all. The Teacher got up to go meet them. He hugged Andrew, then *Jesus looked at Simon and said, "You are Simon the son of John. You shall be called Cephas"* *(which means Peter).*

The day after, they departed together with Jesus to return to Galilee and stopped in Bethsaida. There, the Nazarene met Philip, a lanky young man, a childhood friend of the two brothers with whom he had traveled till then.

He said to him, "Follow me." Now Philip was from Bethsaida, the city of Andrew and Peter. Philip found Nathanael and said to him, "We have found him of whom Moses in the Law and also the prophets wrote, Jesus of Nazareth, the son of Joseph." Nathanael said to him, "Can anything good come out of Nazareth?"

Nathanael, also known as Bartholomew, "son of Tolmai," reacted as many others would have. Nazareth, whose name never appears in the Scriptures, was a small village, known for nothing. It was a small speck on the map, a place to be passed over unnoticed. Would the Messiah, announced by the prophets and so long awaited by the people of Israel really come from there? Philip replied exactly as the Teacher would have.

Philip said to him, "Come and see." Jesus saw Nathanael coming toward him and said of him, "Behold, an Israelite indeed, in whom there is no deceit!" Nathanael said to him, "How do you know me?" Jesus answered him, "Before Philip called you, when you were under the fig tree, I saw you." Nathanael answered him, "Rabbi, you are the Son of God! You are the King of Israel!" Jesus answered him, "Because I said to you, 'I saw you under the fig tree,' do you believe? You will see greater things than these." And he said to him, "Truly, truly, I say to you, you will see heaven opened, and the angels of God ascending and descending on the Son of Man."

Nathanael Bartholomew, surprised that he had been "seen" before being seen . . . Peter, Andrew and Philip . . . young John, the son of Zebedee with an open heart, always ready to follow the Teacher. . . . Only a few days had passed. Meeting after meeting, journey after journey, dinner after dinner—Jesus of Nazareth was attracting a small group of friends around himself. They were curious to know him, fascinated by the way he looked at them and by his word, willing to follow after him.

They were sitting in Philip's house having lunch together, enjoying some good roasted fish seasoned with aromatic herbs, when someone knocked franticly on the door. It was Judas Thaddeus, a cousin of Jesus on Joseph's side. He, too, had inherited his physical strength from that side of the family. He had a message from Mary for her son. "She's expecting you, together with your friends, tomorrow in Cana for Susanna's wedding, whom you both know."

The place where the wedding was to be held was Cana of Galilee. It was near Nazareth and Tiberias, where Nathanael Bartholomew was from. Jesus hugged his cousin, who had joined the first group of followers, and invited him to sit down at the table, sharing with him half the food on his plate. "My mother's every wish is mine," Jesus said. "We'll go." So they quickly finished eating lunch to get themselves ready to head out on their way by early afternoon, bringing with them their best tunics in order to participate in the wedding.

∾

Stopping once to eat and rest a few hours at the house of a friend along the way, they arrived in time for the celebration. Mary had already come to Cana a few days earlier to help the bride. The house of the groom, Samuel, was on the outskirts of the town. The main room on the ground floor was decorated with colored fabric, flowers, and green branches. Since daybreak the women had been putting honey cakes and bread fresh out of the oven on the long table in the middle. Meat was being roasted in the back of the house. The celebration would last a few days. A friend of the groom, who was designated the "master of the feast," was supervising the preparations. Six jars filled with water for the purification rituals were leaning against a wall of the room next to a serving table where the sauces were arranged.

In the meantime, just over a mile away, the bride was being assisted by some friends. She was all dressed up, wearing the family jewels. When she was ready, she was accompanied in procession from her own house to the groom's house. Thus, she left her family of origin forever so as to form a new one. Together with the other women, Mary followed Susanna, remembering her own wedding thirty years before when everything had been much simpler. While she had walked that short distance to Joseph's house, her joy had mingled with the questions within her regarding the baby she was already carrying in her womb after the angel's annunciation.

The wedding procession advanced, and the entire town emptied into the street to see the bride go by, accompanying her with songs, acclamations, and blessings. The Nazarene and his friends awaited the arrival of the bride at the groom's house. Then the celebration began. Jesus sat at table next to his mother, who was seeing him again for the first time after nearly two months. They had much to tell each other, but they did not speak only among themselves. Both of them participated good humoredly in the celebration. Mary was radiant next to her son because of the authority and fascination he exerted over the people around them. But she did not forget the prophecy about the sword that would pierce her heart.

The feast continued for hours. Moments at table alternated with pauses during which they danced together. Jesus appeared to be at ease at every moment during the celebration. He was with his mother, with his first disciples, participating in the great joy of his friends. Then something happened.

When the wine ran out, the mother of Jesus said to him, "They have no wine."

There was food in abundance. But due to an unforeseen error on the part of the "master of the feast," who was a leather worker, not a wedding planner by trade, there was not enough wine. They had used it all. How could the banquet continue? Mary, with her attentive eyes, followed the servants' and the cooks' every movement. She was the first to realize that something was not right.

"Mary is attentive during the wedding feast that had already begun. She is concerned for the needs of the newlyweds. She is not isolated in herself, centered only on her own world. Rather, her love makes her be for others. She does not even seek out her friends to comment on what is happening, and to criticize the poor organization of the wedding feast. And since she is attentive, she discreetly notices that there is no wine. Wine is a sign of joy, love, and abundance."[22]

Jesus turned to her and said, "Woman, what does this have to do with me [and you]? My hour has not yet come."[23]

He had told her that it was not the time to manifest himself. The look in his eyes and the tone of his voice seemed to Mary to be identical to when, as a twelve-year-old, after they had found him among the doctors in the temple and she had reproved him, he had reminded his parents of the reason why he had come into the world—his mission. Jesus's eyes were filled with love for his mother. Despite his response, it was already evident that he would surrender to her. No other words passed between them, only looks. His mother's eyes did not turn away from her son's. She did not lower her eyes. She looked at him like a mother does when she asks a child to something, certain to be obeyed. Since that moment, for centuries and centuries, and still today, the most rapid and secure way to open the heart of Jesus has been, is, and always will be, to ask Mary to open the way.

These were the only words Mary said to the servants: "Do whatever he tells you."

Now there were six stone water jars there for the Jewish rites of purification, each holding twenty or thirty gallons. Jesus said to the servants, "Fill the jars with water." And they filled them up to the brim. And he said to them, "Now draw some out and take it to the master of the feast." So they took it. When the master of the feast tasted the water now become wine, and did not know where it came from (though the servants who had drawn the water knew), the master of the feast called the bridegroom and said to him, "Everyone serves the good wine first, and when people have drunk freely, then the poor wine. But you have kept the good wine until now."

---

22. Homily, Mass at Samanes Park, Guayaquil (Ecuador), July 6, 2015.
23. The two words in brackets have been added. This translation essentially means, "Why are you talking to me about this?" It is closer to the Greek text, as found in the ancient Coptic versions, and is attested to in Greek uses of the text in the Patristic era.

Everything happened in a few minutes without the guests even noticing anything. Mary's eyes had provoked Jesus.

"The words Mary addresses to the servants crown the wedding at Cana: 'Do whatever he tells you.' It is curious—these are her last words recounted in the Gospels. They are the legacy she hands down to us. Today too, Our Lady says to us all, 'Whatever Jesus says, do it.'"[24]

The servants distributed that superb wine, a wine that had not been created from nothing. Jesus had needed water from the purification jars, where the guests would wash their hands. In those jars, in addition to their impurity, they would "leave" their sins as well.

"In the family . . . miracles are performed with what is there, with what we are, with what is on hand. And many times, it is not the ideal. . . . There is one detail that makes us think: the new wine, that good wine, as the master of the feast at the wedding at Cana calls it, comes from the jars used for purification, that is to say, from the place where everyone had left their sin. It originates out of the worst, 'where sin abounded, grace abounded all the more.' In each of our families, and in the common family that all of us form, nothing is thrown away, nothing is useless."[25]

With this wondrous sign, known by very few, the Nazarene had begun to manifest his glory. *And his disciples believed in him.*

The celebration continued, blessed by that exquisite and abundant wine. When the wedding feast was over, Jesus went down from Cana to Capernaum for a few days.

---

24. General Audience, June 8, 2016.
25. Homily, Mass at Samanes Park, Guayaquil (Ecuador), July 6, 2015.

Return to Jerusalem and a Meeting at the Well

Year AD 28, April—May.

*Cleansing of the Temple. Visit with Nicodemus.
Water and the Samaritan Woman.*

In Capernaum, the rapport with the disciples was consolidating, and soon the call Jesus had addressed to them would become more explicit. But Passover was drawing near, and the Nazarene and his first followers set out again on the road, this time toward Jerusalem. When they arrived in the city, they found it filled with people. Many were fulfilling the prescribed pilgrimage.

Late in the morning, Jesus broke away from his followers and headed to the temple alone. Crossing the threshold leading to the outer court of God's house, he found himself before a sight that was not unusual during the feast. The air was thick with the stench of dung, because of the presence of so many animals. There were people selling sheep and doves. Money-changing booths could be found at almost every column since money bearing the emperor's image could not be used as offerings in the temple. In the distance, the strains of the sacred hymns to the Almighty could just barely be heard, while everything else had the air of a noisy village fair.

Jesus remembered coming upon this scene other times as well, on the occasion of the Passover pilgrimages, including the time when he was twelve years old and his parents had found him after three days while he was dialoguing intensely with the doctors in the temple. But this time it was different, not because there were more people and money changers doing business, or because there were more animals on sale than usual. It was different because he had now begun to reveal himself. He had begun his public life.

And making a whip of cords, he drove them all out of the temple, with the sheep and oxen. And he poured out the coins of the money-changers and overturned their tables. And he told those who sold the pigeons, "Take these things away; do not make my Father's house a house of trade."

He had made a whip in a flash and had begun to overturn all the counters and merchants' tables. His disciples, in the meantime, had entered the outer courtyard and saw him in action. He was so angry that they kept their distance, frightened.

His disciples remembered that it was written, "Zeal for your house will consume me."

Why was he acting this way? What would the consequences be for such a radical, overt action? Seeing him overturning the merchandise and whip the wooden cloth-covered frames, his disciples were surprised not so much at his unusual anger, but at his authoritativeness. Whether he was preaching quietly around a fire, speaking to larger groups with a thundering voice, approaching people with his gentle and merciful look, or throwing out of the temple those who were profaning it, he did everything with an innate, mysterious authority. His every word, every action, every look testified to a profound unity. "Truly, he speaks like no one else has ever spoken," his first followers thought to themselves, half-hidden behind the columns.

The uproar he had caused could certainly not have gone unnoticed. Some scribes, Pharisees, doctors of the law, and priests came toward him, alerted by the shouts of the merchants, the cries of the people, the noise of the frightened animals.

They approached Jesus, whip still in hand, asking, *"What sign do you show us for doing these things?" Jesus answered them, "Destroy this temple, and in three days I will raise it up." The Jews then said, "It has taken forty-six years to build this temple, and will you raise it up in three days?"*

Three days had gone by before Mary and Joseph, anxious because their young son had vanished from their sight, found him again in the temple. Now, Jesus was speaking of three days as the time it would take him to rebuild that monumental building, created with great effort and expense in little less than half a century. What did he intend to say? He was not referring to the walls, to the huge blocks of white rock that had been raised to mark off the sacred space. Nor was he speaking of the highest pinnacle that towered over the Holy City. He was speaking of himself, the temple of his body, that would know the darkness of the grave for three days before being "reconstructed" in the Resurrection. Despite the whip he was still swinging from his hands, he said those words in a voice that had now become quiet and peaceful, while looking the doctors of the temple straight into their eyes. Those who interrogated him heard him, but at that moment they did not understand. They were not able to understand.

Only three years later would his disciples remember that phrase and understand its meaning.

"These chief priests, these scribes were attached to money, to power, and had forgotten the spirit. And to justify themselves, and say that they were just, that they were good, they had exchanged the Lord's spirit of freedom with rigidity. . . ."[26]

"The people would go there on pilgrimage to ask the Lord's blessing, to make a sacrifice. Those people were exploited there! The priests did not teach them to pray, they did not give them catechesis. . . . It was a den of robbers—you pay, you enter. . . . They performed empty rituals without devotion."[27]

⁓

During those days spent in Jerusalem, many believed in Jesus, having been struck by his words, by his authority, by the signs he was performing. Among those who witnessed the cleansing of the temple was a Pharisee, one of the leaders of the Jews, a member of the Sanhedrin. His name was Nicodemus. He was fascinated, and at the same time frightened, by what he had seen that afternoon in the temple's outer court. Not having the courage to approach Jesus, he left to others the task of interrogating Jesus to understand the motivation behind his action.

Two days later, he waited for sundown. Then, after disguising himself a bit, wrapping himself in a tattered cloak that did not belong to him, he drew near the house where the Nazarene was staying, to speak to him. Because of his role, he did not feel free to go to him in broad daylight. He was afraid of being seen, and above all, of being numbered among Jesus's disciples. That would have meant calling into question the religious and social position he had fought so hard to attain. The power he had won conditioned him in some way, but not to the point of foregoing the opportunity of satisfying his desire of personally knowing this Nazarene about whom so many people were speaking—some with enthusiasm and some with concern.

"This man Nicodemus is one of the leaders of the Jews, a man with authority. He felt the need to go to Jesus. He went by night because he had to be careful, since those who went to talk with Jesus were not looked upon well. . . . He was a just Pharisee. He felt restless since he was a man who had read the prophets and knew that what Jesus was doing had been foretold by the prophets."[28]

26. Homily, Santa Marta, November 20, 2015.

27. Homily, Santa Marta, May 29, 2015.

28. Homily, Santa Marta, April 20, 2020.

Nicodemus went in. John, the youngest disciple, welcomed him at the door. He found Jesus as he was sitting awake. The faint light of a lamp dimly illuminated the small room where they were sitting, one in front of the other, on mats covering the hard earth floor. A small window let in the cold night air, along with gusts of wind every now and then.

Nicodemus got straight to the point, without wasting words. There was only one crucial question. It was the same for him as it was for the multitudes of Israel: Who was this man really? One of many teachers, or the Messiah, the One the people had been waiting for?

Nicodemus recognized in Jesus a connection with heaven. He said, *"Rabbi, we know that you are a teacher come from God, for no one can do these signs that you do unless God is with him."* Jesus's response was both elusive and unsettling.

"Truly, truly, I say to you, unless one is born again he cannot see the kingdom of God."

It was obvious that these words had nothing to do with natural birth. The Nazarene was referring to spiritual rebirth from above. But Nicodemus, who had not understood completely what he had just heard, preferred to play dumb to try to get a clearer explanation.

"How can a man be born when he is old? Can he enter a second time into his mother's womb and be born?"

Jesus answered, "Truly, truly, I say to you, unless one is born of water and the Spirit, he cannot enter the kingdom of God. That which is born of the flesh is flesh, and that which is born of the Spirit is spirit. Do not marvel that I said to you, 'You must be born again.' The wind blows where it wishes, and you hear its sound, but you do not know where it comes from or where it goes. So it is with everyone who is born of the Spirit." "Spirit" and "wind" are the same word in Hebrew.

"To be born from on high, to be born from the Spirit. This is the leap that Nicodemus's confession needs to make and does not know how. Because the Spirit is unpredictable. The definition of the Spirit Jesus gives here is interesting: 'The wind blows where it wishes, and you hear its sound, but you do not know where it comes from or where it goes. So it is with everyone who is born of the Spirit,' that is, free. A person who allows him or herself to be brought from one place to another by the Holy Spirit—this is the freedom of the Spirit. . . . Being a Christian means letting the Spirit enter within you, and lead you, lead you where he wants."[29]

Nicodemus's dialogue with Jesus had led this leading Pharisee into unknown territory.

---

29. *Ibid.*

Nicodemus said to him, "How can these things be?"

Jesus answered him, "Are you the teacher of Israel and yet you do not understand these things? Truly, truly, I say to you, we speak of what we know, and bear witness to what we have seen, but you do not receive our testimony. If I have told you earthly things and you do not believe, how can you believe if I tell you heavenly things? No one has ascended into heaven except he who descended from heaven, the Son of Man. And as Moses lifted up the serpent in the wilderness, so must the Son of Man be lifted up, that whoever believes in him may have eternal life."

There was a reference to his divinity in the words of the Nazarene as well as to the serpent lifted up by Moses that prefigured the not-too-distant future of the cross. Words that the leader of the Pharisees did not understand. Their dialogue continued for quite a while, as it had eighteen years earlier, when the twelve-year-old Jesus had taught the doctors in the temple. Suddenly, Nicodemus remembered. He, too, had witnessed that dialogue but had kept his distance, not hearing distinctly either the questions or the responses of that extremely wise young boy. Jesus read the amazement in the eyes of the leader of the Pharisees, limiting himself to repeating the words he had addressed to his parents at that time, "I must occupy myself with my Father's affairs."

Their meeting was interrupted just before dawn. Nicodemus left the same way he had come, wrapped in the ragged cloak, hiding his faced framed with his thick gray beard, his eyes red because of the sleepless night. He left the house cautiously to walk back to his own home, quickly mingling in the bustle that had already begun in the streets of Jerusalem. Almost running to release the tension he had accumulated, he reached his home in a matter of minutes, exhausted. But he could not sleep. He had gone to the Nazarene curious, restless, full of questions. On his return, he was still full of questions and even more fascinated by the Teacher, but not to the point of exposing himself completely, putting his duties and his religious authority on the line. Jesus had planted a small seed in his heart even though he was not capable of understanding everything he had heard. It would blossom little by little. For Nicodemus, too, the day would come when he would expose himself publicly, coming to Jesus's defense after he had been dragged before the Sanhedrin.

~

The days they had spent in Jerusalem for the Passover had made the Teacher known in the Holy City. What the Pharisees had heard the people saying reached his ears: *Jesus was making and baptizing more disciples than John.* In reality, Jesus was not baptizing, his disciples were. But the time had come for them to close the curtains there and return to Galilee. The temple, which he had defined as the "house of my Father," and the Jewish capital in general, would always be the stage of brief stays for the son of the carpenter of Nazareth.

To return to the places from whence he had come, he chose the route most frequented by Galileans—the one that crossed through Samaria. It led from a narrow valley closed to the north by Mount Ebal, and to the south by Mount Gerizim. Just a short distance into the valley, "Jacob's well" could be found, a well-known location from the time of the Hebrew patriarchs. Of ancient Semitic lineage, the Samaritans were considered "heretics," people to avoid. In fact, they preached that their temple on Mount Gerizim, and not the one in Jerusalem, was the legitimate place to worship God. For this reason, some preferred to avoid Samaria and its people and would travel to Galilee taking a route more to the east along the Jordan River. But there were no "heretic" souls, no one was excluded from coming into contact with Jesus, who was eager to announce the kingdom of God to everyone.

Jesus came to a town of Samaria called Sychar, near the field that Jacob had given to his son Joseph. Jacob's well was there; so Jesus, wearied as he was from his journey, was sitting beside the well. It was about the sixth hour.

He remained alone at the well because his disciples had gone into the city to procure food after the fatigue of the journey they had begun before dawn. So it was that he saw her arrive with a large terra-cotta jar on her head, her face veiled. She zigzagged along. Her steps were quick, and she kept looking around, as if she wanted to remain hidden, even though the only things around were rocks and sand.

Midday was certainly not a suitable time to leave home to fetch water. The burning sun was scorching the stones, throats burned with thirst. Usually, the women went there in the morning when it was cooler. It gave them the opportunity to meet one another and converse with their friends and acquaintances. Instead, this woman went out under the sun, on the sly, so as not to meet others along the way or subject herself to the judging looks of those who knew about her "irregular" situation.

No sooner had she raised her eyes (she was accustomed to keeping her eyes down while walking) than she became aware of him and paused for a moment. Then she decided to keep moving forward. She saw he was not someone she knew, but a stranger, so she got up her courage and approached the well. Never would she have spoken to him. Never would she have expected Jesus to speak to her. Men traditionally did not speak to women in public. In any case, observant Jews never spoke to the "heretic" Samaritans. And yet, it happened. The Teacher spoke first.

A woman from Samaria came to draw water. Jesus said to her, "Give me a drink."

He entered into dialogue with her, making it known that he was the first to need something. It was he who was thirsty. It was he who asked for something, placing himself on the same level as the woman. Their communication did not begin with a list of the Samaritan woman's sins, nor was it a revelation about the Messianic identity of the Nazarene.

The Samaritan woman said to him, "How is it that you, a Jew, ask for a drink from me, a woman of Samaria?" . . .

Jesus answered her, "If you knew the gift of God, and who it is that is saying to you, 'Give me a drink,' you would have asked him, and he would have given you living water."

Thus, he began revealing something about his origins.

The woman said to him, "Sir, you have nothing to draw water with, and the well is deep. Where do you get that living water? Are you greater than our father Jacob? He gave us the well and drank from it himself, as did his sons and his livestock."

Jesus said to her, "Everyone who drinks of this water will be thirsty again, but whoever drinks of the water that I will give him will never be thirsty again. The water that I will give him will become in him a spring of water welling up to eternal life."

The woman said to him, "Sir, give me this water, so that I will not be thirsty or have to come here to draw water."

Jesus was certainly infinitely greater than Jacob. But for now, to make her understand who he truly was, he needed to give the woman a sign. *Jesus said to her, "Go, call your husband, and come here."*

That hit her. Her heart began beating a mile a minute and her forehead was beaded with sweat. This "stranger" knew. This "stranger" knew her. In an instant, she decided not to lie. Neither did she avoid the Nazarene's eyes. There was such a light in his eyes.

The woman answered him, "I have no husband."

Jesus said to her, "You are right in saying, 'I have no husband'; for you have had five husbands, and the one you now have is not your husband. What you have said is true."

The woman said to him, "Sir, I perceive that you are a prophet. Our fathers worshiped on this mountain, but you say that in Jerusalem is the place where people ought to worship."

Jesus said to her, "Woman, believe me, the hour is coming when neither on this mountain nor in Jerusalem will you worship the Father. You worship what you do not know; we worship what we know, for salvation is from the Jews. But the hour is coming, and is now here, when the true worshipers will worship the Father in spirit and truth, for the Father is seeking such people to worship him. God is spirit, and those who worship him must worship in spirit and truth."

This dialogue under the sun was about to reach its conclusion.

"When the woman realizes that the man with whom she is speaking is a prophet, she confides her own life to him and asks him religious questions. Her thirst for affection and a full life had not been satisfied by the five husbands she had had. Instead, she had experienced disappointment and deceit. Thus, the woman was struck by the great respect Jesus had for her, and when he actually spoke to her of true faith . . . she perceived that this man could be the Messiah."[30]

Hearing him speak this way, the Samaritan woman got to the point.

The woman said to him, "I know that Messiah is coming (he who is called Christ). When he comes, he will tell us all things."

Jesus said to her, "I who speak to you am he."

He revealed himself as the Messiah, as the Christ. And he did so, conversing with a Samaritan.

It is a *"historical dialogue—it is not a parable, this happened—an encounter of Jesus with a woman, with a sinner. It is the first time in the Gospel that Jesus declares his identity. And he declares it to a sinner who had the courage to tell him the truth."*[31]

⁓

In the meantime, his disciples had returned, bringing a bag of bread they had picked up in the city. They saw him speaking with the woman and were amazed. But no one had the courage to ask him why he was doing it. It would be difficult for them to get used to the fact that Jesus went beyond their traditions, their customs, the unwritten codes of conduct regarding what could and could not be done.

30. Angelus, March 19, 2017.
31. Homily, Santa Marta, March 15, 2020.

The woman left her water jar and went away into town and said to the people, "Come, see a man who told me all that I ever did. Can this be the Christ?"

Heedless now about the looks and judgment of the people, she ran off to tell everyone that he had seen what was in her heart. Without hiding the sins she had committed, but rather through those sins, she proclaimed who Jesus was.

They went out of the town and were coming to him. . . .

Many Samaritans from that town believed in him because of the woman's testimony, "He told me all that I ever did." So when the Samaritans came to him, they asked him to stay with them, and he stayed there two days. And many more believed because of his word. They said to the woman, "It is no longer because of what you said that we believe, for we have heard for ourselves, and we know that this is indeed the Savior of the world."

She had spoken about him beginning with the truth about herself, and in so doing she piqued the curiosity of others.

The Samaritan woman did not approach her fellow villagers *"with theological arguments—as she perhaps wanted in her dialogue with Jesus: 'On this mountain, on the other mountain.' . . . She goes with her truth. And her truth is what sanctifies her, justifies her. It is her truth that the Lord uses to proclaim the Gospel.*

"We cannot be Jesus's disciples without our own truth, with who we are. . . . We cannot be disciples of Jesus with argumentation alone. . . . This woman had the courage to dialogue with Jesus because these two peoples did not communicate with each other. She had the courage to be interested in Jesus's proposal, in that water, because she knew she was thirsty. She had the courage to confess her weaknesses, her sins. What's more, she had the courage to use her own story as a guarantee that he was a prophet. . . ."

"The Lord always wants transparent dialogue, without hiding things, without dual intentions."[32]

Before the people from the city arrived to get to know him, Jesus remained for a while with his disciples next to the well. His disciples had begged him to eat. Seeing that he did not do it, that he took none of the bread they could still smell since they had just purchased it, they began to ask each other if someone had brought him some food in their absence.

---

32. *Ibid.*

Jesus said to them, "My food is to do the will of him who sent me and to accomplish his work."

~

They spent two days at Sychar. Then the little band set out again, finally heading for Galilee.

7

Fishers of Men and Healings in Galilee

Year AD 28, summer.

*The Son of the King's Official. In the Synagogue of Nazareth.
Miraculous Catch of Fish. The Possessed Man at Capernaum.
Peter's Mother-in-Law. A Leper Is Purified.
The Paralytic Let Down through the Roof. Matthew's Calling.*

As the days passed, people spoke of him more and more. Many had seen him in Jerusalem during the Passover. Now, having returned to Galilee, they were recounting what had happened in the Holy City. Jesus was going to synagogues, speaking with the leaders, performing miracles, like the one that took place at Cana not too far from the house where he had transformed water into wine. Here, one of the king's officials went to him. His son was near death, and he asked Jesus to go with him to save him. The Teacher's reaction was, *"Unless you see signs and wonders you will not believe."* He said it with a firm voice, looking the other man in the eyes, almost as if to provoke him.

The official said to him, "Sir, come down before my child dies."

Overcome with emotion by the imploring look of this now desperate father, Jesus responded, *"Go; your son will live." The man believed the word that Jesus spoke to him and went on his way.*

As he was nearing his house, his servants came to meet him to tell him that his son had been cured at the exact hour the Nazarene had said, "Your son will live." News of what had happened spread like wildfire.

Every time he performed these wondrous signs, Jesus felt his heart overflow with gratitude to his Father. It is true, he had not come primarily to perform miracles but to proclaim the kingdom of God, taking the sins of the world on himself. This he did, repeating everywhere he went, *"Repent, for the kingdom of heaven is at hand."* But he could not resist the imploring eyes of fathers and mothers who were asking him to have compassion on their children.

~

Having returned home to Nazareth for several days, he went as usual one Sabbath to the small synagogue he had frequented as a child and where Joseph had had him educated.

He stood up to read. And the scroll of the prophet Isaiah was given to him. He unrolled the scroll and found the place where it was written,

> *"The Spirit of the Lord is upon me,*
> *because he has anointed me*
> *to proclaim good news to the poor.*
> *He has sent me to proclaim liberty to the captives*
> *and recovery of sight to the blind,*
> *to set at liberty those who are oppressed,*
> *to proclaim the year of the Lord's favor."*

And he rolled up the scroll and gave it back to the attendant and sat down, remaining silent. *And the eyes of all in the synagogue were fixed on him.* So he began to speak, attributing the prophecy to himself:

"Today this Scripture has been fulfilled in your hearing."

"Let us imagine ourselves too entering the synagogue of Nazareth, the village where Jesus grew up until he was about thirty years old. What happens is an important event, which delineates Jesus's mission. . . . He addresses the Good News to everyone, excluding no one, favoring instead those who are most distant, the suffering, the sick, those cast out by society. . . . In Jesus's time these people were probably not at the center of the community of faith."[33]

What was the reaction to these words the Nazarene had spoken? *And all spoke well of him and marveled at the gracious words that were coming from his mouth. And they said, "Is not this Joseph's son?"*

His authority, the depth of his gaze, his capacity to read the soul of whoever was in front of him, the signs he was performing. . . . It was so evident, so completely evident. But it was neither that easy nor obvious to surrender to that evidence, even though he spoke differently than the scribes. With such few words, Jesus knew how to derive such new things from the Scriptures, offering authentic treasures for everyone's life. He was not wearily parroting words from tradition but opening horizons. He was shaking deeply rooted and hardened certainties, while at the same time awakening great hope in many

---

33. Angelus, January 24, 2016.

hearts. But there, in the homes of that small village where he had grown up, the objection easily resurfaced: He is Joseph's son. How can he pretend to be the Messiah we are waiting for?

Jesus noticed the reserve in their eyes even before they began murmuring the name of his earthly father and guardian. With a calm voice, looking them in the eye, he began to cite examples taken from Scripture.

"No prophet is acceptable in his hometown. But in truth, I tell you, there were many widows in Israel in the days of Elijah, when the heavens were shut up three years and six months, and a great famine came over all the land, and Elijah was sent to none of them but only to Zarephath, in the land of Sidon, to a woman who was a widow. And there were many lepers in Israel in the time of the prophet Elisha, and none of them was cleansed, but only Naaman the Syrian."

He had come for everyone, not only for Israel. He had come for everyone, knowing that his own people would not accept him. A ripple of indignation seized those present, then exploded.

They rose up and drove him out of the town and brought him to the brow of the hill on which their town was built, so that they could throw him down the cliff. But passing through their midst, he went away.

No one had the courage to kill him. No one had the courage to stop him. Nazareth, little Nazareth, where someone had once looked with disapproval on his mother, who had become pregnant before going to live with her betrothed spouse; Nazareth, which had seen him carefree at play with the other children, then as he grew up, taking Joseph's place in the workshop, working with wood and stone; that Nazareth, home to his former playmates, now looked at him hostilely.

~

The umbilical cord connecting him to Nazareth was now broken. *And he went down to Capernaum*, where he would live near the sea.

Everything was simpler in Capernaum. The low rock and brick houses were piled one on top of the other until they reached the banks of the Sea of Galilee. Some called it a "sea" because it was large, deep, and filled with fish. It was really a lake, the Lake of Gennesaret. There was a flood of people in the narrow and unpaved alleys—fishermen and merchants selling their products, money changers, tax collectors, Roman soldiers, beggars, groups of noisy children engrossed in their games. The smell of fish mixed with the smell of spices and the aroma of tasty bread. It was very different from Jerusalem, where the presence of the religious authorities and the occupying Romans was perceived in a much more all-encompassing way. Here, a variety of humanity from diverse ethnicities and languages made this crossroad a "globalized" center.

It was also very different from Nazareth, where he would have remained only "the son of Joseph" to everyone. Capernaum was a hinterland, where Asia and Europe connected along the "way of the sea" that crossed through it. In the upper part of the city were the customs and tax-revenue offices. The lower part was where the fishermen were, along with everyone working in the fishing industry, day laborers, those who lived by their wits, the poor.

Here, on the banks of the great lake, everything appeared less problematic, including the meetings with Jesus that took place during those long summer days both in the streets and in the homes of his friends who had welcomed him.

Simon Peter, his brother Andrew, and the others who had accompanied Jesus to Jerusalem, had continued to carry out their own work in their small fishing business. Until that Thursday morning. They had just come back from an uneventful night—hours and hours of casting their nets, hauling in little or nothing. Exhausted after the sleepless and difficult night, and discouraged by the poor results, they had begun to wash their nets after mooring the two boats along the bank.

Jesus arrived on the shore, accompanied by a throng of people who wanted to listen to his word. He looked at the two brothers, his friends, and *getting into one of the boats, which was Simon's, he asked him to put out a little from the land. And he sat down and taught the people from the boat.*

And when he had finished speaking, he said to Simon, "Put out into the deep and let down your nets for a catch." And Simon answered, "Master, we toiled all night and took nothing! But at your word I will let down the nets." And when they had done this, they enclosed a large number of fish, and their nets were breaking.

They went out a short distance from the shore. The sea that had just been very stingy with them was now suddenly populated with fish that seemed to be in competition with each other to end up in their nets. *They signaled to their partners in the other boat to come and help them. And they came and filled both the boats, so that they began to sink.*

They could not recall such a large catch of fish. On seeing this, Simon Peter, who had chosen to bet on the generosity of the Teacher's word despite his exhaustion going out into the deep again, *fell down at Jesus's knees, saying, "Depart from me, for I am a sinful man, O Lord." For he and all who were with him were astonished at the catch of fish that they had taken, and so also were*

James and John, sons of Zebedee, who were partners with Simon. And Jesus said to Simon, "Do not be afraid; from now on you will be catching men." And when they had brought their boats to land, they left everything and followed him.

His clothing dirty, his forehead bathed in sweat, Peter did not completely understand these words. What did it mean that they would become "catchers of men?" The other word Jesus spoke was comforting. The Teacher had said, "Do not be afraid." Peter felt understood. That reassurance, accompanied by a paternal smile, would remain etched in his memory throughout his entire life.

"The disciples were fishermen. Jesus had called them right as they were at work. Andrew and Peter were working with their nets. They left their nets and followed Jesus. The same with John and James. They left their father and the others who worked with them, and followed Jesus. The call came precisely in their work as fishermen."[34]

~

The following Sabbath, Jesus went into the synagogue in Capernaum with his disciples. Jesus's eyes immediately met the eyes of a young, handsome man possessed by a demon, eyes that betrayed immense suffering. When the spirit living in him prevailed, his features would change, assuming the ferocious characteristics of a beast. He began to get agitated. The Nazarene did not move his eyes off him. The possessed man *cried out with a loud voice: "Ha! What have you to do with us, Jesus of Nazareth? Have you come to destroy us? I know who you are—the Holy One of God."*

The powers of evil knew well who Jesus was and why he had come to earth. *Jesus rebuked him, saying, "Be silent and come out of him!" And when the demon had thrown him down in their midst, he came out of him, having done him no harm.* A spasm contorted him—everyone thought it lasted too long—until he was freed. *And they were all amazed and said to one another, "What is this word? For with authority and power he commands the unclean spirits, and they come out!" And reports about him went out into every place in the surrounding region.*

It was not easy for him to continue walking the streets of Capernaum without people coming up to him bringing the sick and others who were disturbed or possessed by demons. Everyone wanted to ask him something, but they also wanted to see him speak, to listen to his word, even if they could perceive only a few phrases, even though they could not understand that well what he was saying.

---

34. Homily, Santa Marta, April 17, 2020.

~

Jesus took refuge in Peter's house, to spend a few hours away from the sun and to refresh himself. He saw the look of palpable concern on the faces of Peter's relatives. Seraphina, Peter's mother-in-law, the real supporting pillar of this family of fisherman and an exceptional cook as well, *was ill with a high fever, and they appealed to him on her behalf.* Immediately, Jesus headed toward the room in the back of the house and found the tall, stout woman curled up on the floor on a straw mattress. She was trembling and delirious, almost unaware of what was happening. *He stood over her and rebuked the fever, and it left her, and immediately she rose and began to serve them.*

One instant, she seemed to be at death's door. The next instant, Seraphina was on her feet helping her daughter prepare lunch for Jesus and his friends. She did not stop thanking the Teacher for curing her. Once again, Peter was left without words. An exchange of glances with Jesus was all that was necessary to express his gratitude. That woman, who daily sacrificed herself for others, was truly important for her family. Peter's wife, a slender woman with long dark hair, who had inherited her determination and strength of soul from her mother rather than her physical characteristics, drew near to Jesus as well to whisper her thanks, her eyes fixed on the ground, almost as if she wanted to apologize for that household healing "stolen" from the Nazarene before he could sit down to eat.

~

Meanwhile, news was spreading. People were coming in search of him not only from the city and surrounding areas but also from Jerusalem and the Decapolis. The Teacher tried to welcome everyone. Whenever he left the house, he would impose hands on the sick and the possessed, healing them.

"Jesus's day in Capernaum begins with the healing of Peter's mother-in-law and ends with the scene of townspeople gathered outside the house where he was staying to bring him all who were sick. Marked by physical suffering and spiritual misery, the crowd comprises, so to speak, 'the lively environment' in which Jesus accomplishes his mission made up of healing and comforting words and actions. Jesus had not come to bring salvation in a laboratory. He does not preach from a laboratory, detached from the people. He is in the midst of the crowd! In the midst of the people! Just think that most of Jesus's public life took place on the streets, among the people, to preach the Gospel, to heal physical and spiritual wounds." [35]

---

35. Angelus, February 4, 2018.

The crowd was uncontrollable at this point, and besieged him at every step, stopping to wait for him at the door of the houses he would go into. Jesus said to his disciples that they would set out again on the road to visit other places. And to his friends who tried to keep him in Capernaum, he replied, *"I must preach the good news of the kingdom of God to the other towns as well; for I was sent for this purpose."*

~

During one of their journeys, at the first light of dawn, while he was walking with his disciples toward a city, a leper came up to meet him. He had violated the rules. The Mosaic law prohibited lepers from going near those who were healthy. They were considered impure. Clad with filthy rags, the leper's disfigured body gave off a bad odor. Leaning on a sturdy stick taller than he was, he could hardly walk. Before contracting leprosy, he had been a potter in Sepphoris but had been forced to abandon everything to live in isolation. Leprosy was a social death, a curse. His wife and children would take turns bringing him something to eat. There were days, however, when they themselves struggled to put the bare minimum on the table for themselves to eat. This is why the man, in the grip of desperation, had mustered up the courage to violate the law. That Nazarene, whom he had heard about from some wayfarers, was his last resort. He implored Jesus, *and kneeling said to him, "If you will, you can make me clean."*

This time, too, Jesus allowed himself to be touched by the cry of that wounded person. He did not keep his distance, but he, too, broke the conventions and traditions. Approaching the leper, he entered into contact with the disfigured man in front of him. *Moved with pity, he stretched out his hand and touched him and said to him, "I will; be clean." And immediately the leprosy left him, and he was made clean.*

After freeing him from leprosy, Jesus warned him and asked him to fulfill what was prescribed by the law for his healing. *"See that you say nothing to anyone, but go, show yourself to the priest and offer for your cleansing what Moses commanded, for a proof to them."* But he did not do this. Rather, *he went out and began to talk freely about it, and to spread the news, so that Jesus could no longer openly enter a town, but was out in desolate places, and people were coming to him from every quarter.*

"Compassion involves. It comes from the heart and involves and leads you to do something. Compassion is suffering with, taking the other person's suffering on yourself to resolve it, to heal it. This is Jesus's mission. Jesus did not come to preach *the law and then go away. Jesus came in compassion, that is, to suffer with and for us and to give his own life."* [36]

He returned once again to Capernaum, and news of the works he had accomplished preceded him. One afternoon, while the sun was still high and a hot wind gripped the entire city, Jesus was in the house of Amos, one of Andrew's friends. He was a merchant who purchased sizable quantities of fish from the two brothers, covering it in salt and selling it to the Romans. His house on the outskirts of Capernaum had a large central room, open on one side, and was covered with a tiled roof. The Teacher was sitting there teaching. In the audience, some *Pharisees and teachers of the law were sitting there, who had come from every village of Galilee and Judea and from Jerusalem. And the power of the Lord was with him to heal. And behold, some men were bringing on a bed a man who was paralyzed, and they were seeking to bring him in and lay him before Jesus.*

There were so many people in front of the open side that it was not possible to get through. So, *finding no way to bring him in, because of the crowd, they went up on the roof and let him down with his bed through the tiles into the midst before Jesus.* They had climbed up the stone stairs. It was not difficult. Little effort was needed to open a hole in the roof. The Nazarene stopped speaking, silently taking in the scene. He was struck by the creative proactiveness of the men.

And when he saw their faith, he said, "Man, your sins are forgiven you." The paralytic remained speechless, continuing to look at Jesus. His friends had worked hard to bring him here, and they expected that he would be healed. The Teacher first healed his soul, uttering words that certainly had not passed unnoticed.

Hearing Jesus make that statement, the scribes and Pharisees looked at one another in utter shock. Then they began to talk among themselves, darting strange glances at Jesus. They were saying, *"Who is this who speaks blasphemies? Who can forgive sins but God alone?"*

Expecting that reaction, Jesus responded, *"Why do you question in your hearts? Which is easier, to say, 'Your sins are forgiven you,' or to say, 'Rise and walk'? But that you may know that the Son of Man has authority on earth to forgive sins"*—he said to the man who was paralyzed—*"I say to you, rise, pick up your bed and go home."*

---

36. Homily, Santa Marta, January 16, 2020.

It was just a matter of seconds. The man's contorted limbs began to stretch as previously non-existent muscles began to take on form again. For the first time, the Teacher had performed a miracle explaining why he was doing it. He had come to heal souls, to save souls, to free them from all the many paralyses that afflict them. This physical healing was just a sign, a confirmation of this.

~

And immediately he rose up before them and picked up what he had been lying on and went home, glorifying God. And amazement seized them all, and they glorified God and were filled with awe, saying, "We have seen extraordinary things today."

The crowd separated and let the healed paralytic pass through. These were the same people who, just a little while before, had not made space for the small group trying to carry him to Jesus. Many of them knew that man and his family. He had remained immobile in his bed for years due to an illness that had struck him when he was still young. His wife, informed about what had happened by some teens who had run to her house, ran to meet her husband and threw her arms around him.

"The people who followed Jesus took risks . . . they took risks to meet Jesus, to find what they wanted. Unable to bring the paralytic in front of Jesus because of the crowd, they removed the roof above him and, after making an opening, lowered the bed. These men took a risk when they made the hole in the roof—they risked the owner of the house suing them, taking them before the judge who would make them pay. They took a risk, but they wanted to go to Jesus. . . . Following Jesus is not easy but it is beautiful, and there are always risks, and many times it becomes ridiculous. But you find something important—your sins are forgiven. . . . Behind that grace that we ask for—health or the resolution of a problem, or whatever—is the desire that our soul be healed, to be forgiven."[37]

~

Jesus disappeared for two days after that healing, taking refuge not far from Capernaum to pray. He left the house under cover of night to avoid the crowd. When he returned to the city, it was Thursday morning. As he had done other times, he passed in front of the tax collectors' booths. These were short, square structures made of white stone, different from the stone made of tufa, used for the other dwellings surrounding them. This place, so highly hated by the

---

37. Homily, Santa Marta, January 13, 2017.

Israelites, symbolized the power of the occupiers under the standard of Rome. Two soldiers guarded the tax collectors. Everyone looked at tax collectors with disgust. They were considered collaborators, impure, traitors to the Jewish people's cause for independence.

In the preceding weeks, Jesus's eyes had rested on one of them several times—a stout, handsome young man, skillful and quick at counting money. His eyes had never crossed Jesus's gaze. Matthew Levi had heard about the Teacher who was healing the sick and freeing the possessed. But he had never left his workplace to go and listen to Jesus. This time, Jesus took the initiative, looked at Matthew, and called him as he was hunched over counting and dividing dozens of coins. *He saw Levi the son of Alphaeus sitting at the tax booth, and he said to him, "Follow me." And he rose and followed him.*

It was because of the power of Jesus's gaze more than the abruptness of his invitation that Matthew Levi, who felt that he was being looked on and loved like never before in his life, found it natural to get up and follow him, turning his back on the tax collector's booth, that hated place where even Peter and Andrew had gone to pay their taxes. His friends' faces betrayed a mixture of shock and bewilderment, perhaps because tax collector Matthew Levi—the sinner Matthew Levi—had been "caught" unexpectedly, and after Jesus's own style of breaking the traditions, customs, social mores, and unwritten rules of society.

To be called according to Jesus's style meant not only welcoming an invitation to follow him, but to welcome him, to sit down to eat with him. That day the Nazarene went to eat in the house of a tax collector. In front of everyone, his call to that young man bent over counting money was not everything. Jesus had also given Matthew the courage to invite him to dinner. In fact, Matthew also wanted his friends, his not-all-that-presentable daily dinner companions, to meet the gaze of the Teacher so they could speak with him. *Matthew Levi made him a great feast in his house, and there was a large company of tax collectors and others reclining at table with them. And the Pharisees and their scribes grumbled at his disciples, saying, "Why do you eat and drink with tax collectors and sinners?" And Jesus answered them, "Those who are well have no need of a physician, but those who are sick. I have not come to call the righteous but sinners to repentance."*

He had not come for the healthy, for the righteous, but for the sick, for sinners—for everyone. And he had come especially for those sinners who would never have thought of such a concrete and powerful possibility of redemption, of mercy, of forgiveness, of acceptance. No one was unworthy or rejected from eating with him. Nobody was tossed aside, he considered no one beneath him. Instead, his merciful gaze sought those who did not feel "like they had it all together," those who did not feel "all right."

"Jesus looked at him. What powerful love was in Jesus's look to have moved Matthew like it did! What power must have been in his eyes to make him get up! . . . Jesus stopped. He did not continue quickly on by. He looked at Matthew without being in a hurry, he looked on him with peace. He looked at him with merciful eyes. He looked at him as no one had ever looked at him before. And that look opened Matthew's heart, it set him free, it healed him, it gave him hope, a new life. . . . Even if we dare not raise our eyes to the Lord, he always looks at us first. This is our personal story. Like that of so many other people, each one of us can say: I, too, am a sinner, on whom Jesus's eyes have rested. . . . His love precedes us, his look anticipates our needs. He knows how to see beyond appearances, beyond sin, beyond failures or unworthiness."[38]

～

The group of disciples and followers was consolidating. They had begun to divide the tasks, even while being aware of the unpredictability of their Teacher, so different from the messiah all of Israel was waiting for, and the many political expectations the people had projected onto this figure. One night, Jesus went off by himself to pray. Then, when it was day, *he called his disciples and chose from them twelve, whom he named apostles: Simon, whom he named Peter, and Andrew his brother, and James and John, and Philip, and Bartholomew, and Matthew, and Thomas, and James the son of Alphaeus, and Simon who was called the Zealot, and Judas the son of James, and Judas Iscariot.* The latter was a short, quick young man. He had already been chosen a short time before to manage the group's money and nurtured tremendous hope in Jesus, convinced that the Teacher would be made a leader of the people of Israel.

Peter and Andrew remembered Jesus's words that day on the banks of the Sea of Galilee, and his promise to make them "catchers of men." They still did not know what this would mean in their lives that had been turned upside down because of their meeting with him. This understanding would come little by little as they remained in his company, exchanging looks with him, listening to his word, sharing every instant of their lives with him.

---

38. Homily of the Mass at the Plaza de la Revolución, Holguín (Cuba), September 21, 2015.

8

"Blessed . . . Blessed . . ." The Kingdom of God That Raises Up the Lowly

Year AD 28, August.

The Sermon on the Mount. The Our Father, a Simple Prayer.

The crowd was following him because they were looking for miracles. The poorest were going to him, those who lived only on alms, the outcasts, those who did not fit in, the ones who felt like everything was going wrong. Some had sick ones at home. There were even some evildoers and others who were deemed unrespectable in public. They recognized in the Teacher an authority never seen before, so different from so many self-proclaimed "messiahs."

His eyes struck them even before his words. It was striking the way he looked at you, making you feel welcome, understood, loved, while at the same time, laying bare the truth of life, of sin, of human misery. Many followed him, staying at a distance, able to catch only a few words. But then they would run into someone who had been forgiven and healed. The personal testimony of those who had been healed in body and spirit piqued their interest, their curiosity, their desire to meet the Nazarene. In those days, in the daily hustle and bustle of the cities of Galilee, something new had erupted; new hope had dawned.

~

Who was Jesus of Nazareth really? The Twelve, his apostles, followed him wherever he went, making sure he did not lack food or a roof to sleep under. His disciples, a few dozen in number, tried to stay with him when he went out, when he encountered the people, when he preached. No one was yet able to say who he really was, or where his power came from. They had decided to stake everything, their entire lives, on that attraction he held over them. It was beautiful to be with him, to watch him speak, to listen to him comment on the Scriptures in such an authentic but, at the same time, new way, capable of breaking down prejudices, conventions, and above all, hypocrisy.

That day, as he looked at them with eyes filled with love, compassion, friendship, Jesus understood that the moment had finally arrived to say more, to proclaim the kingdom of God to everyone, not only to his followers. So after calling the Twelve and spending some time with them, he decided to speak to the crowd that was waiting for him.

~

It was morning. The sun was already shining high, casting brilliant reflections on the waters of the Sea of Galilee on that very calm summer day. It was not that hot. All of the nature surrounding them seemed predisposed to welcome what he was about to say. Behind them was the "mount," a green hill. A light breeze coming down from the top of the mount helped carry his words to those farther away. In front of him was an impressive expanse of people who had arrived not only from Capernaum and other cities in Galilee, but also from Jerusalem, Sidon, and Tyre.

They were standing in groups seeking refuge under the shade of some of the taller bushes. Some were dressed only in rags; others seemed to be in better condition. Their faces spoke louder than their tunics, their rags, their knapsacks—each face manifested a question, an unspoken anguish, a doubt, some pain, a desire, restlessness, a wound. None of them would have considered themselves satisfied or at peace. These were the crowds that always succeeded in soliciting Jesus's compassion, a visceral compassion that was contemporaneously divine and human. Seeing him arrive with his eyes fixed on them, many would rise to their feet; others tried to get closer to him; still others raised their hands in greeting. Mothers would lift up the smallest children so he might look at them, bless them. For many of these women, their little children were everything they had. Jesus rested his eyes on them, knowing how they would grow up, who they would become, how their lives would turn out. He prayed to his Father for each of these children so that the gates of heaven might be open to them.

After looking at the crowd a long time, he signaled to everyone to sit down so they could listen better. Then he began to shout that word, repeating it many times: "Blessed . . . blessed . . . blessed." The people who were the farthest from him, on the edge, could distinguish only that word, but they understood that the Teacher was speaking about being happy, about a happiness for them. Jesus said:

"Blessed are the poor in spirit, for theirs is the kingdom of heaven.

Blessed are those who mourn, for they shall be comforted.

Blessed are the meek, for they shall inherit the earth.

Blessed are those who hunger and thirst for righteousness, for they shall be satisfied.

Blessed are the merciful, for they shall receive mercy.

Blessed are the pure in heart, for they shall see God.

Blessed are the peacemakers, for they shall be called sons of God.

Blessed are those who are persecuted for righteousness' sake, for theirs is the kingdom of heaven.

Blessed are you when others revile you and persecute you and utter all kinds of evil against you falsely on my account. Rejoice and be glad, for your reward is great in heaven, for so they persecuted the prophets who were before you."

A surreal silence enveloped that hill, from the banks of the lake to its summit. Even the sobbing and crying of the little ones had ceased. To the right of the plateau, under cover of an olive tree, was a woman who had been divorced by her husband when she became pregnant with his child. Rebecca was her name. She was still extremely beautiful despite the hardships she had been forced to live since then. Ashamed, she kept her eyes downcast, not having the courage to raise them toward Jesus, not even from afar, almost afraid of meeting his gaze. Before she could hold him back, her son Yehoshua ran up to get closer to the Nazarene. He wanted to hear Jesus better. As the Teacher began to speak, he sat down just beside his feet. Yehoshua was not able to touch them only because Peter grabbed him, reaching out his hand as if to catch a fish that had jumped out of the water, and held Yehoshua next to him.

Yehoshua was six years old, with two bright eyes and chestnut curls filled with sand and sweat. The little one was impressed by only a few of Jesus's words—"Blessed are those who mourn, for they shall be comforted." "Those who mourn," like his mother who had nothing to live on and spent her days in search of a scrap of food in exchange for some menial service, ashamed because of her condition as a repudiated wife. Before Peter could stop him, the little one got up all of a sudden and ran to his mother. Jesus followed him out of the corner of his eye. Yes, he had said that also for him, for that child; even for her, for that mother. . . .

"Mamma, *Imma . . .*" the little one went up to her saying, "Even you are blessed. Why are you crying? He's the one who said it! He said you'll be comforted!"

Her tears became joy; her poverty, wealth. The kingdom was promised to the losers, the meek, the merciful, the hungry, those with broken and wounded hearts, the outcasts, the persecuted, the castaways, those deemed unworthy of presenting themselves in public.

Those words babbled by her son were a promise, redemption, hope. "There is really nothing wrong with me," Rebecca thought. "I'm not cursed," she repeated, trying to hold onto Jesus's words that were completely one with his look of mercy. Only by contemplating that look did his words take on their liberating and revolutionary meaning. Only by fixing her gaze on the face of the Nazarene did she understand that his teaching was not an umpteenth doctrine, a new exegesis of Scripture. Nor was it a prophecy. It was true. The Beatitudes promised something for the future. But she could already sense consolation because Jesus had looked at her. Feeling loved and understood like she had never felt until that moment in her troubled life, Rebecca finally felt the courage to lift up her eyes to contemplate the Teacher who was speaking. He was speaking for her too, just for her.

"Jesus begins to proclaim his way of happiness with a paradoxical proclamation—'Blessed are the poor in spirit, for theirs is the kingdom of heaven.' Poverty is a surprising path and a strange condition for beatitude. . . . What does it mean to be poor in spirit? . . . They are the ones who are and who feel poor, like beggars, in their inmost being. Jesus proclaims them blessed because the kingdom of Heaven belongs to them. How many times have we been told the opposite! You have to be something in life, be someone. . . . Loneliness and unhappiness stem from this—if I have to be 'someone,' I am in competition with others and I live worrying excessively about my ego. If I do not accept that I am poor, I hate everything that reminds me of my frailty. . . . The kingdom of God belongs to the poor in spirit. . . . Those who truly reign, are those who know how to love what is truly good more than themselves."[39]

Jesus began to speak again, inviting everyone listening to be *salt of the earth* and *light of the world*. Then he told them what he had come to do. Many were thinking that this original "Rabbi," the son of the carpenter of Nazareth, had come to institute a new law. They had seen him challenging the Pharisees and the doctors; they had heard how he responded to their subtle objections; they had at times observed how he kept silent so as not to fall into the insidious dialectical "traps" of those who had made the interpretation of the word of

---

39. General Audience, February 5, 2020.

God nothing more than a job and were imposing unnecessary burdens on the shoulders of the people.

"Do not think that I have come to abolish the Law or the Prophets," Jesus clarified. *"I have not come to abolish them but to fulfill them. For truly, I say to you, until heaven and earth pass away, not an iota, not a dot, will pass from the Law until all is accomplished. Therefore, whoever relaxes one of the least of these commandments and teaches others to do the same will be called least in the kingdom of heaven."*

He had not come to abolish but to fulfill or, better, to reveal the authenticity of God's will in all its purity. And so, while the crowd hung on his words, Jesus began to teach again, stretching his eyes out on the horizon over the lake that, because of a play of light, had ended up blending in with the heavens Never before this moment had heaven and earth seemed to be united in an embrace.

Jesus began to cite the commandments, revealing their origin. *"You have heard that it was said to those of old, 'You shall not murder; and whoever murders will be liable to judgment.' But I say to you that everyone who is angry with his brother will be liable to judgment."*

So not only physical killing, killing the body, but also the moral type, the one caused by anger, by gossip, by calumny—to the point that being reconciled with one's brothers and sisters became the prerequisite for approaching God.

"So if you are offering your gift at the altar and there remember that your brother has something against you, leave your gift there before the altar and go. First be reconciled to your brother, and then come and offer your gift."

～

He also said some pretty exacting words about adultery, calling for purity of heart.

"You have heard that it was said, 'You shall not commit adultery.' But I say to you that everyone who looks at a woman with lustful intent has already committed adultery with her in his heart. . . . It was also said, 'Whoever divorces his wife, let him give her a certificate of divorce.' But I say to you that everyone who divorces his wife, except on the ground of sexual immorality, makes her commit adultery, and whoever marries a divorced woman commits adultery."

Only a few fragments of his words reached Rebecca, who was being hugged by little Yehoshua. This time, too, she understood he was speaking to her and for her, that he was speaking of her, a woman and mother who had been divorced through no fault of her own.

As Jesus's words continued to flow, the most shocking message was the one in which he invited them to love not only their friends and people who were good to them but also their enemies.

"You have heard that it was said, 'An eye for an eye and a tooth for a tooth.' But I say to you, Do not resist the one who is evil. But if anyone slaps you on the right cheek, turn to him the other also. And if anyone would sue you and take your tunic, let him have your cloak as well. And if anyone forces you to go one mile, go with him two miles. Give to the one who begs from you, and do not refuse the one who would borrow from you.

"You have heard that it was said, 'You shall love your neighbor and hate your enemy.' But I say to you, Love your enemies and pray for those who persecute you, so that you may be sons of your Father who is in heaven. For he makes his sun rise on the evil and on the good, and sends rain on the just and on the unjust. For if you love those who love you, what reward do you have? Do not even the tax collectors do the same? And if you greet only your brothers, what more are you doing than others? Do not even the Gentiles do the same? You therefore must be perfect, as your heavenly Father is perfect."

"It was said . . . But I say to you . . ." These demanding words overturned everything! How was it possible to love enemies, adversaries, opponents?

The apostle who was smiling the most was Matthew Levi, who could not take his eyes off Jesus even for an instant. For so long he had been accustomed to calculating, to exacting every last coin, dividing the world between friends and enemies. . . . For so long his eyes had looked down only on piles of money, on accounting sheets.

Now, the look on the Teacher's face, along with his words, was resounding in him—a consequence of the call he had received as he sat in the tax collector's booth. Pure gift was this radically different way of looking at others, at things, at the world. A superabundance of love was the key to it all. A revolution otherwise unimaginable except in the company of that man.

∽

Through his message, Jesus was asking the people who had come to listen to him to move from the rule written to their hearts toward the norms of their consciences, from clinging to exterior observance to clinging to an interior, higher good.

"Jesus does not give importance simply to disciplinary observance and exterior conduct. He goes to the law's roots, focusing first and foremost on the intention, and so, on the human heart, from which our good and bad actions originate."[40]

Everyone perceived how liberating and unheard of his teaching was. It would have sounded absurd on anyone else's lips, especially those of the professional lawyers, whose speeches hardly moved the people who longed for liberation. His teaching, instead, poured out of him so naturally. Jesus did not need to enhance his discourses, backing himself up continually with Scripture passages or citing the law. He was renewing its interpretation, finally making it authentic, just as it had come out of his Father's mouth. It was not easy to accept the teaching to love the people who hate you, to pray for those who persecute you.

Every one of the people intent on listening to him carried ancient incrustations in their hearts, knots of enmity, bleeding wounds that had never closed. How could someone welcome such a precise, specific, and disturbing invitation, this logic "from another world?" And yet, no one got up to go away. Everyone sensed a deep liberation. To not have enemies lightened their hearts suddenly, it made them happier. The Commandments ceased to be inscriptions on stone, heavy stones of condemnation for those who were unable to observe them. The people were becoming a "mirror image" of Jesus's face.

"Looking at Christ we see beauty, goodness, truth. . . . In this way we better discover why the Lord Jesus did not come to abolish the law but to fulfill it, to develop it. And while the law according to the flesh was a series of prescriptions and prohibitions, according to the Spirit this same law becomes life, because it is no longer a rule but the very flesh of Christ who loves us, seeks us out, forgives us, consoles us, and in his Body recreates communion with the Father, lost through the disobedience of sin. In Christ, and in him alone, the Decalogue ceases to be condemnation and becomes the authentic truth of human life."[41]

⁓

---

40. Angelus, February 16, 2014.
41. General Audience, November 28, 2018.

Jesus started speaking and once again surprised everyone, inviting the people to be authentic, not to show off, and not to seek public recognition even for good deeds done.

"*When you give to the needy, sound no trumpet before you, as the hypocrites do in the synagogues and in the streets, that they may be praised by others. Truly, I say to you, they have received their reward. But when you give to the needy, do not let your left hand know what your right hand is doing, so that your giving may be in secret. And your Father who sees in secret will reward you.*

"*And when you pray, you must not be like the hypocrites. For they love to stand and pray in the synagogues and at the street corners, that they may be seen by others. Truly, I say to you, they have received their reward. But when you pray, go into your room and shut the door and pray to your Father who is in secret. And your Father who sees in secret will reward you.*"

∽

"Pray to your Father. . . ." Using what words? Jesus advised not to waste words like the pagans, who *"think that they will be heard for their many words."* He said, *"Your Father knows what you need before you ask him"* and taught them to pray like this:

> "*Our Father in heaven,*
> *hallowed be your name.*
> *Your kingdom come,*
> *your will be done,*
> *on earth as it is in heaven.*
> *Give us this day our daily bread,*
> *and forgive us our debts,*
> *as we also have forgiven our debtors.*
> *And lead us not into temptation,*
> *but deliver us from evil.*"

"It's a simple prayer, the prayer of a beggar," Peter thought at that moment, struck by the phrase that was an invitation to ask God to forgive his "debts" so he would be able to do the same with his brothers. The apostles and disciples were looking at each other, filled with astonishment by the simplicity and extraordinary power of this new prayer Jesus had pronounced while his eyes were lifted beyond the horizon. God's forgiveness took into account the forgiveness that people offer each other.

"For if you forgive others their trespasses," the Teacher continued, *"your heavenly Father will also forgive you, but if you do not forgive others their trespasses, neither will your Father forgive your trespasses."*

It was the mercy people were experiencing when they came into contact with the man who was speaking that made this new way of interacting possible. "I could never do it on my own," Simon Peter said to himself. "But with you, even this seems possible!"

Jesus continued to speak. Regarding fasting and penance, his invitation was not to make oneself seen, not to focus on the exterior.

"And when you fast, do not look gloomy like the hypocrites, for they disfigure their faces that their fasting may be seen by others. Truly, I say to you, they have received their reward. But when you fast, anoint your head and wash your face, that your fasting may not be seen by others but by your Father who is in secret. And your Father who sees in secret will reward you."

~

His words were an invitation to go to what was essential, to what matters, to what can last. He said, *"Do not lay up for yourselves treasures on earth, where moth and rust destroy and where thieves break in and steal, but lay up for yourselves treasures in heaven, where neither moth nor rust destroys and where thieves do not break in and steal. For where your treasure is, there your heart will be also."*

Among the apostles, Matthew was the one who was more capable of understanding the breadth of the message. He had been dealing a long time with the treasures consumed by rust. . . . The Nazarene's words were liberating for all the others too. Very few of those present belonged to the category of those who amassed wealth, although what Jesus meant to say was not connected solely to amounts of money or possessions, but also to being attached to those possessions that become a "treasure" capable of robbing the heart, of becoming the center of life.

The Teacher continued, *"You cannot serve God and money. Therefore, I tell you, do not be anxious about your life, what you will eat or what you will drink, nor about your body, what you will put on. Is not life more than food, and the body more than clothing? Look at the birds of the air: they neither sow nor reap nor gather into barns, and yet your heavenly Father feeds them. Are you not of more value than they? And which of you by being anxious can add a single hour to his span of life?"*

For some who were listening, this was not easy to understand, especially for those who were used to getting up in the morning without knowing if they would find something to eat for themselves or their own children during the day. Yet even these people sensed the truth in the words they had just heard. They no longer felt like strangers to one another. Everyone was looking with new eyes at the person sitting next to them, regardless of social standing. Even a Roman who was in the employ of the army, recognizable by his short garb and shoes, was greeted with smiles. The more fortunate shared what they had, opening their pouches and knapsacks.

But Jesus had not yet finished what he wanted to proclaim. After having taught the prayer of the "Our Father" and having warned about exterior appearances and attachment to money and wealth, the Nazarene called the people to another conversion of heart.

"Judge not, that you be not judged. For with the judgment you pronounce you will be judged, and with the measure you use it will be measured to you. Why do you see the speck that is in your brother's eye, but do not notice the log that is in your own eye?"

He also said not to condemn so as not to be condemned in our turn. Jesus was not speaking only about other human beings, of a reciprocity among people. He was talking about how God acts. . . .

"If I want to be merciful like the Father, as Jesus tells me, I should think: How many times a day do I judge? And you will not be judged. What I do to others, others will do to me! And in the end, the Lord will do that to me."[42]

~

The Nazarene was still speaking. It was the hottest time of day by now, but everyone was hanging on his words and did not want him to stop teaching. A bit of the kingdom of God proclaimed by the Son was present that day on the mount overlooking the Sea of Galilee.

"Ask, and it will be given to you; seek, and you will find; knock, and it will be opened to you." If a father knows how to give good things to his children, *"how much more will your Father who is in heaven give good things to those who ask him!"* "Your Father. . . ." It was John, the youngest of the Twelve, who picked up that nuance. Jesus had taught those women and men how to pray, calling God "our Father." But when he was speaking about his relationship with the Father, he was always making a distinction, "My Father and your Father," as

---

42. Homily, Santa Marta, March 18, 2019.

if to emphasize that his relationship was not the same as that between other human beings and the Almighty.

Then Jesus repeated the golden rule to them. *"So whatever you wish that others would do to you, do also to them."* To be loved, forgiven; not to feel judged but accepted. . . . Isn't this what the heart of every person present on the mount that day wanted? The way to being treated this way was to treat others that way. The way to be looked at in this way was to look at others in that way.

Then Jesus concluded his sermon. *"Not everyone who says to me, 'Lord, Lord,' will enter the kingdom of heaven, but the one who does the will of my Father who is in heaven."*

And before taking his leave of the crowd, still amazed and happily listening to him, Jesus spoke about how his words could be received. He did so using one of the examples he had often learned from the lips of Joseph the carpenter, who was often found working at the construction sites of nearby Sepphoris.

"Everyone then who hears these words of mine and does them will be like a wise man who built his house on the rock. And the rain fell, and the floods came, and the winds blew and beat on that house, but it did not fall, because it had been founded on the rock. And everyone who hears these words of mine and does not do them will be like a foolish man who built his house on the sand. And the rain fell, and the floods came, and the winds blew and beat against that house, and it fell, and great was the fall of it."

∼

When he finished speaking, the apostles and disciples looked at one another in silence. They had not received a new handbook of rules to accept, prescriptions to follow, things to do. They had learned who Jesus was, had seen his face manifesting the face of the Father. They did not sense that what they had heard was an obligation but a new way of being, made possible by the extraordinary authority of the Teacher. The Twelve understood that only by remaining with him could those words become their experience of life as well.

And when Jesus finished these sayings, the crowds were astonished at his teaching, for he was teaching them as one who had authority, and not as their scribes.

9

The Centurion, the Widow, and the Sinner

Year AD 28, September—October.

The Healing of the Servant. The Miracle at Nain.
Perfume for His Feet Bathed with Tears. Jesus's New Family.

After he had finished all his sayings in the hearing of the people, he entered Capernaum.

It was already late afternoon. The temperature was mild. The Teacher had taken leave of the crowds and had headed down to Capernaum accompanied by only eleven of the twelve apostles. John was not with them. He had been detained by a family of friends who had emigrated to Sidon and was helping them find lodging for the night along the banks of the Sea of Galilee but not near the populated area. The apostles were exchanging thoughts and opinions among themselves regarding what they had heard, on that overturning of worldly criteria that had enkindled so much hope in the people who had gone out to meet the Nazarene. Jesus was walking ahead of them, listening to their reasoning and questions, praying to the Father.

Arriving in Capernaum, the small group was heading for Peter's house. As soon as they entered the city, they found a small crowd waiting for them. There were still men and women asking for a prayer, a blessing, a healing.

Standing off to the side, away from the crowd, was a Roman centurion, Servius Emilius Felicitus. He was a small, stocky man in his forties, with a wide, square jaw and skin darkened by the sun. He was wearing a military uniform, which usually provoked extreme hatred in the Israelites, since it was a sign and symbol of the occupation that oppressed them. Yet this man was not being regarded with contempt by those around him. You could see esteem in everyone's eyes.

Centurions, chosen from among the legionaries, were high ranking and represented the backbone of the Roman army. They were paid up to five times more than a simple legionary. Servius Emilius Felicitus was not only a good commander but was also astute and combative, a great leader for the Roman soldiers who guarded the crossroads along the *Via Maris*. Although the emperor Tiberius had never shown any sympathy toward the Jewish religion, this centurion had shown that he was attentive to the religious traditions of the people at Capernaum. This was manifested through the friendship that several influential elders had forged with him, especially after Servius Emilius had actively collaborated on the construction of the new synagogue.

The man in uniform kept his distance, not even seeming to have the courage to raise his eyes toward Jesus. A tremendous sorrow gripped him—his faithful servant Filone, whom he loved like a son and brother, was ill. This servant, who had been in his service many years and had become part of his family, had been in bed, paralyzed, for weeks now, suffering from a fever and pain in his bones. He was at the point of death, after all the attempts of the doctors he had consulted to cure him had been of no avail. For that man, Jesus was his last hope.

When Servius Emilius Felicitus had heard the Nazarene's words on the mount, he had not been wearing his uniform because he did not want to be recognized. The Roman was curious about this man everyone in Capernaum was talking about, and had wanted to personally hear what he was saying and see what he was doing. Even though he had stayed at a distance so he would not be recognized, which meant he could not hear everything Jesus said, he had nevertheless been unsettled by the message of the Beatitudes. Because of this, once he had returned to the town and knew the Teacher was headed in that direction, he had decided to wait for him along the way. Not believing himself worthy to approach Jesus and speak to him directly, he had asked a few elders of the town who were his friends to act as his ambassador. They were the ones who first told Jesus about the centurion's servant.

And when they came to Jesus, they pleaded with him earnestly, saying, "He is worthy to have you do this for him, for he loves our nation, and he is the one who built us our synagogue."

Without saying a word, the Nazarene unexpectedly headed quickly toward the centurion. When Servius Emilius Felicitus saw Jesus coming toward him, he said, *"Lord, my servant is lying paralyzed at home, suffering terribly."*

Jesus replied, *"I will come and heal him."* But the centurion replied, *"Lord, I am not worthy to have you come under my roof, but only say the word, and my servant will be healed. For I too am a man under authority, with soldiers under me. And I say to one, 'Go,' and he goes, and to another, 'Come,' and he comes, and to my servant, 'Do this,' and he does it."*

The commander of the Roman legionaries of Capernaum did not feel worthy to welcome the Teacher who had said he was willing to pay him a visit to heal his servant. This sentiment, flowing from humility, together with his determination in asking for an impossible healing, surprised Jesus and touched him deeply.

"This man felt the need of prayer. Why? Surely because he loved, but also because he was aware that he was not the master of everything, that he was not the last resort."[43]

A few moments of silence followed. Jesus's compassionate gaze was mirrored in the centurion's.

When Jesus heard this, he marveled and said to those who followed him, "Truly, I tell you, with no one in Israel have I found such faith. I tell you, many will come from east and west and recline at table with Abraham, Isaac, and Jacob in the kingdom of heaven, while the sons of the kingdom will be thrown into the outer darkness. In that place there will be weeping and gnashing of teeth."

That Roman's faith, the faith of that man who did not belong to the people of Israel, pierced the heart of the Nazarene who had come for the salvation of many, not just a few.

"The Lord marveled at that centurion. He marveled at the faith he had. The centurion had undertaken a journey to meet the Lord, but he had made it in faith. Because of this, he not only met the Lord, but he felt the joy of being met by the Lord. And this is precisely the sort of encounter we desire, the encounter of faith. To encounter the Lord, but to allow him to encounter us."[44]

Jesus looked at the centurion and said, *"Go; let it be done for you as you have believed."* And the servant was healed at that very moment.

The Roman could not say even one word. His eyes, filled with tears, thanked Jesus. He ran home so quickly that some of his servants following him could hardly keep up. Throwing open the wooden doors, he found Filone healed, squatting on a mat on the floor, without a fever, eating and drinking, to the amazement of everyone who lived in that house, who until a few minutes previously, had been assisting him on his deathbed.

~

---

43. Homily, Santa Marta, September 18, 2017.
44. Homily, Santa Marta, December 2, 2013.

In the days that followed, Jesus and his followers set out again, traveling through the villages of Galilee. They were a close-knit group by now—the disciples provided for their daily needs and the apostles assisted Jesus more closely. Seeing how he was moving about and the decisions he was making, it was clear to everyone that he had a great mission to accomplish within a limited amount of time. They all became accustomed to not living a stable life. Prior to meeting the Christ, the scope of their activities had been limited, with Jerusalem being a pilgrimage destination every now and then. Now, instead, they found themselves constantly on the go. They were following Jesus without understanding his plan. They understood that his proclamation, his words, and his gestures were one and the same, and that the center of his proclamation was not writings or theories, nor was it about a simple exterior observance of the law. The center of his proclamation was himself and his relationship with his Father. So they tried to keep up with him, each with his own thoughts, dreams, expectations, hopes. It still was not clear what type of "kingdom" he would inaugurate in that proud land, so intolerant of any foreign rule.

It was a dry, cold November day. Just over seven miles from Nazareth was a tiny city called Nain, which stood at the foot of Little Hermon. The village was surrounded by a wall and had only one city gate. As the Teacher and his disciples, together with a sizeable crowd that was following him, approached the gate of Nain, *behold, a man who had died was being carried out, the only son of his mother, and she was a widow, and a considerable crowd from the town was with her.*

Two processions were crossing paths: the one with the people following the Nazarene to hear him and ask for his help, the other a funeral procession bringing the body of Ezekiel to his sepulcher in the grottoes just outside the town. Fourteen-year-old Ezekiel had died in a few days from an infection that left him no chance. He was the only son of Jael, a young woman who had already been widowed for a decade. Her husband, a potter by trade, had been killed when a wall in his workshop collapsed. Ezekiel had become the only reason his mother lived. Never wanting to remarry, she struggled to secure the bare necessities for her family.

Now she was taking the boy to a sepulcher hewn out of the rock, next to his father's. She was desperate. How many times over the years had she traversed this short passage from the town to the cemetery, never ever thinking that one day she would do it bidding farewell to her son. She was wrapped in a black mantle that seemed to weigh like a two-hundred-pound yoke on her shoulders. Hunched over with her hands stretched out like a beggar, she moved forward. But there was nothing left to beg for in the face of the ultimate sentence of death. Her older sister and two other friends supported her, while all of her and her husband's relatives around them were weeping, along with many of Ezekiel's friends. The woman's eyes were red and swollen from crying. She no longer had the energy to cry out her pain and desperation.

And when the Lord saw her, he had compassion on her and said to her, "Do not weep."

In just a matter of seconds, the two processions met each other—the noisy one following Jesus, and the desperate one accompanying the boy to his grave. At that moment, the Nazarene's eyes saw nothing but her, bowed over in excruciating pain, still incapable of accepting this cruel destiny that deprived her of her only reason for living, her only means of support in old age. Jesus was deeply moved, and seeing her, he could not but think of his own mother and what she would have to suffer before too long. Leaving his own procession, he started over to the funeral procession under the surprised and suspenseful looks of everyone on both sides.

Then he came up and touched the bier, and the bearers stood still. And he said, "Young man, I say to you, arise." And the dead man sat up and began to speak, and Jesus gave him to his mother.

Ezekiel got up as if waking from a light sleep. He raised the shroud he was wrapped in and began to free himself from the bands of cloth sticking to him because of the perfumed ointments. "Mamma!" he cried out several times. Then he asked the people carrying him to help him unravel the cloths. To him it seemed like he had awakened from a dream. He, too, was incapable of comprehending what had happened in that moment.

Jael's eyes remained wide open. Thinking she was dreaming, she could not take her eyes off her son, who had suddenly come back to life. She touched him continuously as if wanting to assure herself that it was all true. Then she turned toward Jesus, who was smiling at her. First, she bowed her head; then she fell on her knees, still incapable of speaking. He tenderly put his hand on her veiled head and whispered to her, "Don't weep anymore. Ezekiel is alive!" The black, heavy mantle of mourning became Ezekiel's makeshift clothing once he was finally freed from the shroud.

This is *"a truly great miracle of Jesus, the resurrection of a young man. And yet, the core of this narrative is not the miracle, but Jesus's tenderness toward the mother of this young man. Here, mercy takes the name of tremendous compassion toward a woman who had lost her husband and is now accompanying her only son to the cemetery. This deep sorrow of a mother moves Jesus and causes him to perform the miracle of resurrection. . . . Tremendous compassion guides Jesus's actions—touching the bier he stops the procession, and, moved by profound mercy for this mother, decides to confront death face to face, so to speak. And he will confront it definitively, face to face, on the cross."*[45]

The two processions remained immobile for several minutes.

Fear seized them all, and they glorified God, saying, "A great prophet has arisen among us!" and "God has visited his people!" And this report about him spread through the whole of Judea and all the surrounding country.

∽

Jesus and his disciples entered Nain preceded by the news of what had just happened moments before at the city gates. Jael was a woman who was well liked by everyone. Her son's coming back to life was the talk of the town. Now even more people flocked around the Teacher as he passed by. Each person had a problem, a family tragedy, a request.

Among the eyewitnesses of the resurrection of Ezekiel was a Pharisee named Simon, who invited Jesus to dinner after the Sabbath prayer in the synagogue. Jesus accepted his invitation as always. All the other guests around the sumptuous table were men. Simon had truly wanted to honor the Nazarene the best he could. Jesus was accompanied only by John.

He went into the Pharisee's house and reclined at table. And behold, a woman of the city, who was a sinner, when she learned that he was reclining at table in the Pharisee's house, brought an alabaster flask of ointment, and standing behind him at his feet, weeping, she began to wet his feet with her tears and wiped them with the hair of her head and kissed his feet and anointed them with the ointment.

The young woman's name was Miriam. An extremely tender expression covered her face. Until that moment, she had led a dissolute life, just as much being subject to public ridicule as being sought out by night by some of the same men who mocked her during the day. She had never married and had no children.

Miriam came in without asking permission, taking advantage of the hustle and bustle of the cheerful confusion that reigned in Simon's house that special evening. All of them had seen her enter. Some of them had looked at her with hungry eyes. Her comely beauty certainly did not go by unnoticed. She was wearing a fine dress and jewels. A light veil covered her thick, light hair. She

---

45. General Audience, August 10, 2016.

had stealthily approached Jesus, accomplishing that act of love. No one dared throw her out seeing that the Nazarene had neither stopped her nor shown a sign of impatience.

Now when the Pharisee who had invited him saw this, he said to himself, "If this man were a prophet, he would have known who and what sort of woman this is who is touching him, for she is a sinner." It was only a thought. It is true, what he had seen the day before was astounding, impossible. A dead man awakened from the dead in the blink of an eye! If this man, so captivating and revolutionary, were truly a prophet sent by God, would he have accepted the amorous attention of this sinner? Why hadn't he realized who was in front of him and how improper it was to accept her attention in public? This was the thought crossing Simon's mind as he dipped a piece of bread into the sauce. The Pharisee did not have the courage to say anything out of respect for his guest.

And Jesus answering said to him, "Simon, I have something to say to you."

And he answered, "Say it, Teacher."

The Pharisee had not spoken. Reading his heart, Jesus had understood everything.

He said, *"A certain moneylender had two debtors. One owed five hundred denarii, and the other fifty. When they could not pay, he cancelled the debt of both. Now which of them will love him more?"*

Simon answered, "The one, I suppose, for whom he cancelled the larger debt."

And he said to him, "You have judged rightly."

Until that moment, the Pharisee believed the Teacher had intended to tell him a parable. He had not connected Jesus's words to his behavior toward Miriam.

Then turning toward the woman [Jesus] said to Simon, "Do you see this woman? I entered your house; you gave me no water for my feet, but she has wet my feet with her tears and wiped them with her hair. You gave me no kiss, but from the time I came in she has not ceased to kiss my feet. You did not anoint my head with oil, but she has anointed my feet with ointment. Therefore I tell you, her sins, which are many, are forgiven—for she loved much. But he who is forgiven little, loves little."

And he said to her, "Your sins are forgiven."

The master of the house remained speechless. Even the other guests reclining around the table were mute before the determination of the Teacher who was looking with compassion on the woman who was still clinging to his feet.

Then those who were at table with him began to say among themselves, "Who is this, who even forgives sins?"

And he said to the woman, "Your faith has saved you; go in peace."

His mercy, his forgiveness, his grace, were offered to whoever was seeking him with a sincere heart. It made no difference if the person who approached him was righteous or a hardened sinner. On the contrary. The sinners who encountered him, aware of their condition, of what they were lacking, of their spiritual sickness, were inundated with a superabundant, unexpected, liberating outpouring of love. It was a love greater than any sin, any fault, any sense of guilt. It was a love that loosened every chain.

The woman *"is told that her sins are forgiven. Jesus only points out and explains the actions to the others, including the actions not done, that is, what they have not done for him. . . . There was so, so much love in her. But concerning his dinner companions, Jesus does not say they lack love, but he makes it understood. As a result, he says the words of salvation—'Your faith has saved you!'—only to the woman, who is a sinner. And he says that to her because she was able to weep for her sins, to confess her sins, to say, 'I am a sinner.' He does not say it, instead, to those people who, although they were not bad, actually believed they were not sinners. For them, everyone else were sinners—the publicans, the prostitutes."*[46]

At dawn the following morning, Jesus left Nain together with his apostles and disciples. Among them was also a group of women whom Jesus had cured. They were helping him, making what they had available to him. *Mary, called Magdalene, from whom seven demons had gone out, and Joanna, the wife of Chuza, Herod's household manager, and Susanna, and many others, who provided for them out of their means.*

～

As Jesus's fame grew, so also did aversion to him. Some hated him; others envied him. Still others were incapable of surrendering before the reality or the impossibility of undoing long-standing human traditions that had been passed off as divine law. So a group of scribes, led by one of the dignitaries at court, after having heard the news and testimony about Jesus, decided to set out, going down from Jerusalem to Galilee to try to dissuade people from following him. Their accusation was that Jesus was possessed by a demon. They met up with him at the gates of Capernaum. Keeping their distance, they shouted at him.

"He is possessed by Beelzebul," and *"by the prince of demons he casts out the demons."*

---

46. Homily, Santa Marta, September 18, 2014.

Not allowing them to intimidate him, Jesus *called them to him and said to them in parables, "How can Satan cast out Satan? If a kingdom is divided against itself, that kingdom cannot stand. And if a house is divided against itself, that house will not be able to stand. And if Satan has risen up against himself and is divided, he cannot stand, but is coming to an end. But no one can enter a strong man's house and plunder his goods, unless he first binds the strong man. Then indeed he may plunder his house."*

Their argument caved in like a flimsy straw castle hit by the first gust of wind. Jesus continued, *"Truly, I say to you, all sins will be forgiven the children of man, and whatever blasphemies they utter, but whoever blasphemes against the Holy Spirit never has forgiveness, but is guilty of an eternal sin."*

Mute and defeated, the scribes went away.

"Jesus reacts with strong and clear words. He does not tolerate this because those scribes, perhaps without realizing it, are falling into the gravest sin—denying and blaspheming against God's Love present and operative in Jesus. And blasphemy, the sin against the Holy Spirit, is the only unforgivable sin, as Jesus says, because it comes from closing one's heart to God's mercy at work in Jesus.

"But this episode contains a warning that is useful to all of us. Indeed, it can happen that strong jealousy of a person's goodness and good works can drive one to falsely accuse him or her. There is true, lethal poison here—the malice by which, in a premeditated manner, someone wants to destroy the good reputation of another. May God free us from this terrible temptation!"[47]

As he was going from one village to another, Jesus and his disciples were joined by Mary, Jesus's Mother, and by several of his relatives who had come from Nazareth. *They could not reach him because of the crowd. And he was told, "Your mother and your brothers are standing outside, desiring to see you." But he answered them, "My mother and my brothers are those who hear the word of God and do it."*

After he had finished speaking and healing, he welcomed his family. Two cousins with whom Jesus was very close were with Mary.

"Jesus formed a new family no longer based on natural bonds, but on faith in him, on his love, which welcomes us and unites us to each other in the Holy Spirit. All those who welcome Jesus's word are children of God and brothers and sisters among themselves."[48]

---

47. Angelus, June 10, 2018.
48. *Ibid.*

10

The Parables of the Kingdom, and the Journey by Night

Year AD 28, November—December.

The Sower, the Weeds, and the Mustard Seed.
The Nocturnal Storm on the Lake.
The Possessed Man and the Herd of Pigs.

Winter was approaching. Jesus and his disciples continued to journey from city to city, village to village. People held differing attitudes regarding him, his deeds, and his words. Some welcomed him as a prophet; some allowed themselves to be touched and wounded by his words; some were awestruck witnessing the signs he performed. There were some who judged him as well, using the traditions, customs, and attitudes of the people of Israel at the time as their litmus test. Some were scandalized because the Nazarene went into the houses of the people whose presence was unacceptable in public; he was seen in the company of sinners; he did not turn away from those with the "mark of impurity."

In his Sermon on the Mount, proclaimed before a huge crowd gathered on the foot of the hill that faced the Sea of Galilee, Jesus had described the necessary characteristics to enter the kingdom of God. Now the time had come to proclaim the characteristics of this kingdom, so different from the one many Israelites were expecting.

It was a cold November morning. The air was clear, and the streets of Capernaum were bustling with activity as usual. Jesus and his followers had returned to the city the previous day, accompanied by many people who camped out overnight in whatever way they could. For a few weeks already, even the disciples had been animatedly discussing among themselves the fate of their own people and their liberation. In fact, several of Jesus's followers were impatiently looking forward to the time when he would be made head of the people—an invincible leader—to liberate them. Of the twelve apostles, it was Judas Iscariot who observed every sign, every one of the Teacher's words, waiting for that moment. He believed in Jesus and was waiting for him to reveal himself as the Messiah, to avenge the oppressed. Judas was hoping Jesus would finally use the power received from the Father to begin something extraordinary.

In Peter's house that morning, there was a strange feeling of expectancy they had never felt before. John and Andrew had seen Jesus keeping vigil, praying during the night. Then when everyone had woken up, the Nazarene had invited them to go out immediately with him into the street. There was a group of children waiting for him outside the threshold of the house. As they went through the maze of streets heading toward the sea, other groups of people who had waited during the night set out along with them. Jesus's footsteps were quick. Yet every now and then someone would appear in front of him, asking for something. He would stop, bless, pray.

Once he arrived on the banks of the Sea of Galilee, Jesus first sat down on the shore. Then, because of the large crowd that was quickly gathering, he headed toward Peter's boat, moored a few meters away. *He got into a boat and sat down. And the whole crowd stood on the beach.*

This way everyone could see him better, even if it meant he would have to raise his voice even more so those farther away could hear him. The apostles got into the boat with him.

And he told them many things in parables, saying:

"A sower went out to sow. And as he sowed, some seeds fell along the path, and the birds came and devoured them. Other seeds fell on rocky ground, where they did not have much soil, and immediately they sprang up, since they had no depth of soil, but when the sun rose they were scorched. And since they had no root, they withered away. Other seeds fell among thorns, and the thorns grew up and choked them. Other seeds fell on good soil and produced grain, some a hundredfold, some sixty, some thirty. He who has ears, let him hear."

The people listened. His own followers did not understand.

Then the disciples came and said to him, "Why do you speak to them in parables?" And he answered them, "To you it has been given to know the secrets of the kingdom of heaven, but to them it has not been given. For to the one who has, more will be given, and he will have an abundance, but from the one who has not, even what he has will be taken away. This is why I speak to them in parables, because seeing they do not see, and hearing they do not hear, nor do they understand. . . . But blessed are your eyes, for they see, and your ears, for they hear. For truly, I say to you, many prophets and righteous people longed to see what you see, and did not see it, and to hear what you hear, and did not hear it."

He continued to speak only to them as they stood with him in the boat. In fact, he lowered his voice to explain it to them. The crowd continued looking at him even though they could not hear his words now. He explained to the apostles the meaning of the parable he had just told.

"Hear then the parable of the sower: When anyone hears the word of the kingdom and does not understand it, the evil one comes and snatches away what has been sown in his heart. This is what was sown along the path. As for what was sown on rocky ground, this is the one who hears the word and immediately receives it with joy, yet he has no root in himself, but endures for a while, and when tribulation or persecution arises on account of the word, immediately he falls away. As for what was sown among thorns, this is the one who hears the word, but the cares of the world and the deceitfulness of riches choke the word, and it proves unfruitful. As for what was sown on good soil, this is the one who hears the word and understands it. He indeed bears fruit and yields, in one case a hundredfold, in another sixty, and in another thirty."

They remained captivated and awestruck. The comparison with the sower was immediately understandable to them. Around Capernaum, too, there were small plots of land, or depressions in the land, where families struggled to grow some fruit. The difficulty of getting plants to germinate, the different types of soil, the amount of seed sown that would never take root because it would fall onto the dirt paths, was a common experience. Listening was not enough to understand the message about the kingdom of heaven. It was necessary to allow the proclamation to take root in the heart, to make room for it. The good soil of pure and humble hearts was needed. Jesus's message would transform those who welcomed it in the same way as new life is protected in a mother's womb.

"With what dispositions do we receive it? We can ask ourselves, 'What is our heart like? What type of soil does it resemble: a path, a rock, a thornbush?' It is up to us to become good soil without thorns or stones, but tilled and cultivated carefully, so it might bear good fruit for us and for our brothers and sisters."[49]

"Let us find the courage to reclaim the soil, to reclaim our hearts through a beautiful conversion, bringing our rocks and our thorns to the Lord in confession and prayer. By doing this, Jesus, the good sower will be happy to carry out an

---

49. Angelus, July 13, 2014.

additional task—to purify our hearts, removing the rocks and the thorns that choke his Word."[50]

Then Jesus turned again toward the crowd who was watching him from the shore. He continued to speak in a loud voice so everyone could hear him.

"The kingdom of heaven may be compared to a man who sowed good seed in his field, but while his men were sleeping, his enemy came and sowed weeds among the wheat and went away. So when the plants came up and bore grain, then the weeds appeared also. And the servants of the master of the house came and said to him, 'Master, did you not sow good seed in your field? How then does it have weeds?' He said to them, 'An enemy has done this.' So the servants said to him, 'Then do you want us to go and gather them?' But he said, 'No, lest in gathering the weeds you root up the wheat along with them. Let both grow together until the harvest, and at harvest time I will tell the reapers, "Gather the weeds first and bind them in bundles to be burned, but gather the wheat into my barn."'"

What did these words about the weeds mean? This harmful plant could not be distinguished from the wheat. The difference became evident only after the ears of grain had formed. To take action before that would harm the good plants. Why was Jesus saying this?

The Teacher could see question marks in many peoples' eyes, beginning with those closest to him. But he did not explain himself. Instead, he continued to speak about the kingdom using comparisons connected to everyday life.

"The kingdom of heaven is like a grain of mustard seed that a man took and sowed in his field. It is the smallest of all seeds, but when it has grown it is larger than all the garden plants and becomes a tree, so that the birds of the air come and make nests in its branches."

Another parable, another comparison to explain that the kingdom he was proclaiming to them was different from the one many were expecting. As everyone listening to him knew, the mustard tree had extremely small seeds that could generate shrubs up to three or four feet tall.

He told them another parable. "The kingdom of heaven is like leaven that a woman took and hid in three measures of flour, till it was all leavened."

A seed, a grain, a bit of yeast. . . . But what "kingdom" was this man speaking of? He was not proclaiming a conquest, exalting the use of power or demonstrations of force. It seemed Jesus was choosing his every word to avoid being misunderstood by those who were expecting a mighty leader, a political liberator, a leader who would trample down the enemies of the people of Israel.

---

50. Angelus, July 16, 2017.

He was speaking in parables to keep his message from being twisted into the human objectives of those who wanted to rebel against the Romans, of those who wanted to bring an end to the reign of the "collaborationists" and corrupt rulers, of those who wanted political change.

When he finished speaking, he dismissed the crowd and disembarked. Then he returned to Peter's house with his followers. There, around the table, the disciples asked him to explain the parable of the weeds. They were curious and full of questions.

He answered, "The one who sows the good seed is the Son of Man. The field is the world, and the good seed is the sons of the kingdom. The weeds are the sons of the evil one, and the enemy who sowed them is the devil. The harvest is the end of the age, and the reapers are angels. Just as the weeds are gathered and burned with fire, so will it be at the end of the age. The Son of Man will send his angels, and they will gather out of his kingdom all causes of sin and all law-breakers, and throw them into the fiery furnace. In that place there will be weeping and gnashing of teeth. Then the righteous will shine like the sun in the kingdom of their Father. He who has ears, let him hear."

They were beginning to understand. The separation of the good from the bad was expected in this world. They were awaiting the vindication of the good and the victory over the evildoers to take place on this earth before long. Instead, Jesus explained that the wheat had to coexist with the weeds while awaiting the final judgment.

Frowning, Judas remained the most perplexed, for with the explanation of the parable, he saw certain of his messianic expectations waning, constructed by the human imagination and shared by a part of the people. The kingdom of God had begun. It was slowly making headway. But it bore the face of an unarmed prophet who was not imposing himself, not leading armies, not forming a revolt—a prophet who had difficulty being recognized even by his own relatives, in his own village—a meek man whom everyone by now knew was "the son of the carpenter" of Nazareth. The kingdom he was announcing would not grow by mowing down enemies and the corrupt. It was, instead, a small, defenseless seed, at the mercy of events. It was not human might he was promising to the men and women following him. Besides, had he not already stated this clearly when he had repeatedly cried out those "beatitudes?" The reversal of human criteria contained in the Sermon on the Mount was reflected now in the parables he was telling.

He continued to speak to them using other examples. As he watched them, he felt compassion for them. All of them tried to understand what he meant regarding the nature of the proclamation he had come to bring. They were doing well with him, even though they felt torn by his words. Being near him was more important than understanding. One day, they would understand.

"The kingdom of heaven is like treasure hidden in a field, which a man found and covered up. Then in his joy he goes and sells all that he has and buys that field.

"Again, the kingdom of heaven is like a merchant in search of fine pearls, who, on finding one pearl of great value, went and sold all that he had and bought it.

"Again, the kingdom of heaven is like a net that was thrown into the sea and gathered fish of every kind. When it was full, men drew it ashore and sat down and sorted the good into containers but threw away the bad. So it will be at the end of the age. The angels will come out and separate the evil from the righteous and throw them into the fiery furnace. In that place there will be weeping and gnashing of teeth."

The image of the good and bad fish complemented the one of the wheat and the weeds, expressing the same reality. But Peter and Andrew smiled at this practice Jesus had hinted at that they knew so well. Every time they used to haul in their nets, they would separate the edible fish and throw away the bad fish.

"Today, the Lord, who is Wisdom incarnate, helps us understand that good and evil cannot be identified with neatly defined boundaries or specific human groups—'These are the good ones, those are the bad ones.' He tells us that the boundary between good and evil passes through each person's heart. It passes through each of our hearts, that is, we are all sinners. . . . Jesus teaches us a different way of looking at the field of the world, of observing reality. We are called to learn God's timing—which is not our timing—and how God sees things too. Thanks to the beneficial influence of anxious waiting, what were weeds, or seemed to be weeds, can become a good product. It is the reality of conversion. It is the prospect of hope!"[51]

⁓

Evening was drawing near. The crowd was still waiting for Jesus. People were going out into the streets on their way back again to the lakeshore.

---

51. Angelus, July 23, 2017.

He said to them, "Let us go across to the other side." And leaving the crowd, they took him with them in the boat, just as he was. And other boats were with him.

They loaded just a little bit of food and quickly put out to sea as night descended. A little after pulling away from shore, Jesus fell asleep in the boat's stern. Although the crossing was a matter of just a few miles, it was not without risks because of the cold winds that could suddenly come down from Hermon's snowy summit, causing violent storms. Fishermen were familiar with them. Some had even lost their lives, never to return home. While they were still at sea, toward the center of the lake, *a great windstorm arose, and the waves were breaking into the boat, so that the boat was already filling.*

Jesus remained in the stern *asleep on the cushion.* He was in a deep sleep, clinging to the "cushion," a canvas sack stuffed with rags. His body lay there abandoned to sleep, intertwined with a cable rolled up next to him. It seemed that the high waves and water that were coming violently into the boat, that had suddenly become so vulnerable, were not touching him. The apostles who were expert seafarers were scrambling to keep the boat from sinking and shouting orders at the less experienced among them. Everyone was running to and fro, according to the rapid succession of waves, the gusts of cold wind, the splashing water that chilled their faces. Every now and then they glanced over toward Jesus who remained immobile, untouched by what was going on around him.

Finally, driven by exasperation, his followers shook him out of his torpor, which they considered unexplainable.

And they woke him and said to him, "Teacher, do you not care that we are perishing?" And he awoke and rebuked the wind and said to the sea, "Peace! Be still!"

Standing in the ship's stern, arms outstretched before him, he had imparted an order to the forces of nature.

And the wind ceased, and there was a great calm.

All of a sudden, Lake Tiberius became completely still. The wind, the waves, the rain, the thunder and lightning had vanished. It was as if the sudden storm had never taken place. Philip was assailed by the doubt that maybe he had been dreaming and was asking himself if he had just awakened from an awful nightmare. But his wet garments and freezing body brought him immediately back to reality. No, he had not been dreaming. A minute before, they had been drowning; the next, the forces of nature had all calmed down at the same instant, obeying Jesus's order.

He said to them, "Why are you so afraid? Have you still no faith?" And they were filled with great fear and said to one another, "Who then is this, that even the wind and the sea obey him?"

Peter took up the helm again to guide the boat toward the mooring on the other shore. The others remained astonished, petrified by the manifestation of power over the elements of nature.

"What is harder to understand is Jesus's attitude. While his disciples are quite naturally alarmed and desperate, he is in the stern, right in the part of the boat that sinks first. And what does he do? In spite of the tempest, he sleeps on soundly, trusting in the Father. This is the only time in the Gospels we see Jesus sleeping. When he is woken up, and after calming the wind and the waters, he turns to the disciples in a reproaching voice, 'Why are you afraid? Have you still no faith?'

"Let us try to understand. In what does the lack of the disciples' faith consist, as contrasted with Jesus's trust? They had not stopped believing in him. In fact, they called on him. But we see how they call on him, "Teacher, do you not care if we perish?" Don't you care—they think Jesus is not interested in them, does not care about them. One of the things that hurts us and our families most is when we hear it said, "Don't you care about me?" It is a phrase that wounds and unleashes storms in our hearts. It would have shaken Jesus too. Because he, more than anyone, cares about us. Indeed, once they called on him, he saved his distrusting disciples.

"The storm exposes our vulnerability and uncovers those false and superfluous certainties around which we have constructed our daily schedules, our projects, our habits and priorities. It shows us how we have allowed the very things that nourish, sustain, and strengthen our lives and our communities to become dull and feeble. . . . Lord, you are calling to us, calling us to faith. Which is not so much believing that You exist, but coming to You and trusting in You."[52]

It was late at night by now. Everyone except Jesus was exhausted, cold, and hungry. The boat came to shore on the eastern side of the lake.

They came to the other side of the sea, to the country of the Gerasenes.

On the hills near the shore, near the mouth of the river, stood the village of Gergesa, not far from a cliff that overlooked the waters of the lake. The people living there were not Israelites and did not follow the precepts and traditions of the Jewish religion. From the beginning of the foundation of the village, the Gerasenes had hewn tombs into the sides of the lower part of the cliff, and made use of some natural caves for the same purpose.

---

52. Extraordinary Moment of Prayer, March 27, 2020.

A short distance from there, Jesus and his friends disembarked and set up camp, lighting a fire to warm themselves and to rest. The glowing flames reflected off the rock, taking on grotesque shapes.

Immediately there met him out of the tombs a man with an unclean spirit. He lived among the tombs. And no one could bind him anymore, not even with a chain, for he had often been bound with shackles and chains, but he wrenched the chains apart, and he broke the shackles in pieces. No one had the strength to subdue him. Night and day among the tombs and on the mountains, he was always crying out and cutting himself with stones.

He was dressed in rags, his face was disfigured, and he was shouting like a madman. The man was still young, imposing, and sturdy. His hair was long, and his thick beard was matted with blood and filth. *And when he saw Jesus from afar, he ran and fell down before him. And crying out with a loud voice, he said, "What have you to do with me, Jesus, Son of the Most High God? I adjure you by God, do not torment me."*

The Teacher was not disturbed. It was as if he had been expecting that visit. He ordered the demon to leave his victim in peace.

"Come out of the man, you unclean spirit!" And Jesus asked him, "What is your name?"

He replied, "My name is Legion, for we are many."

The demons were cursing and begging Jesus not to cast them out of the area. Gergesa had become their home!

Now a great herd of pigs was feeding there on the hillside, and they begged him, saying, "Send us to the pigs; let us enter them." So he gave them permission. And the unclean spirits came out and entered the pigs; and the herd, numbering about two thousand, rushed down the steep bank into the sea and drowned in the sea.

One after the other, as if in the grip of an unforeseen instinct, the pigs threw themselves off the cliff, ending up drowned or crushed on the rocks. After the shock of the storm, the apostles were even more shaken by the unexpected "visit" of the demoniac and the slaughter of the animals. In the meantime, dawn had broken.

Startled by their grunting, the herdsmen guarding the pigs tried in vain to stop them. Then they fled into the village, informing their fellow villagers about what they had seen.

The herdsmen fled and told it in the city and in the country. And people came to see what it was that had happened.

They knew the man possessed by the unclean spirits and feared his wrath. Who had succeeded in curing him?

And they came to Jesus and saw the demon-possessed man, the one who had had the legion, sitting there, clothed and in his right mind, and they were afraid. And those who had seen it described to them what had happened to the demon-possessed man and to the pigs. And they began to beg Jesus to depart from their region.

The Gerasenes, or rather the few dozen of them who had taken the trouble of going to personally verify the story of the angry herdsmen, were so shaken that they decided to ask this mysterious and powerful prophet to immediately move on somewhere else.

"When the herdsmen saw that they had lost their pigs because of that miracle, they made some calculations and said, 'Yes, it's true. This man performs miracles, but it's not convenient for us. We're losing money over this!' And they kindly said to him, 'Go away! Go home!'" [53]

Their journey to the other side of the Gennesaret had lasted but a few hours. And as Jesus *was getting into the boat, the man who had been possessed with demons begged him that he might be with him.*

His liberation had completely changed the deformed features of that man, the son of a rich oil merchant from Gergesa. His face had become human again. At peace and reconciled with himself and with others, his previously threatening mountainous muscles now evoked compassion as he begged Jesus to take him with him. The Nazarene, however, still seeing the reflection of the frightened Geresenes in his eyes, desired that this living and powerful sign of God's mercy remain on that strip of land, giving witness to what had happened. Thus, the former demoniac became a missionary.

And he did not permit him but said to him, "Go home to your friends and tell them how much the Lord has done for you, and how he has had mercy on you." And he went away and began to proclaim in the Decapolis how much Jesus had done for him, and everyone marveled.

---

53. Homily, Santa Marta, April 16, 2018.

11

Extraordinary Deeds in Galilee, and the First Mission

Year AD 29, January—February.

*The Daughter of Jairus. A Woman with a Hemorrhage.
Two Insistent Blind Men.
The Disciples Are Sent to Proclaim the Kingdom of God.*

By now, it was impossible for the Nazarene and his friends to walk about Capernaum without being surrounded by a crowd. Everyone was talking about the signs Jesus had performed in the last months. So when they returned to the other side of the Sea of Galilee that winter morning when the air was unusually warm, they found people waiting for them on the shore.

The Nazarene stepped quickly out of Peter's boat as soon as it docked. Jesus began to walk along the shore together with his companions, who were trying to contain the pressure of the people a little too brusquely and aggressively at times. As always, there were many children darting in and out among the people who managed to reach Jesus without the apostles being able to keep them at bay.

At a certain point, as they were nearing the populated part of the village, someone shouted, "Let him pass! Make way!" They recognized the man who was coming toward them. He had a dark face, his head was wrapped in a large white cloth, and his black tunic reached down to his feet. He was fifty years old. His name was Jairus, the head of the synagogue, the person who held the responsibility of maintaining the sacred building in the town and organizing religious functions. The inhabitants of Capernaum esteemed him, considering him a moderate and just administrator.

He was finally able to approach Jesus, and *seeing him, he fell at his feet and implored him earnestly, saying, "My little daughter is at the point of death. Come and lay your hands on her, so that she may be made well and live."* Jairus was well aware of what the Nazarene had done for the centurion's servant. Good father that he was, he knew he could ask for the healing of his only daughter, Zara, who was the family's true joy. With her smile, she alone could take the edge off of certain harsh aspects of Jairus's character. Since he had had that child, he lived the precepts of the law differently. He had learned from her to consider the heart of the matter more than the exterior form.

Jesus looked with compassion at the leader of the synagogue. He, a dignitary, had humiliated himself, throwing himself to the ground. He was no longer the man to be seen, the important person. He was a father who was fighting with all his might to save his daughter. Jesus lifted him up, reassuring him with a look that said more than words could. He took Jairus by the hand and headed with him toward his home. *A great crowd followed him and thronged about him.*

∼

While they were walking, people continued to press on him. At a certain point, Jesus stopped, and for a few seconds did not move.

There was a woman who had had a discharge of blood for twelve years, and who had suffered much under many physicians, and had spent all that she had, and was no better but rather grew worse. She had heard the reports about Jesus and came up behind him in the crowd and touched his garment.

Her name was Samarah. She lived in a small village not far from Capernaum. That illness had truly become her curse. Because of it, her husband had divorced and abandoned her. Consultations with the doctors and so-called healers had been to no avail. The herbal remedies had had no effect whatsoever, and no one was able to restore her health, and with that, her dignity. In a short time, the exhaustion the continual bleeding caused her, together with the social exclusion, had destroyed her. She was dressed in rags and seemed much older than her thirty-five years.

She had no aspiration of exchanging any words with the Teacher or of appearing in front of him. All she wanted to do was to touch, even if only for an instant, a part of his tunic, one of the four tassels on Jesus's garment, which the Nazarene, like any Israelite, wore according to the precepts of their tradition. Samarah was certain of one thing. This man, this prophet, was her last resort.

For she said, "If I touch even his garments, I will be made well."

It was a matter of seconds. Crawling through the crowd, she managed to reach out her hand and brush against one of the tassels of Jesus's mantle that was touching the ground. At that very moment, *the flow of blood dried up, and she felt in her body that she was healed of her disease. And Jesus, perceiving in himself that power had gone out from him, immediately turned about in the crowd and said, "Who touched my garments?"*

The Master's eyes looked unusually hard. He scrutinized the faces of the people surrounding him but was not able to identify the one who had "stolen" a miracle.

Surprised, the disciples said, *"You see the crowd pressing around you, and yet you say, 'Who touched me?'"*

But Jesus *looked around to see who had done it.* After a few moments that seemed interminable, Samarah, who was hunched over on the sand, finally got up the courage to identify herself. *But the woman, knowing what had happened to her, came in fear and trembling and fell down before him and told him the whole truth.*

The hard look in Jesus's eyes melted into compassion and admiration.

And he said to her, "Daughter, your faith has made you well; go in peace, and be healed of your disease."

Her eyes swollen from tears, without ceasing to thank him and bow to him, the woman walked away, finally cured after bleeding for more than a decade. She kept looking over her shoulder every now and then, looking at Jesus and the group headed toward Jairus's house.

"More than her health, it was her affections that were compromised. . . . She was hemorrhaging blood and, therefore, according to the mindset of the time, was deemed impure. She was a marginalized woman who could not have stable relationships, a husband, a family. And she could not have normal social relationships because she was 'impure.'. . .She lived alone, with a wounded heart. . . . The greatest illness in life is the lack of love, not being able to love. This poor woman was sick, yes, with the loss of blood, but she lacked love as a consequence, because she could not be with others socially.

"That woman is looking for direct contact, physical contact with Jesus. . . . At times we content ourselves by observing some precept and repeating prayers. . . . But the Lord waits for us to come into contact with him, that we open our hearts to him, that we, like that woman, touch his garment to be healed. Because, by entering into intimacy with Jesus, our affections are healed.

"Jesus goes beyond sins. Jesus goes beyond prejudices. He does not stop at appearances. Rather, Jesus reaches the heart. And he heals the very one who had been rejected by everyone else, an impure woman. He tenderly calls her 'daughter.' Jesus's

style was closeness, compassion, and tenderness—'daughter' . . . *and he praises her faith, restoring her self-confidence."*[54]

∾

A sad bearer of news had already left the house toward which they were heading. He had to inform the leader of the synagogue that the unavoidable fate awaiting little Zara had unfortunately taken place. *"Your daughter is dead. Why trouble the Teacher any further?"*

Jairus knew his daughter's condition was desperate and that her death was only a matter of time. But he was not expecting the sudden outcome right at the moment, when a hand—Jesus's hand—had grabbed hold of his, giving him new hope. On hearing the news, it was as if his heart were torn asunder. Jesus then, looking tenderly at him, said to him, *"Do not fear, only believe." And he allowed no one to follow him except Peter and James and John the brother of James.*

The others remained there, keeping the crowd back.

They came to the house of the ruler of the synagogue, and Jesus saw a commotion, people weeping and wailing loudly.

The wailing over the body of the deceased young girl had just begun. Her mother was slumped over in an adjacent room, huddled in a corner, her head in her hands. She was crying desperately. No one could console her. Everyone else around her was busy preparing the little girl's body. Jairus went over to his wife to embrace her. Before he reached her, Jesus addressed all those present with surprising words, to put an end to their mourning. *"Why are you making a commotion and weeping? The child is not dead but sleeping."*

One of the child's uncles began to ridicule him. Zara was unmistakably dead, and the Nazarene's words rang in their ears like foolishness, a bad joke.

But Jesus *put them all outside and took the child's father and mother and those who were with him and went in where the child was.*

Even though she had died in spasms, Zara's face was now delicate and relaxed, her skin was extremely white. *She's so beautiful,* Jairus thought to himself, holding his wife even more tightly to himself since she was unable to keep standing, so great was her pain.

Jesus, *taking her by the hand said to her, "Talitha cumi," which means, "Little girl, I say to you, arise." And immediately the girl got up and began walking (for she was twelve years of age), and they were immediately overcome with amazement.*

---

54. Angelus, June 27, 2021.

And he strictly charged them that no one should know this, and told them to give her something to eat.

The little girl seemed to blossom again. She began to eat a dish of bread and cheese with oil and wild herbs her mother had prepared but which no one had touched yet.

This miracle, like the others, did not remain a secret within the walls of Jairus's house. Despite Jesus's order, the same relatives who had first ridiculed him, after seeing the little girl resuscitated, walking, and eating, began to run about in shock recounting what they had witnessed.

"When we pray, many of us do not believe that the Lord can work miracles. I am reminded of the story—which I witnessed—of a father who was told by the doctors that his nine-year-old daughter would not survive the night. She was in the hospital. And he took a bus and went about 40 miles to the Shrine of Our Lady. It was closed and, clinging to the gate, he spent the whole night praying, 'Lord, save her! Lord, give her life!' He prayed to Our Lady all night long, crying out to God, crying out from his heart. Then when he returned to the hospital in the morning, he found his wife weeping. And he thought, 'She's dead.' And his wife said, 'No one understands, no one understands! The doctors say it's a strange thing. She seems to be healed.' That man's cry that asked for everything was heard by the Lord who gave him everything." [55]

Jesus left Jairus's house and found the crowd waiting for him again. He headed toward Peter's house. *As Jesus passed on from there, two blind men followed him, crying aloud, "Have mercy on us, Son of David."*

To address someone like this on the streets of Judea or Galilee was not a matter of small importance. In fact, it meant that someone was attributing typically messianic qualities to that person. And at that moment, this mode of address risked igniting undue hopes among the people galvanized by the miracles they had witnessed.

The ones who had lifted their voices were two men very different from each other. Reuben was older, very tall in stature, but physically frail. Asher was younger, very short in stature, and stocky. They were both beggars, helping each other. Thanks to the reciprocal protection they provided each other, they managed to survive, having the street for their home and the heavens as their roof.

---

55. Angelus, October 24, 2021.

Asher had been blind from birth. Reuben had lost his sight when he was fifteen years old. Every now and then, he still seemed to glimpse a glimmer of light or some shape with indistinct outlines. Together they helped each other, and together they managed to approach the group following Jesus, who had just entered Capernaum, hoping to be able to attract his attention.

The Nazarene heard their cry but did not respond. He did not stop, nor did he turn around. Having been called the messiah under these circumstances would have had unforeseeable consequences. It would have above all distracted the people from what he wanted to communicate—the proclamation of the kingdom of God, which is not imposed but which operates like yeast in dough, like a mustard seed.

The two blind men, however, did not give up. They continued calling out loudly. Having reached the wooden door of Peter's house, that was only a short distance from shore, they would not admit defeat. They grabbed hold of James's arm and, pushing right and left, managed to make room so they could ask for the grace of being healed.

When he entered the house, the blind men came to him, and Jesus said to them, "Do you believe that I am able to do this?" They said to him, "Yes, Lord." Then he touched their eyes, saying, "According to your faith be it done to you." And their eyes were opened.

Their healing took place in the presence of a few witnesses. Peter's mother-in-law was frozen, holding a pitcher of water in her hand. The two men continued to look at their hands. Then they looked all around them, noticing every detail of the faces of Jesus and his apostles, surprised by the unexpected sight. Then they, too, fell at the feet of the Teacher to thank him.

"See that no one knows about it." These words came from his heart, he was almost choked up. Whoever asked his compassionate heart for anything with a tiny bit of faith managed to "steal" a sign, a miracle. But these signs were meant to help people recognize the mission the Father had entrusted to him. They were not meant to nurture false hopes of a political redemption which the most extreme fringes of the population clung to. This is why he begged the two men who had been blind not to tell anyone about it.

But they went away and spread his fame through all that district. Events like this could not be hidden by the people they happened to. The two mendicant blind men could not pretend nothing had happened. Speaking about it was a form of gratitude, so great was the joy that Jesus had given them.

"There are two blind men. They are together on the roadside. They share the pain of their condition. Together they desire that a light might begin to glow in the heart of their night. . . . They do everything together—both of them follow Jesus, both cry out to him and ask for healing—not each for himself, but together. What they say to Christ is significant, 'Have mercy on us.' They use 'us,' they do not say 'me.' They do not think of their own blindness, but they ask for help together. This is an eloquent sign of the Christian life . . . to think, to speak and to act as 'we,' moving beyond individualism and the pretension of self-sufficiency that makes the heart sick."[56]

When Jesus went out of the house again after having eaten and rested a while, he found himself in front of a mute demoniac. Jesus freed him from the devil and gave him back the gift of speech. The people there were saying, *"Never was anything like this seen in Israel."*

But together with the awe felt by those who allowed their hearts to be touched at the sight of these extraordinary deeds, there were others who murmured and, on the basis of prejudice, "judged" Jesus. *But the Pharisees said, "He casts out demons by the prince of demons."*

In these last few weeks of that winter, it had become evident how many people were following Jesus—how many beggars, how many sick people, how many "outcasts," how many people considered "impure"; but also, how many people who were high up in society, how many dignitaries, men of the law, functionaries. A need, a hope, an expectation, simple curiosity, or even the fear of something new and uncontrollable that could upset the balance of power, were the motivations that moved people in his direction. The seed was being planted in every heart. The grace of that message combined with actions, looks, tenderness, and closeness, flowered wherever it found fertile soil. Often, that fertile soil was found in the least expected places—the places considered least expected by those who considered themselves to be already just, already perfect, already saved, those who were accustomed to look down on others.

And Jesus went throughout all the cities and villages, teaching in their synagogues and proclaiming the gospel of the kingdom and healing every disease and every affliction.

---

56. Homily during Mass at GSP Stadium in Nicosia (Cyprus), December 3, 2021.

As the number of people around him was increasing little by little, so did the heartfelt compassion that the Teacher felt within him for that wounded humanity.

"Compassion makes you see reality as it is. Compassion is like the lens of the heart, making us truly understand dimensions. In the Gospels, Jesus is often moved by compassion. Compassion is also God's language. . . . Our God is a God of compassion, and we can say that compassion is God's weakness, but also his strength. He gives us what is best for us because it was compassion that led him to send us his Son. Compassion is God's language."[57]

So *when he saw the crowds, he had compassion for them, because they were harassed and helpless, like sheep without a shepherd.*

There was an expectation that deserved a response. This is why Jesus gathered his friends and asked them to follow him to a secluded place not far from Capernaum. The apostles had organized everything and had brought along something to eat.

Still having before his eyes the suffering multitudes who were wandering about like a flock without a guide, he said, *"The harvest is plentiful, but the laborers are few; therefore pray earnestly to the Lord of the harvest to send out laborers into his harvest."*

And he called to him his twelve disciples and gave them authority over unclean spirits, to cast them out, and to heal every disease and every affliction.

Jesus sent them out, asking them not to go among the pagans or the Samaritans, inviting them to go instead after the *lost sheep of the house of Israel.*

He gave them very specific directions. *"And proclaim as you go, saying, 'The kingdom of heaven is at hand.' Heal the sick, raise the dead, cleanse lepers, cast out demons. You received without paying; give without pay. Acquire no gold or silver or copper for your belts, no bag for your journey, or two tunics or sandals or a staff, for the laborer deserves his food."*

He had spelled out every smallest detail regarding the basic equipment for those who set out on the journey—money well-hidden and ready when needed, a sack with some food, one change of clothing, appropriate shoes.

He instructed them to enter the houses and, if they were not welcomed, to shake the dust off their feet, adding that on the Day of Judgment those cities would be harshly treated. Then he spoke words foretelling that his missionary disciples would experience the same treatment that would befall him before long. *"Behold, I am sending you out as sheep in the midst of wolves, so be wise*

---

57. Homily, Santa Marta, September 17, 2019.

as serpents and innocent as doves. Beware of men, for they will deliver you over to courts and flog you in their synagogues, and you will be dragged before governors and kings for my sake, to bear witness before them and the Gentiles. When they deliver you over, do not be anxious how you are to speak or what you are to say, for what you are to say will be given to you in that hour. For it is not you who speak, but the Spirit of your Father speaking through you."

Then he added that they would be hated because of his name. He exhorted them to have no fear. *"What I tell you in the dark, say in the light, and what you hear whispered, proclaim on the housetops. And do not fear those who kill the body but cannot kill the soul. Rather fear him who can destroy both soul and body in hell. Are not two sparrows sold for a penny? And not one of them will fall to the ground apart from your Father. But even the hairs of your head are all numbered. Fear not, therefore; you are of more value than many sparrows. So everyone who acknowledges me before men, I also will acknowledge before my Father who is in heaven, but whoever denies me before men, I also will deny before my Father who is in heaven."*

Once more astonished and confused, they looked around at each other as they sat around the fire they had lit in the meantime. They understood that they had received a huge mission, but each of them considered himself absolutely inadequate to accomplished it. How could they totally imitate the Teacher in every way? With what power would they be able to replicate the signs he performed?

They also found the words that followed equally hard and difficult and accept.

Jesus said, *"Do not think that I have come to bring peace to the earth. I have not come to bring peace, but a sword. For I have come to set a man against his father, and a daughter against her mother, and a daughter-in-law against her mother-in-law. And a person's enemies will be those of his own household. Whoever loves father or mother more than me is not worthy of me, and whoever loves son or daughter more than me is not worthy of me."*

He said all this in a calm tone of voice, looking them in the eye. The Twelve, who had left everything to follow him, perceived the significance of his words regarding family bonds. He was asking them for everything. Only in this way, immersed in his love, could they be witnesses of his message.

Peter and Andrew thought of their wives, who were used to seeing them leave to go out fishing, knowing they might never return. And now they needed to accustom themselves to seeing their husbands leave, following after Jesus and remaining away from home for weeks. Their type of fishing had changed. And yet the presence of that man who performed miracles, who looked at you with a depth never experienced before, who could not remain indifferent before the ever-multiplying requests and human cases he encountered, who cast out demons and raised the dead—even they, Peter and Andrew's wives, had capitulated. They had understood, even more than the other disciples, the unprecedented grandeur of what was happening and, at the same time, the enormous responsibility that was falling on the shoulders of these men. In some way, they were even more aware than their husbands since they were observing what was happening from a distance, participating only in those moments when the Nazarene and the apostles returned home.

Those who were following Jesus daily, instead, were immersed in a succession of gestures, words, and powerful signs. This made it difficult to take time to stop and reflect. The unimaginable experience they were living hour after hour, day after day, sharing every moment of life with this prophet, this "Son of Man," was totalizing. The awe and fascination they were experiencing was always more powerful than any doubt or question that surfaced even in the minds of these simple men, well anchored in reality. Among themselves, the one who dreamed and thought the most about the future was Judas. But little by little, Judas Iscariot was substituting his own dream for the reality proclaimed by Jesus.

The Teacher continued, *"And whoever does not take his cross and follow me is not worthy of me. Whoever finds his life will lose it, and whoever loses his life for my sake will find it."*

What did that gloomy reference to the cross, to the most terrible and infamous of torments, mean now? Why did they need to take up their "crosses"? They continued to look at him speaking, aware of their littleness on the one hand, and always more certain of wanting to go all the way on the other hand, staking everything on the hope he had ignited.

"We cannot think about the Christian life apart from this way. There is always this way that he trod first: the way of humility, the way of humiliation as well, of losing oneself, and then rising. This is the way. The Christian style without the cross is not Christian, and if the cross is a cross without Jesus, it is not Christian. The Christian style is to take up the cross with Jesus and move ahead. Not without the cross, not without Jesus. . . . Jesus trod that path of self-emptying in order to give life. The Christian style is precisely this style of humility, meekness, gentleness."[58]

---

58. Homily, "The Christian Way," Santa Marta, March 6, 2014.

Then Jesus added words that encouraged them and made them shiver at the same time. *"Whoever receives you receives me, and whoever receives me receives him who sent me. The one who receives a prophet because he is a prophet will receive a prophet's reward, and the one who receives a righteous person because he is a righteous person will receive a righteous person's reward. And whoever gives one of these little ones even a cup of cold water because he is a disciple, truly, I say to you, he will by no means lose his reward."*

So they left and did what Jesus had asked them. They went two by two, taking different routes, entering the villages. They had no power of their own; they could count only on his word and on the memory of the look in his eyes.

12

From the Multiplication of the Bread
to Life Eternal

Year AD 29, March—April.

The Miracle of the Crowd that Ate Their Fill. Jesus Walks on Water.
The Paralytic at the Sheep Gate.
God's Commandments and Human Traditions.

It was a dress rehearsal for what they would do later, when he would no longer be with them. Because of the way he had looked at them, the disciples sent by Jesus had the courage to enter house after house to speak with the people. Peter took John, the youngest of the group, with him. They precisely followed the directions they had received concerning what to bring, and they did not go far, stopping in Magdala, a town where processing fish was the main industry. Everything seemed more difficult without the Teacher—his fame did not precede them; there were no crowds awaiting them; there was no one who hung on their every word. True, they had been given a mandate. They knew they had to imitate Jesus completely in everything. But without having him beside them, without his eyes reassuring them at times, provoking them at others, they felt lost. Peter tried to reassure John without making evident the turmoil he harbored in his heart.

So they entered the town and walked among the people. What should their first step be? Peter silently asked him, the Teacher, for help, even though he was not present. He stopped a moment, closing his eyes. Then a woman dressed in black drew near him shouting. She was looking for help for her son who was trapped under a wall of their home that had collapsed. Her cries did not interrupt the hustle and bustle of Magdala's main street. John looked at Peter and, without saying a word, both began running where the woman was pointing. She was a widow who lived in a poor neighborhood on the outskirts of town.

While they followed her, struggling to keep up, the two apostles were thinking that the mission of proclaiming the kingdom of God would have to wait because of this mishap. Reaching the place, they managed to free the young man from the rubble. His legs were wounded, but he was still able to move them. The mother did not stop thanking them and begged them insistently to come inside her poor small house for some refreshments. She served them, offering them some water, and asked them where they were from. Peter and John began to tell her about how they had met Jesus, about this man who performed miracles, explained the Scriptures like they had never heard anyone do so before, how he lived every moment in relationship with his Father in heaven, and yet at the same time how his eyes were directly connected with his heart, and how he was capable of demonstrating infinite tenderness for anyone in difficulty, for the wounded, for sinners.

As the woman listened, her eyes grew wider and wider. Lying on a straw mattress, her son, too, was following what they were saying. John let Peter do the talking, intervening only now and then. They began to realize that they did not have to invent words to proclaim the message of salvation they had received. They had only to testify to what they had seen, speak about what they had experienced—the tenderness of God, the proximity of Jesus, the message of the Beatitudes. All this, they transmitted through their eyes. After all, hadn't that already happened to Peter when he had encountered his brother Andrew, who told him he had found the Messiah?

They were about ready to go when the woman, eyes reddened due to her tears, asked, "Does this proclamation that you have spoken to me about apply to me too?" She choked up when they responded yes. Yes, it included her as well. Yes, above all for her, and for her son, who had just barely escaped death.

The apostles came back and told Jesus everything they had done.

James spoke of the hostile encounters he had kept track of. There had been so many of them, he said, that he had stopped shaking the dust from his feet before leaving, such was the compassion he had for those hard-hearted people. In reality, he believed he was inadequate.

Peter recounted what had happened at Magdala. Jesus looked at him, smiling. Peter understood. He and John had never been alone during that mission. Someone had moved their hearts, accelerated their steps, reinvigorated their arms while they were digging through the rubble, inspired their words in the house of the widow. The proclamation had been made through a hug, their closeness, their response to the tragedy the woman was experiencing, worried about her son. The seed had taken root because her heart was fertile terrain.

Peter's eyes met his Teacher's. The apostle had not cast out demons, raised the dead, healed the sick, or calmed storms. But trusting in the word of Jesus, he had reawakened hope in the heart of a poor woman who was sorely tried by life.

All the apostles recounted their own encounters, the difficulties they had met, the surprises that had filled them with amazement.

He then took them with him to the village of Bethsaida, where they could be alone. But a lot of people found out about this and followed him.

Word of mouth made it almost impossible for Jesus and his disciples to move about without being surrounded by people. They even found it difficult to carve out time to eat. The same was true this time. The Teacher did not succeed in spending but a very short time away with his friends, in a deserted area, near the place where the two sets of brothers, Peter and Andrew, James and John, had been born. They had boarded a boat to escape the crowds. After having sailed a short stretch of the lake, they had docked near the shore to walk on foot toward Bethsaida.

The city was on the other side of the Jordan, above its outlet onto the lake. On its eastern side was a large area, almost uninhabited, that could offer refuge and tranquility to the group. His followers needed to rest. Jesus was seeking solitude and silence so as to pray. They also wanted to continue speaking about what had happened those first weeks during the disciples' mission, and to hear about the death of John the Baptist, whom Herod Antipas had ordered decapitated just a few days earlier, to please Salome, the daughter of his companion. This news had shaken everyone, and had particularly saddened Jesus.

Their time alone would prove to be very brief, however. Once again, he was moved by the crowds who had come searching for him, coming to this deserted area outside of Bethsaida, arriving on foot. *Jesus welcomed them. He spoke about God's kingdom and healed everyone who was sick.* After all, he had come into the world for them. So he spoke, he proclaimed, he healed.

Some newly arrived pilgrims, on their way to Jerusalem to celebrate the Passover that year, joined them as well. They took the opportunity to listen to Jesus. It was a sunny but cold afternoon on a day in the middle of March. Jesus spent hour after hour among the people scattered out over the green field.

Late in the afternoon the twelve apostles came to Jesus and said, "Send the crowd to the farms and villages around here. They need to find a place to stay and something to eat. There is nothing in this place. It's like a desert!"

There was nothing to eat. Neither was there shelter for the night. Many of the people who had gone searching for him and had followed him had not brought any provisions with them, and they made no signs of leaving. Seeing the situation, the apostles suggested they tell the people to leave. But what seemed to be sensible advice, motivated by realism and an understanding of the situation, was rejected.

Jesus answered, "You give them something to eat."

But they replied, "We have only five small loaves of bread and two fish. If we are going to feed all these people, we will have to go and buy food." There were about 5,000 men in the crowd.

Jesus's party had only a few loaves of bread and two fish, which they had planned to roast over the fire and consume for dinner. One hypothesis offered was that they themselves, the apostles, would go to the nearby villages to buy some food with the funds in the common purse with which they would buy provisions, give alms, and use for other necessities. But even if they had found someone who could sell them two hundred silver denarii worth of bread—as Philip observed—it would not have been enough. Each person would have had only a small piece. . . . Once again, however, this was not what Jesus had in mind.

Jesus said to his disciples, "Tell the people to sit in groups of 50." They did this, and all the people sat down.

Jesus looked about while the apostles drew near the people in the crowd, asking everyone to sit down on the ground, on the grass. Due to the large number of people present, it took more than a half hour before everyone was seated.

Then Jesus had them give him what little food there was while everyone's eyes were focused on him. But the vast majority of people present could not get a good look at what was taking place.

Jesus took the five loaves and the two fish. He looked up toward heaven and blessed the food. Then he broke the bread and fish and handed them to his disciples to give to the people.

The loaves were broken and broken yet again—the sharing of the bread seemed to have no end. Every piece that was passed along was then broken again and shared. Everyone present received bread and fish for dinner. They lit fires to roast the fish well. No one understood where the enormous quantity of food had come from. In one of the groups a bit farther away, there were two families from Gergesa, the village on the other side of the Sea of Galilee, where Jesus had freed the demoniac from the legion of impure spirits, and where he, too, had been driven out. They had come to look for him, representing those Gerasenes who had not wanted to drive the Nazarene away. There were also many babies in tow. One of them, as slender as a spindle and as quick as a lightning bolt, had rushed toward Philip, who had arrived near them with a basket. He was the first to grab half a loaf of bread. As he was about to run back to his father, mother, brothers and sisters, he heard the apostle say, "Break it and give it to the others. . . ." Without hesitating, the boy obeyed. And that half loaf of bread continued to be divided, and was not completely consumed until everyone in the group had enough bread to feed them sufficiently. The same happened with the fish.

Everyone ate all they wanted. What was left over filled twelve baskets.

In charge of the distribution, it was the apostles who were the first to be aware of the miracle they were witnessing. The crowd understood they were being fed, but in the hustle and bustle of the crowd, people going here and there, some thought everything had been planned and organized ahead of time. The bread did not come from nowhere, but was a miraculous fruit of sharing. Many others, instead, understood they were witnessing something extraordinary. They had been able to feed on spiritual nourishment the entire day. But before night descended, Jesus had also taken into consideration their material condition, providing an overabundance of food of inexplicable origin.

"It is helpful to compare the reaction of the disciples when faced with the tired and hungry people, with Jesus's. They are different. The disciples think it would be better to send them away so they could go and buy food. Jesus instead says, 'Give them something to eat yourselves.' Two different reactions that reflect two contrasting logics—the disciples reason according to the world, by which everyone must think of themselves. . . . Jesus reasons with God's logic, which is that of sharing. How many times do we turn away so as not to see our brothers and sisters in need! . . . Had he sent away the crowds, many people would have been left without anything to eat. Instead, those few loaves and fish, shared and blessed by God, were enough for everyone. . . . It is a sign that invites us to have faith in God, the provident Father, who does not allow us to lack 'our daily bread,' if we know how to share it as brothers and sisters." [59]

Impressed by what had happened, the crowd recognized that Jesus was the long-awaited prophet. A group of people decided to go and take him to proclaim him king. They had been fed and now they were projecting their messianic prototype on the man who had accomplished the miracle before their

---

59. Angelus, August 3, 2014.

very eyes. But Jesus left the place in time to retreat to the mountain by himself and dismissed his disciples, asking them to precede him and to embark toward the other shore, in the direction of Gennesaret, an ancient settlement that had given the lake, that everyone called a "sea," its name.

The apostles did not take their leave of the Teacher willingly. They were concerned about him and feared that the crowds would find him. They continued to talk among themselves about the multiplication of the loaves and fish. It was true, to raise a dead person—as Jesus had done before their eyes at Nain with the widow's son, or at Capernaum with the daughter of Jairus—was a very powerful miracle. To give sight back to a blind man or to make a paralytic walk were equally powerful miracles. In each of these cases, however, there always remained the slimmest possibility of doubt: Was that young man really dead? Was the blind man really blind, or the paralytic really paralyzed? In the case of the loaves and fish that they themselves had distributed, there were no such questions, either individual or collective, to be dealt with. The people had really eaten; they had had their fill of food that was not there before. And this had happened before the eyes of thousands of people. The more the little there was shared, the more that little became so abundant that there were left overs. While they were intent on their discussion, their eyes still filled with amazement for what they had seen happening in their own hands, they almost did not notice a new sudden squall agitating the waters. These were typical, late-spring phenomena, when cold winds blew from the mountains after sunset, growing more intense during the night. Powerful gusts of air hit them, preventing them from moving forward. They had gotten only halfway across.

By this time the boat was a long way from the shore. It was going against the wind and was being tossed around by the waves.

This time, too, Jesus did not leave them alone. As nighttime ended, he joined them, walking on the surface of the lake as if it were a road. His feet skimmed the water, which calmed down as he passed by. James was the first to catch sight of the approaching figure that seemed to be following them, suspended inexplicably over the surface.

When they saw him, they thought he was a ghost. They were terrified and started screaming.

At once, Jesus said to them, "Don't worry! I am Jesus. Don't be afraid."

They recognized the voice but were still too far off to see his face well because of the mist. Light had just begun to dawn.

Peter replied, "Lord, if it is really you, tell me to come to you on the water."

"Come on!" Jesus said.

If it truly was Jesus, he would make the impossible happen. So Peter, in front of the other speechless apostles, climbed overboard and let himself land as if he had already reached the other shore.

Peter then got out of the boat and started walking on the water toward him.

He took a few steps without realizing what force was sustaining him, keeping him from going under. The water had not been transformed into solid ground. It had maintained its consistency. But it was as if the solid weight of the fisherman from Galilee had disappeared all of a sudden, becoming like a twig floating along without ever sinking.

But when Peter saw how strong the wind was, he was afraid and started sinking. "Save me, Lord!" he shouted.

At once, Jesus reached out his hand. He helped Peter up and said, "You surely don't have much faith. Why do you doubt?"

All it took was a gust of wind more powerful than the others. Peter had been walking on the water, keeping his eyes fixed on Jesus, when in an instant he was distracted by the wind and spray. The laws of nature that had till that moment been suspended, gained the upper hand, and he sank. By that time, the Teacher was near. Hearing Peter's cry, he instantly covered the distance between them and offered his secure hand to the trembling hand of the apostle. Peter had believed. Peter had doubted. Peter had asked for help, and had been saved. Certainly, at that moment, the fisherman from Bethsaida could not have imagined the immense number of people in every corner of the earth in the centuries yet to come, who would live that same experience, even without walking on the water. He could not have imagined how many times that test would be repeated in the course of his own life, and how many times he would be saved and raised up by Jesus's hand, and the look in his eyes.

When Jesus and Peter got into the boat, the wind died down. The men in the boat worshiped Jesus and said, "You really are the Son of God!"

If the miracle of the loaves and fish had shocked them, the miracle of seeing him walk on water left them speechless. The only action that was fitting in this situation was to worship him, recognizing him for who he really was.

What happened at the end of that night *"reminds us that faith in the Lord and in his word does not open a way for us where everything is easy and calm, nor does it remove us from life's storms. Faith gives us the assurance of a Presence, the presence of Jesus who pushes us to overcome the existential tempests, the certainty of a hand that grabs hold of us to help us face difficulties, pointing the way for us even when it is dark."* [60]

When the sun was already up, they finally landed at Gennesaret. The people there recognized him. News of his arrival spread, and they *brought all the sick people to Jesus. They begged him just to let them touch his clothes, and everyone who did was healed,* just as had already happened to the woman with the hemorrhage.

Along with those who had come to him, there were several people who had witnessed the multiplication of loaves and had eaten their fill that evening.

"You are not looking for me," Jesus told them, *"because you saw the miracles, but because you ate all the food you wanted. Don't work for food that spoils. Work for food that gives eternal life. The Son of Man will give you this food."*

They responded, requesting new signs and citing the manna that had nourished their fathers, the Israelites, in the desert. The Nazarene reminded them that the Father had given them "bread from heaven." He added, *"The bread that God gives is the one who came down from heaven to give life to this world."*

The people said, "Sir, give us this bread and don't ever stop!"

Jesus replied: "I am the bread that gives life! No one who comes to me will ever be hungry. No one who has faith in me will ever be thirsty."

He told them he had descended from heaven to do the will of the Father. *"My Father wants everyone who sees the Son to have faith in him and to have eternal life. Then I will raise them to life on the last day."*

As could be expected, these words, which more precisely revealed who he was and what his mission was, were received in various ways. Some remained amazed, even though they did not understand. Others did not understand but kept Jesus's expressions in their hearts. Then there were those who began to murmur among themselves, repeating the same objections as the people at Nazareth. *"Isn't he Jesus, the son of Joseph? Don't we know his father and mother? How can he say that he has come down from heaven?"*

Jesus told them: "Stop grumbling! No one can come to me unless the Father who sent me makes them want to come. But if they do come, I will raise them to life on the last day." Then he added: *"I am the bread that gives life. Your ancestors ate manna in the desert, and later they died. But the bread from heaven has come down, so that no one who eats it will ever die. I am that bread from heaven!*

---

60. Angelus, August 13, 2017.

Everyone who eats it will live forever. My flesh is the life-giving bread I give to the people of this world."

The murmuring increased. How could this prophet give his flesh as food? As he was pronouncing those words, Jesus saw what would happen a year later unfold before his eyes—that last supper with his disciples, and then his tortured body, bruised and bleeding, hanging from the cross. . . .

"I tell you for certain, that you won't live unless you eat the flesh and drink the blood of the Son of Man," he explained. *"But if you do eat my flesh and drink my blood, you will have eternal life, and I will raise you to life on the last day. My flesh is the true food, and my blood is the true drink. If you eat my flesh and drink my blood, you are one with me, and I am one with you. The living Father sent me, and I have life because of him. Now everyone who eats my flesh will live because of me. The bread that comes down from heaven isn't like what your ancestors ate. They died, but whoever eats this bread will live forever."*

These were words that could not leave anyone indifferent. Even many of his disciples considered them very difficult, incomprehensible. They murmured, but even more so, they ruminated over their doubts and negative reaction in silence. Jesus knew the thoughts in their hearts. He knew who would betray him, who would abandon him, who would deny him, who would be conquered by fear. *"The words that I have spoken to you are from that life-giving Spirit,"* he said. *"But some of you refuse to have faith in me."*

Then, seeing that many of his followers were leaving him and ceased following him, he turned to the twelve apostles who had remained with him, even though they did not understand, and asked *if they also were going to leave him.*

Simon Peter answered, "Lord, there is no one else that we can go to! Your words give eternal life. We have faith in you, and we are sure that you are God's Holy One." Once again, it was Peter's impetuous courage that came into play. They were not able to totally understand what the Teacher was saying to them. But they had seen and experienced enough to be able to trust him, risking their entire lives.

Peter *"does not say 'where shall we go,' but 'to whom shall we go?' The underlying problem is not about leaving and abandoning the work undertaken, but who to go to. From Peter's question we understand that fidelity to God is a question of fidelity to a person to whom we unite ourselves to walk together on the same road. And this person is Jesus. All we have in the world does not satisfy our infinite hunger. We need Jesus—to be with him, to be nourished at his table, on his words of eternal life! To believe in Jesus means making him the center, the meaning of our lives. Christ is not an accessory. He is the 'living bread,' the essential nourishment."*[61]

After this happened, Jesus and his disciples went up to Jerusalem to celebrate Pentecost, the feast recalling the revelation of God on Mount Sinai. In the northern area of the Holy City, just outside the Sheep Gate, a new neighborhood was under construction. There was a rectangular pool called Bethza'tha, with four porticoes along the sides and another in the center, dividing it in two. Here, waters flowed from an underground spring that people believed contained a special healing power. Every time new water would gush forth from the spring, their eyes of faith saw an angel descend. At that moment, the crowd of the sick, blind, lame, and paralyzed who were in the vicinity competed to immerse themselves, hoping to receive the grace. There was a lot of movement during those feast days.

In one corner, Jonas was lying sheltered under one of the porticoes, flung on the ground like a sack of rags. By this time, he was an old man, disappointed with life. Thirty-eight years earlier, he had been struck with paralysis. Now he would lie on a type of pallet with run-down wheels on one end. He had remained all alone in the world after the death of his parents. A distant relative would reluctantly take him there every morning and bring him back in the evening. He lived off of alms and had resigned himself to his situation. Jesus saw him as he passed by, and reading the suffering and disappointment on his face for all the time he had lived in that condition, asked him, *"Do you want to be healed?"*

His response was not yes, as one might have expected. *The man answered, "Sir, I don't have anyone to put me in the pool when the water is stirred up. I try to get in, but someone always gets there first."*

Jesus told him, "Pick up your mat and walk!" Right then the man was healed. He picked up his mat and started walking around.

At that moment, Jesus was not with his friends. The words just spoken could barely be heard in the general indifference of those who were passing by, seeking to make space for themselves so they would be ready, right next to the edge of the pool, to plunge themselves in at the moment the water began to gurgle.

"That man's attitude makes us think. Was he sick? Yes, perhaps he had some form of paralysis, but it seems he could walk a little. But his heart was sick, his soul was sick, he was sick with pessimism, he was sick with sadness, he was sick with

---

apathy. This is the disease the man had—'Yes, I want to live,' but . . . he stayed there. And his answer is not, 'Yes, I want to be healed.' No, it was to complain."[62]

The incredulous old man stood up, his eyes wide open. He attracted someone's attention in just the split second in which he succeeded in getting up after being bedridden for thirty-eight years. Before that, the poor derelict who had been forever lying down had, in fact, become "invisible." Even now, very few noticed what had happened as he got up, picked up his pallet, put it under his arm, and headed toward the temple. Among those who did notice were some doctors of the law who stopped him, telling him, *"This is the Sabbath! No one is allowed to carry a mat on the Sabbath."*

They did not ask who he was, nor did they try to understand how he had been healed. They were concerned only about the prescriptions of the law.

But he replied, "The man who healed me told me to pick up my mat and walk."

They asked him, "Who is this man who told you to pick up your mat and walk?" But he did not know who Jesus was, and Jesus had left because of the crowd.

Everything had happened so quickly. The now ex-paralytic did not even have time to ask his healer who he was, even though he thought he heard him say, "My name is mercy," as he was leaving.

Jonas reached the temple to give thanks to God. While he was there, Jesus arrived. The man recognized him from afar but waited for Jesus to come nearer. The Nazarene warned him, *"You are now well. But don't sin anymore, or something worse might happen to you."*

As he left the temple, the old man told the doctors of the law who had stopped him that it was Jesus who had cured him. This provoked a new reaction. They persecuted Jesus *because he did things like this on the Sabbath. But Jesus said, "My Father has never stopped working, and this is why I keep on working."* Now the leaders wanted to kill Jesus for two reasons. First, he had broken the law of the Sabbath. But even worse, he had said God was his Father, which made him equal with God.

The words Jesus pronounced increased concern in some, hatred toward him in others. The latter were those who felt their exercise of sacred power threatened since they "regulated" the lives of the people. So some scribes and Pharisees *noticed that some of his disciples ate without first washing their hands. . . . The Pharisees and teachers asked Jesus, "Why don't your disciples obey what our ancestors taught us to do? Why do they eat without washing their hands?"*

---

62. Homily, Santa Marta, March 24, 2020.

Jesus performed miracles on the Sabbath; his disciples did not hold to all the prescribed ablutions. The scribes and Pharisees were asking him to give an account, not so much to understand, but to create trouble for him.

The Teacher responded, citing a great prophet of Israel: *"You are nothing but show-offs! The prophet Isaiah was right when he said that God had said,*

> *'All of you praise me*
> *with your words,*
> *but you never really*
> *think about me.*
> *It is useless for you*
> *to worship me,*
> *when you teach rules*
> *made up by humans.'*

You disobey God's commands in order to obey what humans have taught."

Now he was the one to counter their accusation, exposing their formalism, their exterior observation of the law rather than living it with their heart. He even gave a concrete example:

"You are good at rejecting God's commands so that you can follow your own teachings! Didn't Moses command you to respect your father and mother? Didn't he tell you to put to death all who curse their parents? But you let people get by without helping their parents when they should. You let them say that what they own has been offered to God. You won't let those people help their parents. And you ignore God's commands in order to follow your own teaching. You do a lot of other things just as bad."

If a son did not want to share his possessions with his parents in difficulty, he could declare his possessions as an offering to God. The divine commandment was thus overridden, and the son could continue to benefit from them until he brought the offering to the temple. This was a case of hypocrisy, of rules that were changed according to circumstances, of interpreting the law according to personal interest. Speaking like this, Jesus knew full well that his message would strike home to his listeners.

He did not limit himself, however, to teaching the law of God to the scribes, Pharisees, and doctors. He wanted to speak liberating words to everyone.

Jesus called the crowd together again and said, "Pay attention and try to understand what I mean. The food that you put into your mouth doesn't make you unclean and unfit to worship God. The bad words that come out of your mouth are what make you unclean."

It is not food that contaminates. It is the evil, the sin that lives inside men and women that makes them impure and in need of salvation. As he looked into the eyes of the people who had gathered around him, he knew it was precisely for this that he had come to earth—to make that salvation possible, to provide healing from sin by taking it on himself, to redeem and liberate anyone who would say yes to his message.

That afternoon, even his own followers had been shaken by his words.

After Jesus and his disciples had left the crowd and gone into the house, they asked him what these sayings meant. He answered, "Don't you know what I am talking about by now? You surely know that the food you put into your mouth cannot make you unclean. It doesn't go into your heart, but into your stomach, and then out of your body." By saying this, Jesus meant that all foods were fit to eat.

Then Jesus said: "What comes from your heart is what makes you unclean. Out of your heart come evil thoughts, vulgar deeds, stealing, murder, unfaithfulness in marriage, greed, meanness, deceit, indecency, envy, insults, pride, and foolishness. All of these come from your heart, and they are what make you unfit to worship God."

Evil was unmasked at its root. The original sin had corrupted human nature from what the Father had conceived, willed, and created it to be. This did not come from outside, from food, but dwelt within man and woman. It then followed that formalism or multiplying rules would not "save" the heart of the sinner.

13

Crumbs for Dogs,
and the Revelation about the Cross

Year AD 29, June—August.

Journey to Tyre and Sidon. Healing of the Deaf Man in the Decapolis.
The Pharisees and Sadducees Demand a "Sign from Heaven."
The Blind Man from Bethsaida. The Primacy of Peter.
The Transfiguration on Tabor.

The persistence of the Pharisees and the doctors of the law concerning Jesus was becoming increasingly more aggressive on a daily basis. By now it was clear to many of them that the prophet whom the common people loved represented a threat to them. The Teacher's friends perceived this more and more clearly. It was not a matter of disputes or questions, which in reality were not questions, but attempts to make things difficult for Jesus. Jesus did not shy away from them, even so; being able to read the hearts of those who were in front of him, he did not submit to their interrogation willingly.

In the last few months, the hostility was getting stronger, and someone began to plot to harm the Nazarene. Because of this, after the last dispute, Jesus allowed the apostles to convince him to leave Judea and Galilee for a time so as to distance himself both from danger and from the opposite risk that was daily present of being "crowned" king and messiah by the crowds who were waiting for redemption and liberation.

That summer was the first time he left his country since his flight into Egypt. With his disciples, he withdrew to the area of Tyre and Sidon, in the land the Jews called Canaan, and the Romans, Phoenicia. Its inhabitants were regarded rather negatively by the Jews, who saw them as pagans who were to be avoided, as sinners to be kept away from. They were a people of entrepreneurs, navigators, and merchants. Both of these cities visited by the Nazarene and his friends were port cities overlooking the Mediterranean Sea—a true sea, that had nothing to do with the lake called the Sea of Galilee. He was finally able to spend a few quiet days with his apostles, who had the possibility of interiorizing what they had experienced during the preceding months, asking Jesus questions about his parables and his deeds.

But even in this region, rumors had arrived concerning him, the "healer from Nazareth," who performed miracles. That is how one fine June morning, as they were leaving Tyre along the dusty main road crossing the city, a woman, on seeing him pass by, came out shouting, *"Lord and Son of David, have pity on me! My daughter is full of demons."*

"Son of David" was an expression used mostly as a title for the Messiah. It was often used by beggars who wanted to attract the attention of passersby whose clothing suggested they held a position of authority. That woman was certainly not a beggar, nor did she live on the street. She was still young. Her hair was in place and well groomed. She was dressed in a simple and dignified outfit.

Jesus did not say a word.

Jesus seemed not to have seen or heard her, despite her insistent cries. The woman did not stop moving toward him and continued to shout out her request.

So *his disciples came up and asked him to send her away.*

It was then that the apostles turned to implore the Teacher. They were not so much interested that he fulfill the wish of the Canaanite woman but rather in shutting her up so they could continue on their way in peace, without the fastidious annoyance of her shouting.

Jesus said, "I was sent only to the people of Israel! They are like a flock of lost sheep."

They were in a land considered pagan by the Jews, and Jesus wanted to remind them what the principal objective of his mission was.

The woman came closer. Then she knelt down and begged, "Please, help me Lord!" Jesus replied, "It isn't right to take the food from children and feed it to dogs."

Another difficult response. There was a huge distance between observant Jews and the people who believed in other gods. The Canaanite woman, however, would not surrender. She responded to Jesus, using his own argument. *"Lord, this is true,"* the woman said, *"but even dogs get the crumbs that fall from their owner's table.* If you will not treat me like a daughter, at least treat me like a dog. Don't drive me away, but let me have the crumbs."

Jesus answered, "Dear woman, you really do have a lot of faith, and you will be given what you want." At that moment her daughter was healed.

At the very moment Jesus pronounced those words, Palma, the woman's daughter, was healed. The impure spirit that had infested her left her forever. Everything went back to normal. After years of torment and useless medical consultations, peace returned to that house that had been daily shaken by the gasping and cries of the possessed girl.

"Teacher, why did you listen to her in the end? To make her finally shut up?" James of Zebedee asked.

"No, James," Jesus responded, looking him in the eye. "I heard her because of her faith and her courage as a mother. Would that I could find in Israel such great faith as I found today in this land that welcomed me without casting me out or persecuting me. . . ."

"Turning to Jesus, the woman . . . is courageous, like any desperate mother who is ready to do anything when the health of her child is concerned. They had told her that there was a good man, a prophet, and so she went to look for Jesus, even though she did not believe in the God of Israel. For her daughter's sake, she was not ashamed of the stares of the apostles, who might have been saying among themselves, 'What is this pagan woman doing here?' . . . The woman . . . did not respond to Jesus with her intelligence, but with her mother's gut, with her love. And so she said, 'Even the dogs under the table eat the children's crumbs.' It was as if she were saying, 'Give these crumbs to me!' Moved by her faith, the Lord worked a miracle. . . . It is the story of a mother who . . . coming from paganism and idolatry, found health for her daughter, and the living God for herself."[63]

Jesus and his disciples continued their journey serenely. They passed through Sidon and from there on into the Decapolis, the region of the "ten cities" located close to the eastern frontier of the Roman Empire. These cities were not united among themselves but had been grouped together under that name because of their linguistic, cultural, and political similarities. In fact, they were all centers of Greek and Roman culture, in a territory that was mostly Semitic, inhabited by Nabateans, Arameans, and Jews. Each of the cities enjoyed a degree of autonomy and independence in the Empire. They were cosmopolitan centers with strong commercial ties and open cities.

The Teacher and his apostles felt as if they were back home in Capernaum. Sometimes it took Jesus's friends by surprise to see him praying in silence, staring at the walls of the city, as happened at Pella. They had no way of knowing

---

63. Homily, Santa Marta, February 13, 2014.

what he was seeing—that here, in the Decapolis, the first Christians fleeing from Jerusalem, would find refuge.

Journeying through the Decapolis meant they could remain unrecognized. It was wonderful to be with him without being followed by a crowd, to watch him speak, to contemplate him at prayer and his deep unity with his Father. These weeks were restful and refreshing, despite the daily journey they had to accomplish. But Jesus had not come to remain only with his friends. They resumed the road toward the Sea of Galilee and were drawing near Hippos, the city in the Decapolis closest to the large lake. There, they met a group of men who recognized them.

Some people brought to him a man who was deaf and could hardly talk. They begged Jesus just to touch him.

One of the many requests for healing. This time, too, Jesus was moved and did not draw back, even though he chose an unprecedented way to fulfill the desire of this poor unfortunate who looked double his age and had been kicked out of his family. His name was Greek—Alypius—but he had never been able to utter it and had never heard it uttered.

After Jesus had taken him aside from the crowd, he stuck his fingers in the man's ears. Then he spit and put it on the man's tongue. Jesus looked up toward heaven, and with a groan he said, "Effatha!" which means "Open up!"

He had put a bit of saliva on his fingers and touched the man's tongue with it.

At once the man could hear, and he had no more trouble talking clearly.

He had not performed the miracle at a distance but solely with a verbal command. This time, he had acted on the ailing man's hearing and speech through signs, as if he wanted to prepare him for what was about to happen. It was a way in which he reawakened the deaf man's faith, since he would not have been able to hear what Jesus was saying.

"This action refers back to the Incarnation. The Son of God is a man inserted into human reality. He became man. Therefore, he can understand another man's distressing condition and intervene with an action that involves his own humanity. At the same time, Jesus wants to make it understood that the miracle occurred because of his union with his Father. For this reason, he raised his eyes to heaven."[64]

---

64. Angelus, September 9, 2018.

It was a new birth for Alypius. All of a sudden, he heard the voices of his companions, who were waiting for him at a short distance. He heard the blowing of the wind, the shouts of the beggars, the chatter that rose from the main street of Hippos, teaming with merchants and customers. Reality was speaking, and his heart was no longer burdened by that oppressive cloak of absolute silence. His joy was uncontainable when, for the first time, with a bit of effort, he succeeded in uttering a word and hearing his own voice. "Thank you," he said repeatedly, his eyes fixed on Jesus, while his friends approached him.

The Nazarene *told the people not to say anything about what he had done*, as he had done so many other times. But their joy because of the healing and their contact with Jesus was, however, uncontainable. It was stronger than the words asking them to be discreet.

But the more he told them, the more they talked about it. They were completely amazed and said, "Everything he does is good! He even heals people who cannot hear or talk."

And so, they bore witness to what they had experienced.

～

Returning to Galilee, Jesus and his apostles found themselves once again with the doctrinal experts on their heels. This time, there were not only Pharisees but also the Sadducees, aristocrats who held positions of power. The high priest and the majority of the seventy-member Sanhedrin were Sadducees. They were conservatives who were more interested in politics than in religion at that time. They were also in the good graces of the Roman occupiers. Up till then, they had not given that much importance to the Teacher from Nazareth. Their presence alongside the much more popular Pharisees was an indication that even those supporting the power of Rome had begun to perceive Jesus's preaching as a threat.

The Pharisees and Sadducees came to Jesus and tried to test him by asking for a sign from heaven.

They were aware of Jesus's previous responses and had already been discussing the calm and, at the same time powerful, way in which he spoke about his relationship with his Father and his authority to forgive sins. This time, they pressed Jesus for a "sign," something spectacular, awe striking, and incontrovertible—a supernatural "test" that would confirm the Nazarene's nature and his words.

He told them, "If the sky is red in the evening, you say the weather will be good. But if the sky is red and gloomy in the morning, you say it is going to rain. You can tell what the weather will be like by looking at the sky. But you don't understand what is happening now. You want a sign because you are evil and won't believe! But the only sign you will be given is what happened to Jonah. Then Jesus left."

It was not enough that sick people had been healed, blind people had regained their sight, the dead had been raised, bread had been multiplied. The religious dignitaries, including those closest to the people, manifested that they did not understand their own people. The crowds sought Jesus to be welcomed by him, listened to, healed. They, instead, sought signs to prove the veracity of his words. No sign would have been sufficient to cure the blindness of their eyes, for they harbored the pretense to judge him in their hearts.

Jonah had been in the belly of the whale for three days, just as Jesus, less than a year after these events, would remain for three days in the belly of the earth, in the sepulcher.

"The sign Jesus promises is his forgiveness, through his death and resurrection . . . it is his mercy, the mercy that God had been requesting for some time, 'it is mercy I desire and not sacrifice.' The true sign of Jonah is the one that gives us the confidence of having been saved by the blood of Christ."[65]

~

Confronting the hostility of the religious leaders once again made Jesus decide to head back to Bethsaida, the city where Simon Peter had been born. The fisherman and his brother were well known there. There was not one street corner where they were not greeted and asked for news about their families. Many of the people living there knew about what both brothers had done, how they had left their boats, their small fishing business, their loved ones, and had followed that man, accompanying him during those tiring days among the people and his traipsing around the region. So as soon as they approached, *some people brought a blind man to him and begged him to touch the man.* His name was Terah, like the father of the patriarch Abraham. He was about fifty years old.

Jesus reacted differently from the other times, imagining what reaction the healing might provoke.

---

65. Homily, Santa Marta, October 14, 2013.

Jesus took him by the hand and led him out of the village, where he spit into the man's eyes. He placed his hands on the blind man and asked him if he could see anything. The man looked up and said, "I see people, but they look like trees walking around."

They had remained outside the village, but they were not alone. In the background were the first houses of Bethsaida; a group of disciples was at a distance. All around them, people were coming and going. The blind man needed a few moments before he could reacquire the sight he had lost as a boy from a serious infection. After all, he had been living with the memories he had stored in his mind since infancy. Every day he had tried to imagine the blue sky, the white clouds, the green trees, the ochre stones, the blue Sea of Galilee. So as his eyes miraculously opened once again, it seemed to him he was seeing walking trees. . . .

Once again Jesus placed his hands on the man's eyes, and this time the man stared. His eyes were healed, and he saw everything clearly.

Everything took on shape and color once again. His friends, who had led the Nazarene to him, understood by his reaction that the healing had taken place. Terah continued rubbing his eyes, every now and then raising his arms toward heaven, under the smiling gaze of Jesus, who then *said to him, "You may return home now, but don't go into the village."* He obeyed. But even this time, the news did not remain confined within the walls of the house where the man lived with his brother's family.

⁓

They stayed in Bethsaida just a few days. News of the healed blind man flew from mouth to mouth, and many wanted to make contact with Jesus. At the beginning of July, the Teacher and his apostles set out again, leaving Judea and Galilee once more, heading toward the borders of the Promised Land. Going through Iturea, they arrived near Caesarea Philippi, at the foot of Mount Hermon.

He had wanted to bring them again to a predominantly pagan area, where he was not known. It had now been about a year and a half since they had all known each other and had been journeying together from village to village. The moment had come to be explicit with them so they would understand.

They most certainly knew he was the Messiah. What they did not understand, however, were the reasons behind his reserve, his reluctance to say it openly to the crowds. It was not only Judas who cultivated dreams of grandeur and vindication in his heart, and even more in his mind. Deep down, all of them would not have minded a show of force, to accept a mandate on the part of the people, who were disillusioned by the invaders and by their corrupt leaders and constantly in search of a liberator. During their moments of fraternity in Bethsaida, when he was alone with them at table, he had demolished these expectations more than once. Now the time had come to speak more clearly to them.

It was around midday. They were walking in silence as the heat oppressed them. Caesarea Philippi was already visible in front of them, with the temple of Augustus towering above the rock. They stopped in a deserted place. As they were conversing about the discourses he had made in the last few days, Jesus *asked them, "What do people say about the Son of Man?"*

They were not caught off guard. James, John, and Andrew took the floor. *The disciples answered, "Some people say you are John the Baptist or maybe Elijah or Jeremiah or some other prophet."*

Everyone in the crowd in search of miracles had their own idea they tried to project onto the extraordinary uniqueness of Jesus—a name, a memory, a reference to Israel's religious tradition. . . . The Teacher listened silently, his eyes shifting now to one of his friends, now to another. Their faces were sweaty; they were tired from the journey. They had not imagined that that rest stop to eat some food would be transformed into an annunciation.

He listened to their responses. Then *Jesus asked, "But who do you say I am?"*

There was a moment of silence. Everyone had been invited to look into their own heart, to respond personally. Before anyone else had time to open their mouth, *Simon Peter spoke up, "You are the Messiah, the Son of the living God."*

Silence again. Peter had spoken from his heart.

Jesus told him, "Simon, son of Jonah, you are blessed! You didn't discover this on your own. It was shown to you by my Father in heaven."

Jesus looked at the fisherman from Bethsaida with an intensity that Peter had never experienced before. The apostle felt as he had in that instant when Jesus's hand had grabbed him to pull him out of the dark waters of the Sea of Galilee during the storm.

"So I will call you Peter, which means 'a rock,'" the Teacher added. *"And I tell you,"* the Teacher added, *"you are Peter, and on this rock I will build my church, and the gates of hell shall not prevail against it. I will give you the keys of the kingdom of heaven, and whatever you bind on earth shall be bound in heaven, and whatever you loose on earth shall be loosed in heaven."*

The doors of the kingdom of heaven, the gates of hell, hidden keys, an immense power. . . . *To bind* and *to loose* were terms the Israelites were used to because the rabbis would "bind" when they prohibited, and would "loose" when they allowed this or that to be done. But the vastness of the horizon depicted by Jesus was impressive. Peter felt as if he were once again being sucked under by the waves, even if there was no water near Caesarea Philippi.

What was the meaning of those words? Of what power was Jesus speaking? From that moment on, the other apostles began to view Peter differently. They understood he had been chosen. He, on the other hand, would have preferred to become really little and disappear. Only Jesus's eyes, which remained fixed on his, sustained him. Jesus had brought them to the brink of pagan land to make them understand that his identity was not to be confused with the messianic expectations mingled with politics. Jesus was another type of Messiah, a different Messiah, the only true Messiah.

They ate what little remained after their journey and approached the city. *Jesus told his disciples not to tell anyone he was the Messiah.*

⌣

That same evening, sitting around the fire when they were more rested and refreshed, he spoke again to them, foretelling what would happen in the months ahead.

From then on, Jesus began telling his disciples what would happen to him. He said, "I must go to Jerusalem. There the nation's leaders, the chief priests, and the teachers of the Law of Moses will make me suffer terribly. I will be killed, but three days later I will rise to life."

That the chief priests had begun to hate him was already evident. But to foretell his death . . . and his resurrection . . . no, that was too much. Feeling himself invested with authority and motivated by sincere love, Peter got up, *took Jesus aside and told him to stop talking like that. He said, "God would never let this happen to you, Lord!"*

He had tried to protect Jesus without knowing that in this way, he was tempting Jesus. Jesus's face became unusually hard. *Jesus turned to Peter and said, "Satan, get away from me! You're in my way because you think like everyone else and not like God."*

Jesus had not sent him away but had put him back in his place, the place destined for everyone—behind him, following him, in his footsteps, on his trail. They could not change his destiny, the mission established by his Father. He was asking them to follow him, not protect him. And to be even more clear regarding the way to follow, *Jesus said to his disciples, "If any of you want to be my followers, you must forget about yourself. You must take up your cross and follow me. If you want to save your life, you will destroy it. But if you give up your life for me, you will find it."*

Deny themselves, take up their own cross. . . . Once again, words that were too grand for them. Certainly, they all understood that there would be no tests of strength, no acts of greatness or revenge. Quite the contrary. He had said he would be killed, defeated. He had said he would be raised. But at that moment that last allusion had slipped out of their minds. They understood that to continue to follow him would not be easy, would not involve honors but sacrifices, even the ultimate sacrifice. After having heard these words, the most deluded of them all was Judas.

They went to bed looking around at each other without having the courage to ask anything. They were shaken. Peter struggled to fall asleep as the last reddish glow sparked from the embers and Jesus was praying alone in the distance. He was praying for them and for all those who would come after them.

"We hear Jesus's question directed to each one of us—'And you, who do you say I am?'—to each one of us. And each one of us must give a response that is not theoretical, but one that involves faith, that is, life, because faith is life! 'For me you are . . .' and to confess who Jesus is. A response that demands from us too, as it did from the first disciples, interior listening to the voice of the Father and consonance with what the Church, gathered around Peter, continues to proclaim. It is a matter of understanding who Christ is for us, whether he is the center of our life. . . . Who is Jesus Christ for me? . . . An answer that we should give every day." [66]

They left the region of Caesarea Philippi and returned to Galilee. It took them one day of travel to return to their own land. But they did not enter Capernaum. Jesus, after having revealed the true nature of his mission to his friends, extremely far from the political, messianic projects and expectations of the people, wanted to console them in some way. So in the afternoon, he took the road leading up to Mount Tabor, about a two-thousand-foot climb amid rocky, arid surroundings. He did not allow everyone to come with him.

Jesus took Peter, John, and James with him and went up on a mountain to pray.

---

66. Angelus, August 23, 2020.

They followed behind him at a good pace without asking useless questions. They knew well enough that he needed to go off on his own every day to pray.

They reached the top.

Jesus lifted his eyes toward heaven.

While he was praying, his face changed, and his clothing became shining white. Suddenly Moses and Elijah were there speaking with him. They appeared in heavenly glory and talked about all that Jesus's death in Jerusalem would mean.

In the meantime, the three apostles had not been able to stay awake with him because they were so tired.

Peter and the other two disciples had been sound asleep. All at once they woke up and saw how glorious Jesus was. They also saw the two men who were with him.

They were entranced, enraptured by the vision that appeared before their eyes.

As the two men were about to leave, when Peter said to Jesus, *"Master, it is good for us to be here! Let us make three shelters, one for you, one for Moses, and one for Elijah."*

The supernatural light and peace that reigned estranged them from the world around them, provoking this desire and request to explode in Peter's heart. They would have remained there forever.

But Peter did not know what he was talking about. While Peter was still speaking, a shadow from a cloud passed over, and they were frightened as the cloud covered them. From the cloud a voice spoke, "This is my chosen Son. Listen to what he says!"

It was a voice they had never heard before, another confirmation from heaven of the fact that Jesus was truly the Son of God.

After the voice had spoken, Peter, John, and James saw only Jesus. For some time they kept quiet and did not say anything about what they had seen. They remained shaken by this unique and shocking experience. The other apostles understood that something truly exceptional had happened on Tabor. Jesus had asked Peter, James, and John not to say anything about what they had seen.

~

The next day Jesus and his three disciples came down from the mountain and were met by a large crowd.

He could not escape for long from the people who were looking for him. That climb up to Tabor had been an anticipation of paradise.

Just then someone in the crowd shouted, "Teacher, please do something for my son! He is my only child! A demon often attacks him and makes him scream. It shakes him until he foams at the mouth, and it won't leave him until it has completely worn the boy out. I begged your disciples to force out the demon, but they couldn't do it."

It did not seem that Jesus liked the request. *Jesus said to them, "You people are stubborn and don't have any faith! How much longer must I be with you? Why do I have to put up with you?" Then Jesus said to the man, "Bring your son to me."*

He had responded harshly, while at the same time opening his heart to grant the man's request.

Jethro was the boy's name. The father had entrusted him to two servants to hold him while he tried to get close to Jesus to present his request. Jethro took a few steps toward the Nazarene.

While the boy was being brought, the demon attacked him and made him shake all over.

It was a terrible, impressive sight. Some people could not look at his writhing, shrieking body. The only one who was not repulsed was the Teacher.

Jesus ordered the demon to stop. Then he healed the boy and gave him back to his father. Everyone was amazed at God's great power.

Jethro got up, completely liberated. He ran and hugged his father, who could not take his eyes off Jesus, nor was he able to utter one word.

While everyone was still amazed at what Jesus was doing, he said to his disciples, "Pay close attention to what I am telling you! The Son of Man will be handed over to his enemies."

Once more, he told his followers what was awaiting him. Once more, he foretold a fate far removed from their messianic dreams.

But the disciples did not know what he meant. The meaning was hidden from them. They could not understand it, and they were afraid to ask.

Jesus's disciples were arguing about which one of them was the greatest.

Their Teacher was speaking, but human nature, wounded by original sin, gained the upper hand over these concrete and generous men who were no different from everyone else. They could not and did not want to know anything else about the Nazarene's future. So they ended up discussing the internal hierarchy among themselves. Jesus was not with them at the moment, but he understood what was happening. *Jesus knew what they were thinking, and he had a child stand there beside him. Then he said to his disciples, "When you welcome even a child because of me, you welcome me. And when you welcome me, you welcome the one who sent me. Whichever one of you is the most humble is the greatest."*

He was little, with jet-black hair and a capricious look on his face. Jesus held him close to himself for a few moments. That was enough to teach his followers about the upheaval of human logic testified by the God of Israel, who overturns the mighty from their thrones and lifts up the humble, the poor, the least. They had to become little like that child. They needed to trust in Jesus and entrust themselves completely to him, just as Peter had done when he had taken those few steps on the water.

Then the Nazarene added, *"It will be terrible for people who cause even one of my little followers to sin. Those people would be better off thrown into the deepest part of the ocean with a heavy stone tied around their necks! The world is in for trouble because of the way it causes people to sin. There will always be something to cause people to sin, but anyone who does this will be in for trouble."*

14

Forgiveness and Mercy on the Last Day
of the Feast of Tabernacles

Year AD 29, October—December.

The Lost Sheep. How Many Times to Forgive.
Return to Jerusalem and New Confrontations with the
Pharisees and Chief Priests.
Jesus, the "Light of the World." The Adulteress. The Man Born Blind.

Summer was over by now. The Feast of Tabernacles was drawing near. Having returned to Capernaum, Jesus alternated time spent meeting the crowds and dialoguing with his friends. Day by day, the apostles had the opportunity to observe the completely new behavior of the Teacher who was living and giving testimony to the law in an unprecedented way. He was breaking human patterns and traditions, upsetting people by sitting down at table even with sinners, approaching lepers and other people whose presence in public was abhorrent. Through his actions, even more so than with his words, he was challenging so many of their frivolous certainties. Every day he was making God's loving and merciful face present.

One afternoon, as gusts of cold wind were rattling the old wooden planks that closed off the entrance to Peter's house, Jesus made them understand the power of prayer and, at the same time, assured them that he would always be present among those gathered in his name. *"I promise that when any two of you on earth agree about something you are praying for, my Father in heaven will do it for you. Whenever two or three of you come together in my name, I am there with you."* He was still on the earth; he was still with them, walking with them. But if any of his followers were far away, elsewhere, but gathered in his name, he would be at their side, he would be with them.

He also explained to them the type of attitude to have with someone who may have committed a fault. First, he asked them to admonish the person face-to-face, then in the presence of witnesses. He then repeated the profound reasons why he had come. *"What would you do if you had 100 sheep and one of them wandered off? Wouldn't you leave the 99 on the hillside and go look for the one that had wandered away? I am sure that finding it would make you happier than having the 99 that never wandered off. That's how it is with your Father in heaven. He doesn't want any of these little ones to be lost."*

The apostles who were at table with him listened to these words and looked at each other, question marks on their faces.

"Teacher," Philip said, "I'm no expert at being a shepherd . . . but . . . I'm not so sure I'd leave ninety-nine sheep alone on the mountains to go in search of only one who got lost."

Jesus looked at him, smiling. He had hit the nail on the head—the love and nearness of God to the one who is lost, the one who lost his way, for the one who has strayed, for the one who is a sinner, could appear paradoxical from a human perspective. A superabundance of unconditional love, incomprehensible from a human point of view.

"Philip", Jesus replied, indicating with his eyes the place where Matthew was sitting, "don't you remember that day in the house of our friend the tax collector? I have come for the sick, not for the healthy! I have come for sinners, not for the righteous. . . ." Finally, they understood what type of shepherd the parable they had just heard was about—it was an image of God the Father. Even the last and the most distant sinners were worth every effort to reach. Heaven rejoices for every change of life, every step, however small, toward the Father's House.

This was a revolutionary message. *Peter came up to the Lord and asked him, "How many times should I forgive someone who does something wrong to me? Is seven times enough?"*

Peter thought he was being overly generous suggesting that a person who does another wrong should be forgiven seven times. . . . Once again, Jesus smiled. There was love and understanding in his eyes. Little by little, he was transforming their hearts. Jesus answered: *"Not just seven times, but seventy-seven times!"*—that is to say, always. Just like God does. For the one who has been inundated with mercy is asked to look at his brother or sister in the same way.

"God always forgives, always. But he also requires that I forgive, because if I do not forgive it is like closing the door on God's forgiveness in a certain sense. Instead, this is one door we must keep open—let us allow God's forgiveness to come in so we might forgive others."[67]

In order to explain this to his followers, Jesus began another parable. *"This story will show you what the kingdom of heaven is like: One day a king decided to call in his officials and ask them to give an account of what they owed him. As he was doing this, one official was brought in who owed him 50,000,000 silver coins. But he didn't have any money to pay what he owed. The king ordered him to be sold, along with his wife and children and all he owned, in order to pay the debt. The official got down on his knees and began begging, 'Have pity on me, and I will pay you every cent I owe!' The king felt sorry for him and let him go free. He even told the official that he did not have to pay back the money.*

"But as this official was leaving, he happened to meet another official, who owed him 100 silver coins. So he grabbed the man by the throat. He started choking him and said, 'Pay me what you owe!' The man got down on his knees and began begging, 'Have pity on me, and I will pay you back.' But the first official refused to have pity. Instead, he went and had the other official put in jail until he could pay what he owed.

"When some other officials found out what had happened, they felt sorry for the man who had been put in jail. Then they told the king what had happened. The king called the first official back in and said, 'You're an evil man! When you begged for mercy, I said you did not have to pay back a cent. Don't you think you should show pity to someone else, as I did to you?' The king was so angry that he ordered the official to be tortured until he could pay back everything he owed. That is how my Father in heaven will treat you, if you don't forgive each of my followers with all your heart."

It is not possible to ask God for forgiveness and then have a closed heart toward the brother or sister who asks for forgiveness. "Forgive us our debts, as we also forgive our debtors."

∼

It had been about four months since Jesus had gone to Jerusalem. He had, in fact, visited the Holy City for the Feast of Pentecost. Every now and then, the Teacher's relatives, who did not really believe in him, would come around, expecting to witness more evident signs of his power. The hearts that were the

---

67. Homily, Santa Marta, March 10, 2015.

hardest to touch were those closest to him in terms of family ties. They did not want to be nourished by his presence, his deeds, his words, but were waiting for their own plans to be fulfilled.

Jesus's brothers said to him, "Why don't you go to Judea? Then your disciples can see what you are doing. No one does anything in secret, if they want others to know about them. So let the world know what you are doing!" Even Jesus's own brothers had not yet become his followers.

They wanted Jesus to return to Jerusalem to reveal himself publicly, hoping he would take charge of the crowds of pilgrims already moving toward the Holy City. Chasing their grandiose dreams, they were hoping he would lead the crowds, perhaps reserving a special place for them—his relatives. But the moment had not arrived.

Jesus answered, "My time hasn't yet come, but your time is always here. The people of this world cannot hate you. They hate me because I tell them that they do evil things. Go on to the festival. My time hasn't yet come, and I am not going."

Jesus said this and stayed on in Galilee. He did not join the group. He did not accept their invitation.

After Jesus's brothers had gone to the festival, he went secretly, without telling anyone. He decided to depart after the caravan had already gone on its way, taking a shortcut through Samaria, even though it was riskier since Jews passing through there were often subject to ridicule, and sometimes violence. A year and a half before, Jesus had been well received at Sychar, where he had met the woman at the well. There was nothing, however, that assured him he would find the same willingness to welcome him in other Samaritan cities.

For this reason, having arrived at the gates of a village, he decided to send two disciples ahead. He asked James and John to go and find lodging. As soon as the inhabitants found out where they were headed, they refused. *But he was on his way to Jerusalem, so the people there refused to welcome him. When the disciples James and John saw what was happening, they asked, "Lord, do you want us to call down fire from heaven to destroy these people?"*

They suggested a radical type of punishment for having denied hospitality, asking the Teacher's consent. It was a human reaction, way too human. But *Jesus turned and corrected them for what they had said.* He had not come into the world to set those who rejected him on fire. He had come to seek and to save. So they set out toward Sychar where they had been well received.

Their days on the road were filled with encounters. One young man followed the small group a bit, keeping his distance. He had heard about Jesus from a friend, who in his turn had heard stories about him from a family who had been present at the multiplication of the loaves and fish. He was a scribe and was intrigued by the Teacher. Finally getting up the courage to approach Jesus during a rest stop, he said to Jesus, *"I'll follow you anywhere!"* Jesus looked at the young man, and his response emphasized the itinerant aspect of his earthly life, *"Foxes have dens, and birds have nests, but the Son of Man doesn't have a place to call his own."*

Then there was the time a man who was a little bit older approached him. This time it was the Nazarene who took the initiative. *Jesus told someone else to come with him.*

But the man said, "Lord, let me wait until I bury my father."

Jesus answered, "Let the dead take care of the dead, while you go and tell about God's kingdom."

Deliberately provocative words, *"he intends to emphasize the primacy of following him and of proclaiming the kingdom of God, even over and above the most important realities, such as the family. The urgency of communicating the Gospel, which breaks the chains of death and ushers in eternal life, does not permit delays, but requires promptness and availability."*[68]

A third man came forward after listening to him, saying, *"I want to follow you, Lord, but first let me go back and take care of things at home."*

Jesus answered, "Anyone who starts plowing and keeps looking back isn't worth a thing to God's kingdom!" To follow Jesus, it was not necessary to look back, but to have the same openness of heart as his apostles.

〜

Meanwhile, in Jerusalem, Jesus was the topic of discussion in the places where the crowds were arriving for the feast. Many pilgrims from Galilee and in the city still had a vivid memory of the healing of the paralytic at the pool of Bethza'tha. Scribes and Pharisees were also looking for *Jesus and asked, "Where is he?"* The crowds even got into an argument about him. *Some were saying, "Jesus is a good man,"* while others were saying, *"He is lying to everyone."* But the people *were afraid of their leaders, and none of them talked in public about him.*

A few days later, *when the festival was about half over, Jesus went into the temple and started teaching.*

Listening to him, the scribes and doctors of the law were amazed, and said, *"How does this man know so much. He has never been taught!"* They could not conceive how someone who had not gone to their schools could speak about

---

68. Angelus, June 30, 2019.

the Scriptures and the law in such a profound, pertinent, and at the same time, such a new and liberating way that left everyone—the learned and not-so-learned—open-mouthed.

Jesus responded, recalling where that wisdom came from. He said it in a soft voice, looking them straight in the eye as a large crowd gathered around them. *"I am not teaching something I thought up. What I teach comes from the one who sent me. If you really want to obey God, you will know if what I teach comes from God or from me. If I wanted to bring honor to myself, I would speak for myself. But I want to honor the one who sent me. This is why I tell the truth and not a lie. Didn't Moses give you the Law? Yet none of you obey it! So why do you want to kill me?"*

The crowd did not understand who wanted to kill him. Instead, Jesus knew and, continuing to dialogue with the doctors of the law, added, *"I worked one miracle, and it amazed you. Moses commanded you to circumcise your sons. But it wasn't really Moses who gave you this command. It was your ancestors, and even on the Sabbath you circumcise your sons in order to obey the Law of Moses. Why are you angry with me for making someone completely well on the Sabbath? Don't judge by appearances. Judge by what is right."* He had read their hearts. He knew well that his healing of the paralytic at Beth-za'tha during the Sabbath rest had provoked them into denouncing it as scandalous.

Meanwhile, the crowd continued murmuring and some inhabitants of Jerusalem, accustomed to the constant presence of the doctors of the law, could not explain why the religious leaders allowed him to continue speaking. *"Isn't this the man they want to kill? Yet here he is, speaking for everyone to hear. And no one is arguing with him. Do you suppose the authorities know he is the Messiah? But how could that be? No one knows where the Messiah will come from, but we know where this man comes from."*

Jesus responded, saying, *"Do you really think you know me and where I came from? I didn't come on my own! The one who sent me is truthful, and you don't know him. But I know the one who sent me, because I came from him."*

Some tried to stop him, but in vain. The Pharisees requested that the temple guard be sent to arrest him. Others who were listening to him believed in him instead. This is what had been happening, and continued to happen—no one could remain indifferent, not take a position in his regard.

On the last day of the Feast of Tabernacles, the most solemn day, as Jesus was in the midst of the people, he *stood up and shouted, "If you are thirsty, come to me and drink! Have faith in me, and you will have life-giving water flowing from deep inside you, just as the Scriptures say."* He was speaking of the Holy

Spirit whom those who believed in him would receive after his glorification. His words were becoming more explicit. As his revelation progressed, so, too, did the opposition and risks to his life.

When the crowd heard Jesus say this, some of them said, "He must be the Prophet!" Others said, "He is the Messiah!" Others even said, "Can the Messiah come from Galilee? The Scriptures say that the Messiah will come from the family of King David. Doesn't this mean that he will be born in David's hometown of Bethlehem?" The people started taking sides against each other because of Jesus. Some of them wanted to arrest him, but no one laid a hand on him.

The inhabitants of Jerusalem posed the exact same argument—What good could come from Nazareth, from Galilee? Was not the Messiah supposed to be born of the house of David, in Bethlehem? After thirty years, everyone took him for a Galilean, the son of a carpenter—what did they really know about where he had been born, of the adventure his family had lived through in those days?

Meanwhile, the temple guard returned empty-handed to the chief priests and the Pharisees, who asked them, *"Why didn't you bring Jesus here?"*

They answered, "No one has ever spoken like this man!"

The Pharisees said to them, "Have you also been fooled? Not one of the chief priests or the Pharisees has faith in him. And these people who don't know the Law are under God's curse anyway."

One of their number, Nicodemus, came forward, the same one who, a year and a half earlier, had visited Jesus by night to meet him. He took the floor, making a statement based not only on common sense but also, at the same time, appealing to the law. *"Our Law doesn't let us condemn people before we hear what they have to say. We cannot judge them before we know what they have done."*

By this time, they knew his sympathies leaned toward the Nazarene. Their tempers were overly heated and their reaction too sarcastic. *Then they said, "Nicodemus, you must be from Galilee! Read the Scriptures, and you will find that no prophet is to come from Galilee."*

Everyone else went home.

∽

The feast was drawing to a close, and caravans of pilgrims were preparing to go home. But the next morning, Jesus went to the temple again, and the crowd followed him. *He sat down and started teaching them.* It was a cold day.

A little later, he was interrupted by the sounds of a commotion. The sound of shouting came nearer and nearer until a group of scribes and Pharisees, pushing a woman, entered the courtyard. She was young and she was beautiful. They had found her together with a man other than her husband. Her arms were bruised; her garments, torn; her hair, disheveled and filled with sand, since she had fallen several times while being chased. She lacked the strength to raise her eyes, feeling only immense shame. Unfortunately, she was well aware of the punishment awaiting her, as those who were judging her continued to insult her, spitting at her and shouting, "Whore!" "Corrupt!" "Demoniac!" "Sacrilegious!" "Blasphemer!"

Jesus followed them with his eyes, saying nothing. The crowd surrounding him was quiet. The woman was crying, but not sobbing.

"Teacher, this woman was caught sleeping with a man who isn't her husband. The Law of Moses teaches that a woman like this should be stoned to death! What do you say?" They asked Jesus this question, because they wanted to test him and bring some charge against him. They were not interested in the woman's sins and the punishment to be meted out to her. They wanted to get Jesus into trouble and had answers ready for whatever he might say. If he asked them to be merciful, they would accuse him of not following the Mosaic law. If instead, he incited them to stone her, they would say he was merciless. . . .

But Jesus simply bent over and started writing on the ground with his finger. As one scribe rained accusations down on the woman Jesus wrote, "Usurer." While another attacked her, Jesus wrote, "Liar." He continued writing as he heard each of her accusers—"Thief." "Lustful." "Unworthy father." He exposed each man's sins and hypocrisy. They were all sinners but were standing over this woman as her judges, pronouncing sentence from on top of the pedestals they had built for themselves, while hiding their weakness, their sins, their evil. Jesus continued writing, never lifting up his eyes. It was as if he had always known every one of them, and their vices. One of them began to read . . . .

Finally, Jesus *stood up and said to them, "If any of you have never sinned, then go ahead and throw the first stone at her!" Once again he bent over and began writing on the ground*—more of their sins. *The people left one by one, beginning with the oldest, and Jesus was left alone with the woman standing before him.*

They walked off with their eyes to the ground, saying not one word. They had been exposed by the One who knew the secrets of their hearts. They had come to get him into trouble, to act as judges. They instead had been judged by the only One truly capable of judging. They dropped the stones clenched in their hands, ready to throw at the woman. Only Peter and John, half-hidden behind a column, stayed a short distance away. At this point, the only sound to be heard was that of the cold wind.

Jesus stood up, adjusted his cloak, motioned to the two apostles to head toward the courtyard's exit. Finally, he turned toward the woman slumped on the ground who still continued crying, her eyes still downcast, lacking the courage to lift them up. She was expecting words of condemnation, of reproof. "Woman, look at me," Jesus said instead, bending over toward her. Mercy reverberated on his face and in his words. *"Where is everyone? Isn't there anyone left to accuse you?"*

"No sir," the woman answered.

Then Jesus told her, *"I am not going to accuse you either. You may go now, but don't sin anymore."* He helped her get up and followed her with his eyes as she staggered away trying to walk as close to the wall as possible, hoping to escape notice. She had not been proclaimed innocent, for she was not. He had not said she was without sin, that was not true. Everything about her betrayed mortification and shame. Jesus had lowered himself and raised her up after lowering those who had raised themselves up to judge even though they were no less corrupt, less sinful.

"Jesus forgives. But there is something more here than forgiveness. For as a confessor, Jesus goes beyond the law. In fact, the law said the woman must be punished. . . . But he went beyond. He does not tell her, 'Adultery is not a sin.' But he does not condemn her with the law. This is truly the mystery of Jesus's mercy. . . . How many of us perhaps merit condemnation! And that would even be just. Yet he forgives! How? With this mercy that does not eliminate the sin—it is God's forgiveness that eliminates it, whereas mercy goes beyond. It is like the sky. We see the sky, the many stars, but when the morning sun arrives with all its light, the stars cannot be seen. Such is God's mercy—it is an immense light of love, of tenderness. For God does not forgive with a decree, but with a caress. He forgives by caressing our sinful wounds because he involves himself in forgiveness, involves himself in our salvation."[69]

⁓

The Feast of Tabernacles was over, but Jesus remained for a few more days in the city. There were other confrontational occasions with the Pharisees who prodded and questioned him as he taught in the temple. *Once again Jesus spoke*

---

69. Homily, Santa Marta, April 7, 2014.

to the people. This time he said, "I am the light for the world. Follow me, and you won't be walking in the dark. You will have the light that gives life."

The eyes of those who were questioning him were filled with bewilderment. There was amazement in the eyes of the apostles. Who could ever define himself as the "light of the world"? Jesus was fully revealing himself.

The Pharisees objected, "You are the only one speaking for yourself, and what you say isn't true!"

Jesus replied: "Even if I do speak for myself, what I say is true! I know where I came from and where I am going. But you don't know where I am from or where I am going. You judge in the same way that everyone else does, but I don't judge anyone. If I did judge, I would judge fairly, because I would not be doing it alone. The Father who sent me is here with me. Your Law requires two witnesses to prove that something is true. I am one of my witnesses, and the Father who sent me is the other one."

"Where is your Father?" they asked.

"You don't know me or my Father!" Jesus answered. "If you knew me, you would know my Father."

Jesus said this while he was still teaching in the place where the temple treasures were stored. But no one arrested him, because his time had not yet come.

He explained yet again that he was not from this world like they were, stating one more time who had sent him.

Jesus went on to say, "When you have lifted up the Son of Man, you will know who I am. You will also know that I don't do anything on my own. I say only what my Father taught me. The one who sent me is with me. I always do what pleases him, and he will never leave me."

Hearing these words, many believed in him. *Jesus told the people who had faith in him, "If you keep on obeying what I have said, you truly are my disciples. You will know the truth, and the truth will set you free."*

But instead of calming them down, that mention of freedom rekindled the polemic in some of those who were listening. Since they were descendants of Abraham, they believed they had never been enslaved to anyone and, therefore, were in no need of liberation. But Jesus was speaking of a different kind of slavery. *"I tell you for certain that anyone who sins is a slave of sin! And slaves don't stay in the family forever, though the Son will always remain in the family. If the Son gives you freedom, you are free! I know that you are from Abraham's family. Yet you want to kill me, because my message isn't really in your hearts. I am telling you what my Father has shown me, just as you are doing what your father has taught you."*

To this claim of having only one Father, God, the Nazarene responded, *"If God were your Father, you would love me, because I came from God and now I am here. He sent me. I did not come on my own. Why can't you understand what I am talking about? Can't you stand to hear what I am saying? Your father is the devil, and you do exactly what he wants."*

Once more, they accused him of being possessed by the devil. *Jesus answered, "I do not have a demon, but I honor my Father, and you dishonor me. Yet I do not seek my own glory; there is One who seeks it, and he is the judge. Truly, truly, I say to you, if anyone keeps my word, he will never see death."*

These words about eternal life shocked them. They retorted that Abraham and the prophets had died. Who did this Galilean think he was, to make such claims?

Jesus replied, "If I honored myself, it would mean nothing. My Father is the one who honors me. You claim that he is your God, even though you don't really know him. If I said I didn't know him, I would be a liar, just like all of you. But I know him, and I do what he says. Your father Abraham was really glad to see me."

He had spoken too much using their line of thought. How could he have seen Abraham, when he was not yet fifty?

Jesus's response was definitive, unequivocal, a total revelation of his divinity. *"I tell you for certain that even before Abraham was, I was, and I am."*

"I Am"—Jesus, the "light of the world"—existed before Abraham, before all of Judaism. He had proclaimed himself to be God simply because he was. But his questioners could not tolerate this. They perceived his words as a threat to their power and felt they were authorized to punish him as a blasphemer. It would be easy to stone him, as had already been seen recently with the case of the adulteress woman.

The people picked up stones to kill Jesus, but he hid and left the temple.

~

A few days later, Jesus, together with his disciples, returned to the temple area in Jerusalem. As the small group proceeded along at a fast clip, they came upon a young blind man groping his way along, using the wall as a support. His name was Issachar and he lived off the alms he begged for. He had been blind from birth—born without pupils. Judas Iscariot drew their attention to him, asking Jesus a question based on an old belief, which had already been proven false by the sacred Scriptures themselves, according to which, physical evil was caused by the faults and sins committed by that person or by his parents. *"Teacher, why was this man born blind? Was it because he or his parents sinned?"*

"No, it wasn't!" Jesus answered. "But because of his blindness, you will see God work a miracle for him. As long as it is day, we must do what the one who sent me wants me to do. When night comes, no one can work. While I am in the world, I am the light for the world."

Judas kept silent; the others did not react. For as soon as he finished saying these words, Jesus *spit on the ground. He made some mud and smeared it on the man's eyes. Then he said, "Go wash off the mud in the Siloam Pool."*

Fed by the waters from the Gihon Spring, the pool that flowed through two aqueducts was a well-known place, cited several times in the Bible. Many people would wash themselves in that water before arriving at the temple.

With his face all dirty from the mud Jesus had made, Issachar got there quickly, thanks to the help of a boy who led him through the city's alleys. *The man went and washed in Siloam, which means "One Who Is Sent." When he washed off the mud, he could see.*

He was well known in that neighborhood. So when he showed up again on the street where he used to beg for alms, some of the people in the area asked themselves if it was really him, or only someone who looked like him. The miraculously healed young man answered all of them, crying at the top of lungs with joy, "It's me!"

Many people asked him in disbelief, "How were your eyes opened?"

He responded, telling them exactly what had happened, talking about Jesus and the directions he had given him. He spent hours on the street; everyone was coming up to him.

The miracle was truly too spectacular not to be noticed. News spread by word of mouth. *The day when Jesus made the mud and healed the man was a Sabbath. So the people took the man to the Pharisees. They asked him how he was able to see.*

Issachar responded once again, telling them what had happened—nothing more, nothing less. *"Jesus made some mud and smeared it on my eyes. Then after I washed it off, I could see."* He did not know who the mysterious prophet and healer was. He did not know how he had performed the miracle. He could only recount the facts chronologically, and what had happened.

Some of the Pharisees said, "This man Jesus doesn't come from God. If he did, he would not break the law of the Sabbath." Others asked, "How could someone who is a sinner work such a miracle?" Since the Pharisees could not agree among themselves, they asked the man, "What do you say about this one who healed your eyes?" He responded, "He is a prophet!"

How was it possible that he had healed Issachar in such an incredible way? Not satisfied with the linear responses from the man who had been miraculously healed, and rather than accept the factual evidence, some of the Pharisees began to question whether he had truly been born blind, suggesting it had been a staged event. And so, *they sent for his parents and asked them, "Is this the son that you said was born blind? How can he now see?"*

Issachar's elderly parents responded with the same candor and the same adherence to the facts. *"We are certain that he is our son, and we know that he was born blind. But we don't know how he got his sight or who gave it to him. Ask him! He is old enough to speak for himself."*

Growing increasingly angry, and unable to come to terms with it, *the leaders called the man back* and tried in vain to pit him against Jesus. They said to him, *"Swear by God to tell the truth! We know that Jesus is a sinner."*

Issachar responded again using good sense, speaking about what had happened to him. *"I don't know whether he is a sinner or not. All I know is I used to be blind, but now I can see!"* Once again, he testified, recounting only what had happened.

They could not get him to say what they wanted him to say. Remaining on their feet around him under a portico in the temple area, they continued to ask him questions. *"What did he do to you?" they asked. "How did he heal your eyes?"*

They were insistent, provoking a rather ironic response from the man who had been healed. *The man answered, "I have already told you once, and you refused to listen. Why do you want me to tell you again? Do you also want to become his disciples?"*

That was too much! *The leaders insulted the man and said, "You are his follower! We are followers of Moses. We are sure God spoke to Moses, but we don't even know where Jesus comes from."*

Issachar took the floor again, demonstrating once more that he knew what had happened to him and that he was also capable of arriving at the correct conclusions regarding the miracle he had been granted. *"How strange!" the man replied. "He healed my eyes, and yet you don't know where he comes from. We know that God listens only to people who love and obey him. God doesn't listen to sinners. And this is the first time in history anyone has ever given sight to someone born blind. Jesus could not do anything unless he came from God."*

They reacted furiously, responding, *"You have been a sinner since the day you were born! Do you think you can teach us anything?"* And they kicked him out of the synagogue.

As could be expected, they sent him away badly, blaming the blindness that had afflicted him from birth on his sins. They did not succeed in making him side with them, nor could they get him to say what they wanted. Jesus learned what had happened—the healing and the reaction of the Pharisees were the talk of the town. The next day, Jesus went to the same street and found the young man he had healed speaking with his friends. They were all still filled with amazement. The Teacher asked Issachar, *"Do you have faith in the Son of Man?"*

He replied, *"Sir, if you will tell me who he is, I will put my faith in him."*

"You have already seen him," Jesus answered, *"and right now he is talking with you."*

The man said, *"Lord, I put my faith in you!"* Then he worshiped Jesus.

Jesus made him get up. Meanwhile, a number of people had gathered around them. The Nazarene raised his voice so everyone could hear. *"I came to judge the people of this world. I am here to give sight to the blind and to make blind everyone who can see."*

When the Pharisees heard Jesus say this, they asked, "Are we blind?"

Jesus answered, *"If you were blind, you would not be guilty. But now that you claim to see, you will keep on being guilty."*

Jesus had come for those who could not see, for those who felt there was something wrong with them, for sinners—not for those who were judging others.

"This is a passage of the Gospel that demonstrates the drama of the interior blindness of so many people, even our own, because sometimes we have moments of interior blindness. Our lives are sometimes similar to the blind man's who opened himself to the light, who opened himself to God, who opened himself to God's grace. Sometimes unfortunately, they are similar to the lives of the doctors of the law—from the height of our pride we judge others, and even the Lord!" [70]

---

70. Angelus, March 30, 2014.

15

The Disciples and the Joy of the Mission

Year AD 29, November—December.

The Good Shepherd.
The Sending Out of the Disciples to Preach in Judea.

The healing of the man born blind caused a stir in the city, primarily because of the type of miracle. Despite the clumsy attempts of the doctors of the law to pass Issachar off as fraudulent, everyone knew he had not been able to see since he was born, and his family was well known. Interrogating first him and then his parents, the Pharisees unwittingly contributed to the magnification of the news about what had happened during those days in which Jerusalem was still overflowing with pilgrims.

More than the miracle itself, what struck Jesus's apostles and disciples were the subsequent disputes in the temple. The friends of the Nazarene, after having followed him wherever he went, after having seen with their own eyes and touched extraordinary things with their own hands, were now more desirous of understanding fully who this man was, this prophet who continued to "dare" to define himself as the "Son of God" and to attribute divine prerogatives to himself. Everything about his life—his deeds and his words—ended up shocking and challenging them. While Jerusalem was emptying and caravans were already on the move, Jesus began preaching again in the temple area.

"I tell you for certain only thieves and robbers climb over the fence instead of going in through the gate to the sheep pen. But the gatekeeper opens the gate for the shepherd, and he goes in through it. The sheep know their shepherd's voice. He calls each of them by name and leads them out. When he has led out all of his sheep, he walks in front of them, and they follow, because they know his voice. The sheep will not follow strangers. They don't recognize a stranger's voice, and they run away."

Those words left everyone present perplexed. What did he mean? They did not understand the comparison even though the reality he described was evident, since in that region it was common to see pens closed off by low

155

stone walls that provided shelter in the evening for one, or even several, flocks together. At a certain place in the low wall, a low and narrow door would open, allowing only one sheep at a time to go in or go out. This facilitated counting them at the end of the day. Even if separate flocks shared the same shelter for the night, the sheep were accustomed to recognizing their shepherd's voice and would follow him when they heard his call.

Jesus perceived the questions being transmitted through the eyes of those listening to him. So he added an explanation so they would understand what he was referring to. *"I am the gate for the sheep. Everyone who came before me was a thief or a robber, and the sheep did not listen to any of them. I am the gate. All who come in through me will be saved. Through me they will come and go and find pasture."*

He had said he was the "light of the world" just a few days before, and that he existed before Abraham. He continued to call God Abba, "Father," with a familiarity that made evident an extraordinary bond. Now he was explaining that in order to save oneself it was necessary to go through the "gate" that was he himself. He said he had come so the sheep might have life and have it "abundantly." *"I am the good shepherd,"* he added, *"and the good shepherd gives up his life for his sheep. Hired workers are not like the shepherd. They don't own the sheep, and when they see a wolf coming, they run off and leave the sheep. Then the wolf attacks and scatters the flock. Hired workers run away because they don't care about the sheep. I am the good shepherd. I know my sheep, and they know me. Just as the Father knows me, I know the Father, and I give up my life for my sheep. I have other sheep that are not in this sheep pen. I must also bring them together, when they hear my voice. Then there will be one flock of sheep and one shepherd."*

His mission was universal. It did not concern only the people of Israel, the people of the first covenant, the flock within that "fold." He had come to the world for other sheep as well, for those within other "folds," for those far off. He had come, deeply united to the Father, to voluntarily sacrifice his life. Instead, he did not say who the "robbers" and "hired hands" were, but his friends thought he was referring to the so-called "messiahs" who gathered followings for political purposes, making themselves leaders of revolts. Jesus was not this type of messiah, and he had always distanced himself in time when the people, seeing the miracles he was performing, wanted to make him king.

"Jesus, the Good Shepherd, knows his sheep and the sheep know him. How beautiful and comforting it is to know that Jesus knows us one by one, that we are not anonymous to him, that our name is known to him! . . . Jesus, the Good Shepherd, defends, knows, and above all, loves his sheep. And this is why he gives his

life for them. Love for his sheep, that is, for each one of us, leads him to die on the cross because this is the Father's will—that no one should be lost. Christ's love is not selective; it embraces everyone. . . . He is everyone's shepherd. Jesus wants everyone to be able to receive the Father's love and encounter God."[71]

Those listening to him began to discuss what the Nazarene had just said. Some judged him to be a demoniac, someone who was out of his mind and should not be listened to. Others, instead, even though everything was not completely clear to them, were able to recognize the truth of the facts and, looking at Issachar, the man born blind who had reacquired his sight thanks to Jesus, said, *"How could anyone with a demon in him say these things? No one like this could give sight to a blind person!"*

≈

Over the next few days, moving out of Jerusalem, Jesus and his followers traveled through the villages of Judea. Previously, he had already sent the apostles on their first mission, asking them to proclaim the kingdom of God. This time, *the Lord chose 72 other followers and sent them out two by two to every town and village where he was about to go.* It was no longer only the apostles, but a larger group of disciples as well. If the folds from which to call the sheep were not limited solely to those of the people of Israel, there was a huge, immense mission to accomplish. And it was entrusted to anyone who encountered the Teacher, anyone who had received a grace, a healing.

Before sending the seventy-two disciples out, *he said to them: "A large crop is in the fields, but there are only a few workers. Ask the Lord in charge of the harvest to send out workers to bring it in. Now go, but remember, I am sending you like lambs into a pack of wolves. Don't take along a moneybag or a traveling bag or sandals. And don't waste time greeting people on the road. As soon as you enter a home, say, 'God bless this home with peace.' If the people living there are peace-loving, your prayer for peace will bless them. But if they are not peace-loving, your prayer will return to you. Stay with the same family, eating and drinking whatever they give you, because workers are worth what they earn. Don't move around from house to house. If the people of a town welcome you, eat whatever they offer. Heal their sick and say, 'God's kingdom will soon be here!' But if the people of a town refuse to welcome you, go out into the street and say, 'We are shaking the dust from our feet as a warning to you. And you can be sure that God's kingdom*

---

71. Regina Coeli, April 25, 2021.

will soon be here!' I tell you that on the day of judgment the people of Sodom will get off easier than the people of that town!"

They knew the harvest was abundant and the laborers few—not even the enthusiastic crowds following Jesus in search of his word, his deeds, and above all, his healing, would be enough. And not everyone among those who had been present for the Teacher's public teaching decided to follow him. The disciples remained struck by that comparison that Jesus had already used when he had sent the apostles on their first mission in Galilee—that they were "like sheep in the midst of wolves," that is, helpless, that they would not be able to depend on their own strength, on their own organization or strategy. He asked them to be like him, a helpless lamb doing everything in harmony with the Father. He was asking them to depend on his word and his presence, which he had guaranteed, even when he was not there physically.

This time, too, he suggested they travel light, that they weave relationships from house to house, adapt themselves to the customs of those who would welcome them, and pray for the sick so that God would cure them.

Jesus also said to the disciples, *"Whoever listens to you is listening to me. Anyone who says 'No' to you is saying 'No' to me. And anyone who says 'No' to me is really saying 'No' to the one who sent me."*

He was one with God his Father, his friends were one with him. So they set off to open the way for him, thus going to more villages than Jesus would have been able to visit. It was the first mission for most of them. They headed toward Bethlehem, Ephraim, Emmaus, Ein Karem, doing what he had told them.

Two of them, Amos and Gad, young and accustomed to walking from sunup to sundown without ever stopping, even reached Arimathea. They were brothers and had been born in one of the suburbs of Jerusalem. Up until a few months before, they had been working with their father as textile merchants. While they had been traveling toward Bethsaida, they had come across the crowd following Jesus and had witnessed the multiplication of the loaves and fish. From that day, they had decided to follow the Nazarene, not only because of what they had seen, but also because of the stories they had heard the apostles telling. Both had become used to helping out with the large and small needs of the group surrounding Jesus, but this was the first time Jesus directly involved them on a mission. Amos, who was older, had prepared their knapsacks while reassuring his brother, who was a bit hesitant. Even the apostle Peter had approached them before departing. He said to Gad, "Don't be afraid. You two will never be alone. . . ."

It was almost dusk when the two brothers arrived in Arimathea after a journey lasting a day and a half. Rather than look for lodging, they knocked on the door of one of the first houses they came to in the city. An elderly ailing man opened the door and welcomed them with open arms. He made them feel at home and shared with them the frugal dinner prepared by his wife, who seemed to have more ailments than he. Amos and Gad had no idea how to begin to speak to them about Jesus.

They stayed quite a while, listening to the stories of the elderly couple, about the struggles and disappointments of their lives, about the children who never arrived, about how some of their relatives had betrayed them. Before even beginning to say anything regarding what they had heard, the old man thanked them because, as he said, it was the first time in so long that anyone had listened to him.

Then he asked them about themselves. . . . Gad completely surprised his brother and began. "We're sons of a textile merchant from Jerusalem, but we aren't here to buy or sell. We're here because we have found the Messiah. . . ." He said this with such simplicity that he disarmed his host, who began to ask them questions. Even his wife's eyes, which till that point seemed to be drooping, brightened. They had never heard about Jesus and listened to their stories till late into the night. And thanks to those two unknown pilgrims to whom they had offered dinner and a couple of straw mattresses, their outlook on life changed. They no longer felt cursed because they had never had children to keep their memory alive after their death. Gad's and Amos's words awakened hope. They quoted the Sermon on the Mount and taught the couple to pray the Our Father.

Before going to bed, they asked if there were any needy families in the area. "Oh, yes," the old man responded with a whistling voice. "Here at the end of the road, you'll find a big, beautiful house with two courtyards. The second son of an important man named Joseph lives there. Joseph is a member of the Sanhedrin in Jerusalem. This man's family is beautiful and large, but their youngest son, who is still a boy, has been having convulsions and delirium for three years. Everyone says he's possessed by the devil. His grandfather comes several times from Jerusalem to visit him, but every time, he goes back even more distressed and sad. . . . If you can do something, go there." The brothers exchanged only a fleeting glance. They did not need to talk about it.

Icy wind buffeted Arimathea the next morning. Amos and Gad left the house where they had found hospitality, heading toward the one the old man had indicated to them. They were welcomed by some servants and waited in the entrance hall. The day had not begun well since loud screams were coming from inside the house. A well-dressed, stout man came to meet them. He looked spent, as if his eyes were pierced with pain. "Who are you looking for?"

The two disciples said they had come to visit his family. Moving like a robot, the man invited them in. "You are my guests," he said. Crossing the threshold of the house, they saw a young woman dressed in dark clothing. Her face bore the evidence of tears and lack of sleep. She nodded her head and climbed up a small wooden staircase leading to an upstairs room, holding a jug of water in her hands. Then they heard a terrifying scream similar to that of a wounded animal at the point of death. The man who had allowed them in said to them, "I'm Ishmael, son of Joseph. I'm sorry I can't welcome you as you deserve. What you've heard is . . . is my son, Lot . . . he's very . . . very ill! It seems that an evil spirit has possessed him."

Amos and Gad responded, saying they would pray for him. They explained they were friends of Jesus of Nazareth. "My father, who is in Jerusalem, is a member of the Sanhedrin. He has heard Jesus and has spoken admiringly to me about him," Ishmael responded.

"May we see your son?" the two disciples asked.

The man was paralyzed for a moment. He had not expected a request of that nature. Rather, he had imagined that the two sojourners intended to leave his house as soon as possible. Then, without saying anything, he moved toward the wooden staircase and motioned them to follow him.

On their way up the creaking staircase, they heard another scream even more cavernous than the first. Their blood froze in their veins. The room where Lot was lying was small and dimly lit. The boy was curled up on a small bed. His mother was kneeling at his side. Amos told them they had found the Messiah and they had come to proclaim that the kingdom of God was near. Gad prayed with the words of the Our Father and called down peace and blessings on the family. The boy reacted to the words by jumping up and cursing at them. But when they both invoked the name of Jesus, Lot fell back down on his bed like a marionette whose strings had suddenly all been cut. He lay stunned for a few moments, then reopened his eyes, and for the first time in years, his parents recognized the look in their son's eyes.

"Give him something to eat . . . and we, too, will gladly sit down at table with you," the two disciples said.

It was as if the woman had been reborn and rejuvenated. She asked her son to go down with her to help her, while Ishmael, still speechless, continued to hold the hands of Amos and Gad tightly. He thanked them. They responded that he should not thank them but Jesus. The family shared their food, and the celebration was grand.

Ishmael sent a servant that same day to Jerusalem to tell his father, Joseph, the news. The two disciples visited other families and were well received by everyone. A few days later they returned to Jesus. Not far from Jerusalem, they met up with the other disciples who had been on mission.

When the 72 followers returned, they were excited and said, ."Lord, even the demons obeyed when we spoke in your name!"

Jesus told them: "I saw Satan fall from heaven like a flash of lightning. I have given you the power to trample on snakes and scorpions and to defeat the power of your enemy Satan. Nothing can harm you. But don't be happy because evil spirits obey you. Be happy that your names are written in heaven!"

They had all returned filled with joy, but not inebriated by the power by which they had accomplished wonders.

"Mission is based on prayer, it is itinerant; it is not stationary, it is itinerant; it requires detachment and poverty; it brings peace and healing, signs of the closeness of the kingdom of God; it is not proselytism but proclamation and witness; and it also requires frankness and the evangelical freedom to leave while demonstrating the responsibility of having rejected the message of salvation, but without condemnation and cursing. If lived in these terms, the mission of the Church will be characterized by joy. . . . It is not a matter of an ephemeral joy, which flows from the success of the mission; on the contrary, it is a joy rooted in the promise that, as Jesus says, 'your names are written in heaven.' With this expression, he means inner joy, the indestructible joy that comes from the awareness of being called by God to follow his Son—that is, the joy of being his disciples. . . . Each of us . . . can think of the name we received on the day we were baptized, of that name 'written in heaven,' in the heart of God the Father. And it is the joy of this gift that makes a missionary of every disciple, someone who walks in the company of the Lord Jesus, who learns from him to unsparingly spend oneself for others without reserve, free from oneself and of one's own possessions."[72]

They stayed together, listening to the stories and experiences of the missionary disciples. Jesus, contemplating their happiness, felt *the joy that comes from the Holy Spirit,* and he said: *"My Father, Lord of heaven and earth, I am grateful that you hid all this from wise and educated people and showed it to ordinary people. Yes, Father, this is what pleased you. My Father has given me everything, and he is the only one who knows the Son. The only one who really knows*

---

72. Angelus, July 7, 2019.

the Father is the Son. But the Son wants to tell others about the Father, so they can know him too."

Another manifestation of his union with the Father, once more highlighting the way God acts, the evidence that the apostles, and now the disciples, were beginning to recognize—*"God drags strong rulers from their thrones and puts humble people in places of power."* It had been like this from the beginning, overturning every worldly logic—the Son of Man had come into the world in a shelter for animals; the first people who adored him were poor shepherds; he had lived most of his life hidden in the small village of Nazareth; he had called fisherman to himself. . . . *"You are really blessed to see what you see!"* Jesus continued. *"Many prophets and kings were eager to see what you see and to hear what you hear. But I tell you they did not see or hear."*

How long the wait had been; how many prophecies there had been—a centuries-long history that was stored not only in the memory of the people of Israel. The entire world had waited, was desirous of something new, longing for a revelation, a "bridge" that could unite the unreachable heights of heaven with earth and the struggles of humanity. . . . The Messiah was there. He had been a baby cradled in his mother's arms like every one of them. He was someone who walked with them, who ate with them. He was so similar to them in his humanity, and at the same time, so profoundly different and unique—the forces of nature obeyed him. But in the end, the greatest and most surprising miracle was his capacity to speak to the heart of each person, to surprise them with the unprecedented power of mercy.

They continued speaking and sharing the food they had prepared.

16

"Who Is My Neighbor?"

Year AD 29–30, December—January.

The Good Samaritan. With Martha and Mary in Bethany.
Praying without Growing Tired. Dinner with a Pharisee.
The Woman Who Was Bent Over. Return to Jerusalem.

A few days after the disciples had returned from their mission, Jesus and his followers set out once again visiting various cities in Judea. One late morning on a beautiful sunny day, they stopped a bit in Bethany, a village not too far from Jerusalem. After the Nazarene had spoken to a small group of people, one of those present got up and approached him. He was a doctor of the law who wanted to question him and put him to the test. He asked, *"Teacher, what must I do to have eternal life?"*

Looking at him, Jesus responded with another question, *"What is written in the Scriptures? How do you understand them?"*

The man replied, "The Scriptures say, 'Love the Lord your God with all your heart, soul, strength, and mind.' They also say, 'Love your neighbors as much as you love yourself.'" He knew the commandments; he was familiar with the Scriptures.

Jesus smiled and said to him, *"You have given the right answer. If you do this, you will have eternal life."*

But that was not enough for the scribe. *The man wanted to show that he knew what he was talking about. So he asked Jesus, "Who are my neighbors?"*

Jesus asked him to sit next to him. Then he began to recount a parable. *"As a man was going down from Jerusalem to Jericho, robbers attacked him and grabbed everything he had. They beat him up and ran off, leaving him half dead. . . ."*

Bethany, the village they were in, was located at the end of an almost twenty-mile road connecting Jerusalem with the plain of Jericho, and farther along, with Perea. It was completely downhill, covering a drop in elevation of just over three thousand feet, with long stretches of inhospitable and deserted terrain infested with robbers and brigands who used the rocks for shelter.

Jesus continued, *"A priest happened to be going down the same road. But when he saw the man, he walked by on the other side. Later a temple helper came to the same place. But when he saw the man who had been beaten up, he also went by on the other side. A man from Samaria then came traveling along that road. When he saw the man, he felt sorry for him and went over to him. He treated his wounds with olive oil and wine and bandaged them. Then he put him on his own donkey and took him to an inn, where he took care of him. The next morning he gave the innkeeper two silver coins and said, 'Please take care of the man. If you spend more than this on him, I will pay you when I return.'"*

A priest and a Levite—two dignitaries. They had most likely finished their service in the temple and were returning to their cities. Two men who stood out from the crowd, but both passed by. Perhaps they were in a hurry. Perhaps they said some prayer that the battered man would survive. Neither of the two were moved with pity to the point of taking care of him. The one who did was the least "religious" of the three—a Samaritan merchant, who belonged to a detested people with whom the Jews wanted nothing to do. He did not limit himself to providing him first aid with what he had, soothing oil and wine to disinfect his wounds, bandaging him as best he could with some of the cloth-ing he had with him. The Samaritan picked him up, heedless of the blood, put him on his mount, and took him to the caravan stop, the place where travelers could find safe shelter for the night and could refresh themselves. And he paid the innkeeper two silver denarii, a sufficient amount for a few days' shelter, to look after the wounded man after his departure.

The Nazarene finished his narrative and, staring into the eyes of the scribe, said, *"Which one of these three people was a real neighbor to the man who was beaten up by robbers?"*

The expert in the Law of Moses answered, "The one who showed pity."

Jesus said, "Go and do the same!"

The doctor of the law, who usually stayed within the realm of ideas, heard the need to respond with deeds, and the suggestion to witness to the words of the law concretely through his life. Strictly speaking, and according to reli-gious tradition, the neighbor of the man who had fallen victim to the brigands should have been the priest and the Levite—certainly not the foreigner from whom the Israelites kept their distance. Instead, it was the Samaritan who had compassion, who cared for him as if he were his own kin.

"Maybe he was a merchant who was on a journey to take care of business. He did not look at his watch, he did not think of the blood. He drew near, got down off his mount, bound his wounds, pouring oil and wine over them. He got his hands dirty, got his clothing dirty, and then placed him on his mount and brought him to an inn. He was completely covered in blood—but it was in those conditions that the Samaritan took care of the wounded man. . . . The Samaritan was not a functionary, he was a man who had a heart, a man with an open heart. And there is no doubt that that innkeeper was astounded. He did not understand anything about this stranger, this 'pagan' who was not part of the people of Israel. . . . He may have even thought, 'This man is crazy!' when he booked the room to assist him. . . . Some ancient theologians used to say that the entire Gospel is contained in this passage. Each one of us is that wounded man, and the Samaritan is Jesus. And he has healed our wounds. He has drawn near. He has taken care of us. He paid for us."[73]

The scribe, who had wanted to put Jesus to the test, was himself put to the test. He thanked the Teacher and went away happy. Never before had he heard anyone speak like that.

⁓

Before setting out on the road again, Jesus stopped to eat in the home of his friends in Bethany—Martha, Mary, and Lazarus, three siblings. Lazarus was not around that day. Jesus went into their home. Mary sat at his feet to listen to him, while her elder sister, Martha, *was worried about all that had to be done,* busy preparing lunch for the Nazarene and his friends. Upset at the lack of help, she wanted her sister to help her so she could hurry up and finish, so she, too, could sit next to the Teacher. So she drew near and said, *"Lord, doesn't it bother you that my sister has left me to do all the work by myself? Tell her to come and help me!"* There were still many things to be done.

The Lord answered, *"Martha, Martha! You are worried and upset about so many things, but only one thing is necessary. Mary has chosen what is best, and it will not be taken away from her."* He had reminded her to look at what is essential. Silence descended over the room. The two sisters exchanged glances. Martha sat down next to Mary, and they both continued looking at him as he spoke. Lunch was more frugal than Martha would have wanted, but they feasted on the words of Jesus.

73. Homily, Santa Marta, October 8, 2018.

This afforded him the opportunity to speak once again about prayer, using examples and comparisons that had one goal: to invite them to ask, to beg—always and in any situation—without growing tired.

Then Jesus went on to say: "Suppose one of you goes to a friend in the middle of the night and says, "'Let me borrow three loaves of bread. A friend of mine has dropped in, and I don't have a thing for him to eat.'" And suppose your friend answers, 'Don't bother me! The door is bolted, and my children and I are in bed. I cannot get up to give you something.'

He may not get up and give you the bread, just because you are his friend. But he will get up and give you as much as you need, simply because you are not ashamed to keep on asking. So I tell you to ask and you will receive, search and you will find, knock and the door will be opened for you. Everyone who asks will receive, everyone who searches will find, and the door will be opened for everyone who knocks. Which one of you fathers would give your hungry child a snake if the child asked for a fish? Which one of you would give your child a scorpion if the child asked for an egg? As bad as you are, you still know how to give good gifts to your children. But your heavenly Father is even more ready to give the Holy Spirit to anyone who asks."

His friends frequently asked him questions about prayer because they would often see him pray in profound communion with the Father and they were witnesses to how every one of his prayers was heard. *"Prayer is work, it requires will-power, it requires constancy, it requires determination, without shame. Why? Because I am knocking at my friend's door. God is friend, and I can do this with a friend—constant prayer, invasive."*[74] And, *"When we pray courageously, the Lord not only gives us grace, but he gives us his very self in the grace. For the Lord never gives or sends a grace by mail. He brings it himself, he is the grace!"*[75]

From Bethany, Jesus and his followers began to journey toward other villages in Judea. In Ephraim, *Jesus forced a demon out of a man who could not talk. And after the demon had gone out, the man started speaking, and the crowds were amazed. But some people said, "He forces out demons by the power of Beelzebul, the ruler of the demons!"* This accusation, coupled with the amazement of many, was normal. Faced with the Teacher's miracles, there was always someone who tried to create difficulties for him.

---

74. Homily, Santa Marta, October 11, 2018.
75. Homily, Santa Marta, October 10, 2013.

Others wanted to put Jesus to the test. So they asked him to show them a sign from God. Jesus knew what they were thinking, and he said: "A kingdom where people fight each other will end up in ruin. And a family that fights will break up. If Satan fights against himself, how can his kingdom last? Yet you say that I force out demons by the power of Beelzebul. If I use his power to force out demons, whose power do your own followers use to force them out? They are the ones who will judge you. But if I use God's power to force out demons, it proves that God's kingdom has already come to you. When a strong man arms himself and guards his home, everything he owns is safe. But if a stronger man comes and defeats him, he will carry off the weapons in which the strong man trusted.

Then he will divide with others what he has taken. If you are not on my side, you are against me. If you don't gather in the crop with me, you scatter it."

While the Teacher was speaking, *a woman in the crowd spoke up, "The woman who gave birth to you and nursed you is blessed!"* She was a young woman who, until that moment, had been listening silently after she had tried to get as close as possible to Jesus. At that moment, after an outburst that could have seemed infatuation, he turned his thought to Mary, his mother, from whom he had inherited all his human characteristics. He quickly responded to the woman, *"The people who are really blessed are the ones who hear and obey God's message!"*

～

Over the next few days, their pilgrimage in Judea continued. Jesus and his friends would stop for brief periods of time in one city, and then set out again on their journey. At the end of November, they arrived in Emmaus and stayed in the homes of the disciples Cleopas and Ermas, two young men who lived there with their families. The next morning, while the Teacher was finishing speaking to the crowd gathered outside the synagogue, *a Pharisee invited him home for a meal.* He accepted his invitation and followed him.

The man, who was curious about the Nazarene and about his preaching, wanted to put him to the test. He did not live that far away. Jesus went into the house and was welcomed by other dignitaries and doctors of the law. Jesus greeted them and sat down at the table immediately. *The Pharisee was surprised that he did not wash his hands before eating.* Since the guests had come in off the street, after being in contact with people, pharisaical tradition prescribed ritual-purification washing. What had initially been curiosity regarding this extremely unique prophet changed to disdain, to judgment. This was evident by the expression on the Pharisee's face and the look in his eyes, even before his rebuking words.

So the Lord said to him: "You Pharisees clean the outside of cups and dishes, but on the inside you are greedy and evil. You fools! Didn't God make both the outside and the inside? If you would only give what you have to the poor, everything you do would please God. You Pharisees are in for trouble! You give God a tenth of the spices from your gardens, such as mint and rue. But you cheat people, and you don't love God. You should be fair and kind to others and still give a tenth to God. You Pharisees are in for trouble! You love the front seats in the synagogues, and you like to be greeted with honor in the market. But you are in for trouble! You are like unmarked graves that people walk on without even knowing it."

Still another time he made an appeal to live God's justice and love and not to take refuge behind the exterior adhesion to rules. These were harsh words that provoked another of the invited guests to intervene. He was an elderly man, a doctor of the law, who had already been inside the house when Jesus entered. He said to Jesus, *"Teacher, you said cruel things about us."*

Jesus replied: "You teachers are also in for trouble! You load people down with heavy burdens, but you won't lift a finger to help them carry the loads." This was a shot at the hypocrisy of those who were used to prescribing rule after rule for others, which they themselves never followed.

Jesus continued, *"Yes, you are really in for trouble. You build monuments to honor the prophets your own people murdered long ago. You must think that was the right thing for your people to do, or else you would not have built monuments for the prophets they murdered. Because of your evil deeds, the Wisdom of God said, 'I will send prophets and apostles to you. But you will murder some and mistreat others.' You people living today will be punished for all the prophets who have been murdered since the beginning of the world. This includes every prophet from the time of Abel to the time of Zechariah, who was murdered between the altar and the temple. You people will certainly be punished for all of this. You teachers of the Law of Moses are really in for trouble! You carry the keys to the door of knowledge about God. But you never go in, and you keep others from going in."*

The "main course" of that meal had been served—it was a stinging appeal for authenticity, for truth, for witness. It was an invitation to the men of religion to heed the heart of the law. As could have been predicted, the convivial gathering came to a halt.

Jesus was about to leave, but the teachers and the Pharisees wanted to get even with him. They tried to make him say what he thought about other things, so they could catch him saying something wrong. Jesus had spoken out truthfully.

In so doing, he had provided fresh reasons to those who wanted to accuse him because they considered him a threat.

"There is an attitude the Lord does not tolerate—hypocrisy. They invited Jesus to dinner, but to judge him, not to be friendly. Hypocrisy is appearing one way, but being something else. . . . Outside, you are perfect, even starched with correctness, but you are something else inside. . . . Hypocrisy is the language of the devil. It is the language of evil that enters into our hearts and is sown by the devil. . . . Jesus likes unmasking hypocrisy. He knows that it is precisely this hypocritical attitude that will lead to his death because the hypocrite does not think about whether he is using licit means or not. He just goes ahead."[76]

⁓

Only James had gone in with him. The other apostles were waiting for him at the door of the house together with Cleopas and Ermas. In the meantime, a large crowd had gathered in front of the Pharisee's house. *As the throngs of people were stepping on each other, [Jesus] told his disciples: "Be sure to guard against the dishonest teaching of the Pharisees! It is their way of fooling people. Everything that is hidden will be found out, and every secret will be known. . . . My friends, don't be afraid of people. They can kill you, but after that, there is nothing else they can do. God is the one you must fear. Not only can he take your life, but he can throw you into hell. God is certainly the one you should fear! Five sparrows are sold for only a few cents, but God doesn't forget a single one of them. Even the hairs on your head are counted. So don't be afraid! You are worth much more than many sparrows."*

He was speaking above all to his followers, but the crowd was also trying to listen to him. He told them to be primarily afraid not of those who could only kill the body, but of the devil who could corrupt the soul, leading to eternal damnation.

He continued looking at the faces of his followers one by one. *"If you tell others that you belong to me, the Son of Man will tell God's angels that you are my followers. But if you reject me, you will be rejected in front of them."* Then he added that they should not be anguished should they be brought to judgment before those in authority, saying, *"When you are brought to trial in the synagogues or before rulers or officials, don't worry about how you will defend yourselves or what you will say. At that time the Holy Spirit will tell you what to say."*

---

76. Homily, Santa Marta, October 15, 2019.

⁓

A few days later they were in Hebron. While Jesus was speaking to the people on a main road, a middle-aged man who was hearing him for the first time asked him out loud, *"Teacher, tell my brother to give me my share of what our father left us when he died."*

But Jesus refused. *"Who gave me the right to settle arguments between you and your brother?"* Then he said to the crowd, *"Don't be greedy! Owning a lot of things won't make your life safe."*

Jesus wanted to emphasize the importance of detachment from goods, to remind them about what is essential. So he *told them a parable: "A rich man's farm produced a big crop, and he said to himself, 'What can I do? I don't have a place large enough to store everything.' Later, he said, 'Now I know what I'll do. I'll tear down my barns and build bigger ones, where I can store all my grain and other goods. Then I'll say to myself, "You have stored up enough good things to last for years to come. Live it up! Eat, drink, and enjoy yourself."' But God said to him, 'You fool! Tonight you will die. Then who will get what you have stored up?' This is what happens to people who store up everything for themselves, but are poor in the sight of God."*

That rich man had calculated everything. He had planned where to cram his superabundant possessions and then he would live comfortably and care-freely. He had never become aware that his life was a gift given to him at each instant that could be taken away when he least expected it.

Jesus said to his disciples: "I tell you not to worry about your life! Don't worry about having something to eat or wear. Life is more than food or clothing. Look at the crows! They don't plant or harvest, and they don't have storehouses or barns. But God takes care of them. You are much more important than any birds. Can worry make you live longer? If you don't have power over small things, why worry about everything else? Look how the wild flowers grow! They don't work hard to make their clothes. But I tell you Solomon with all his wealth wasn't as well clothed as one of these flowers. God gives such beauty to everything that grows in the fields, even though it is here today and thrown into a fire tomorrow. Won't he do even more for you? You have such little faith! Don't keep worrying about having some-thing to eat or drink. Only people who don't know God are always worrying about such things. Your Father knows what you need. But put God's work first, and these things will be yours as well."

He continued to speak, looking at his friends.

"My little group of disciples, don't be afraid! Your Father wants to give you the kingdom. Sell what you have and give the money to the poor. Make yourselves moneybags that never wear out. Make sure your treasure is safe in heaven, where thieves cannot steal it and moths cannot destroy it. Your heart will always be where your treasure is. Be ready and keep your lamps burning just like those servants who wait up for their master to return from a wedding feast. As soon as he comes and knocks, they open the door for him. Servants are fortunate if their master finds them awake and ready when he comes! I promise you he will get ready and let his servants sit down so he can serve them. Those servants are really fortunate if their master finds them ready, even though he comes late at night or early in the morning. You would surely not let a thief break into your home, if you knew when the thief was coming. So always be ready! You don't know when the Son of Man will come."

Peter asked him if these words were for the disciples or for everyone else as well. Jesus replied by giving an example of a trustworthy and prudent administrator whose master puts him in charge of all his possessions. If, instead, not seeing the master arrive, he should begin to beat the servants and squander his possessions, he would be punished severely on the master's return.

"If servants are not ready or willing to do what their master wants them to do, they will be beaten hard. But servants who don't know what their master wants them to do will not be beaten so hard for doing wrong. If God has been generous with you, he will expect you to serve him well. But if he has been more than generous, he will expect you to serve him even better."

They began to understand that they were called by grace to a huge responsibility. Having lived with him, shared meals with him, having accompanied him through the streets, in the villages, witnessed his mercy, his miracles, his tenderness—but also the decisive way in which he unmasked hypocrisy—all this represented a calling and clearly laid out their mission.

"With this parable set at night, Jesus proposes life as a vigil of industrious expectation, which heralds the bright day of eternity. To be able to enter there, one must be ready. . . . Come to think about it, this already happens each time we meet the Lord in prayer, or in serving the poor, and above all in the Eucharist, where he prepares a banquet to nourish us with his Word and his Body."[77]

Jesus continued with words that shattered certain diatribes and overanalysis regarding the religious customs and traditions. *"I came to set fire to the earth, and I wish it were already on fire! I am going to be put to a hard test. And I will have to suffer a lot of pain until it is over. Do you think that I came to bring*

---

77. Angelus, August 7, 2016.

peace to earth? No indeed! I came to make people choose sides. A family of five will be divided, with two of them against the other three. Fathers and sons will turn against one another, and mothers and daughters will do the same. Mothers-in-law and daughters-in-law will also turn against each other."

Jesus would have to be the first to pass through the trial. Then his followers. The sign of contradiction he represented would bring discord even within families. It was not hard for his friends to understand this. Each day, they were witnesses of how the Nazarene attracted people, awakened hopes, touched hearts, but also how he provoked divisive reactions, rejection, closure, indignation.

∼

After this, Jesus and his friends left Hebron and began to journey toward Jerusalem. Before arriving in the Holy City, they stopped in Bethlehem. One Saturday morning, Jesus was teaching in the synagogue, *and a woman was there who had been crippled by an evil spirit for 18 years. She was completely bent over and could not straighten up.* She was thirty years old, and her name was Zilpa. Her life had been ruined by the illness. It was not easy for her to move around all hunched up. This infirmity had affected the lives of her entire family. Jesus's gaze rested on her, he *saw the woman, he called her over and said, "You are now well." He placed his hands on her, and at once she stood up straight and praised God.*

The healing took place immediately, in front of everyone who was in the synagogue at that moment, including the woman's father, an old man who had also been deeply affected by his daughter's suffering. Zilpa was not the only one to glorify God and thank the Nazarene. But there were also others there who reacted differently. *The man in charge of the synagogue was angry because Jesus had healed someone on the Sabbath. So he said to the people, "Each week has six days when we can work. Come and be healed on one of those days, but not on the Sabbath."* He wanted to establish the rules and the schedule for miracles, to set in place limits to God's freedom.

After smiling at the woman, happy at seeing her healed, Jesus turned his gaze toward the leader of the synagogue who had just admonished Zilpa. He *replied, "Are you trying to fool someone? Won't any one of you untie your ox or donkey and lead it out to drink on a Sabbath? This woman belongs to the family of Abraham, but Satan has kept her bound for 18 years. Isn't it right to set her free on the Sabbath?"*

These words elicited a surge of approval from the crowd, which *was happy about the wonderful things he was doing,* while *Jesus's words made his enemies ashamed.*

"Jesus was always there with the people rejected by that clerical group. They were there—the poor, the sick, sinners, lepers. They were all there because Jesus had that capacity of being moved when he faced sickness. He was a good shepherd. A good shepherd approaches and has the capacity of being moved. And I would say, the . . . characteristic of the good shepherd is not being ashamed of the flesh, to come into contact with wounded flesh, like Jesus did with this woman—'he touched,' 'he imposed his hands,' he touched lepers, he touched sinners."[78]

Then the Teacher continued speaking, saying, *"What can I compare God's kingdom with? It is like what happens when a woman mixes yeast into three batches of flour. Finally, all the dough rises."* Tiny as a mustard seed, like a pinch of leaven in a huge mass of dough, which has the power of leavening the dough and making it grow. This Jesus of Nazareth himself was an imperceptible speck on the radar of the grand scheme of things, tiny in comparison with the power of King Herod Antipas, let alone that of the emperor Tiberius. Such was the kingdom of God—so far removed from any dream of grandeur or power whatsoever. The Father had chosen to reveal himself through humility and littleness. And that kingdom would grow little by little, slowly progressing through the rubble left behind by the collapse of every other kingdom and potentate.

The next day, *as Jesus was on his way to Jerusalem, he taught the people in the towns and villages. Someone asked him,* "Lord, are only a few people going to be saved?"

Jesus answered: *"Do all you can to go in by the narrow door! A lot of people will try to get in, but will not be able to. Once the owner of the house gets up and locks the door, you will be left standing outside. You will knock on the door and say, 'Sir, open the door for us!' But the owner will answer, 'I don't know a thing about you!' Then you will start saying, 'We dined with you, and you taught in our streets.' But he will say, 'I really don't know who you are! Get away from me, you evil people!' Then when you have been thrown outside, you will weep and grit your teeth because you will see Abraham, Isaac, Jacob, and all the prophets in God's kingdom. People will come from all directions and sit down to feast in God's kingdom. There the ones who are now least important will be the most important, and those who are now most important will be least important."*

---

78. Homily, Santa Marta, October 30, 2017.

This was the same upheaval of perspective as the Beatitudes. This kingdom from another world progressed through littleness, and the invitation was to enter through the "narrow door." *"'Why is this door narrow?' one might ask. Why does he say it is narrow? It is a narrow door not because it is oppressive, but because it demands that we restrain and limit our pride and our fear in order to open ourselves to him with humble and trusting hearts, acknowledging we are sinners in need of his forgiveness. This is why it is narrow—to limit our pride, which puffs us up. The door of God's mercy is narrow but is always wide open for everyone! God does not have preferences, but always welcomes everyone without distinction. A narrow door to restrain our pride and our fear. A door wide open because God welcomes us without distinction."*[79]

At that same time, there were also a few Pharisees who approached him to advise him to go away because Herod wanted to kill him. Jesus sent word to the king through them, *"I am going to force out demons and heal people today and tomorrow, and three days later I'll be through. But I am going on my way today and tomorrow and the next day. After all, Jerusalem is the place where prophets are killed."*

Then, looking sad, his eyes hazy, and fully aware of the fate that awaited him within a few months, Jesus added, *"Jerusalem, Jerusalem! Your people have killed the prophets and have stoned the messengers who were sent to you. I have often wanted to gather your people, as a hen gathers her chicks under her wings. But you wouldn't let me. Now your temple will be deserted."*

After having made their way all over Judea, they finally reached Jerusalem during the days in which the Feast of the Dedication was being celebrated. As had been the case before, this time, too, Jesus's intention was to remain just a short time. *It was winter.* It was raining that day. Jesus *was walking in the part of the temple known as Solomon's Porch.* A small crowd had gathered around him, asking the usual question, *"How long are you going to keep us guessing? If you are the Messiah, tell us plainly!"*

In reality, he had already said it several times. But his words had been in vain for some of them. *Jesus answered: "I have told you, and you refused to believe me. The things I do by my Father's authority show who I am. But since you are not my sheep, you don't believe me. My sheep know my voice, and I know them. They follow me, and I give them eternal life, so that they will never be lost. No one can snatch them out of my hand. My Father gave them to me, and he is greater than all others. No one can snatch them from his hands, and I am one with the Father."*

79. Angelus, August 21, 2016.

He and his Father were one, and he held his flock united—his followers, those who recognized his voice like sheep who recognize the voice of their shepherd. What hurt the sensibilities of the leaders were not the words about the flock but rather that once again he had presented himself as the Christ, the long-awaited Messiah of Israel. *Once again the people picked up stones in order to kill Jesus.*

Jesus answered them, "I have shown you many good things my Father sent me to do. Which one are you going to stone me for?"

They answered, "We are not stoning you because of any good thing you did. We are stoning you because you did a terrible thing. You are just a man, and here you are claiming to be God!"

Jesus replied: "In your Scriptures doesn't God say, 'You are gods'? You can't argue with the Scriptures, and God spoke to those people and called them gods. So why do you accuse me of a terrible sin for saying that I am the Son of God? After all, it is the Father who prepared me for this work. He is also the one who sent me into the world. If I don't do as my Father does, you should not believe me. But if I do what my Father does, you should believe because of that, even if you don't have faith in me. Then you will know for certain that the Father is one with me, and I am one with the Father."

Decades of study or the dexterity of entering into the labyrinth of the laws and traditions was not required to understand, nor was it necessary to be an expert exegete to face the evidence of who he was. It was enough to look at him with a pure heart and, in front of the absolute newness that he represented, allow oneself to be cut to the heart and to try to follow him by making room for his gaze and his word. It was enough to recognize what he was doing before their very eyes.

After the umpteenth unambiguous response, they tried to arrest him once again. But Jesus was able to escape their hands, thanks to the help of some friends. He decided to once again leave the city to go across *the Jordan to the place where John had earlier been baptizing and Jesus remained there.*

17

"I Will Get Up and Return to My Father"

Year AD 30, January—February.

The Man with Dropsy.
The Parables of the Prodigal Son and the Rich Man and Lazarus.

Jesus and his friends were relieved when they left Jerusalem. The atmosphere was really tense in the city. Even if the Nazarene tried to make his interlocutors face the facts, the evidence of what was taking place before their very eyes, it was his own claims that were being examined and scrutinized, sometimes through the lens of prejudice, by those who maintained it was impossible that he could be the Messiah. They finally found a bit of respite beyond the Jordan, in a less populated place. But Jesus, already aware that the end of his earthly life was near, did not want to give up any opportunity to proclaim the kingdom of God and to promote an observance of the commandments from the heart, and not only outwardly.

The second day, as they were passing through Perea across the Jordan, the Teacher had the opportunity of talking again about the Sabbath rest. There had already been several times when he had acted and healed on that day, provoking questions and objections from those who maintained he had violated the law. A year before, while he was crossing some grainfields in Galilee with his apostles, his followers began to pick heads of grain. Some Pharisees had noticed it and had said, *"Look, it is against our Law for your disciples to do that on the Sabbath!"*

Jesus had defended his friends, responding thus, *"Have you never read what David did that time when he needed something to eat? He and his men were hungry, so he went into the house of God and ate the bread offered to God. This happened when Abiathar was the High Priest. According to our Law only the priests may eat this bread—but David ate it and even gave it to his men."* Then he added a phrase that inscribed itself on the minds of his followers: *"The Sabbath was made for the good of human beings; they were not made for the Sabbath. So the Son of Man is Lord even of the Sabbath."*

The Sabbath was for men and women so that they might draw near to God. Every commandment—in fact, every prescription, every devotion, every tradition—made sense only if it led to God. Otherwise, as an end in itself, it risked becoming an idol. Jesus had spoken a lot about this with his disciples as they shared meals together around the fire during their wanderings from one village to another.

That day was a Sabbath, and *Jesus went to eat a meal at the home of one of the leading Pharisees; and people were watching Jesus closely.* And behold, there was *a man whose legs and arms were swollen.* This man was about forty years old. His legs, ankles, and feet were deformed and swollen because of liquid that accumulated but was never absorbed. It was difficult for him to move about, and he was forced to walk barefoot. He had been waiting for the Nazarene at the entrance of the Pharisee's home.

Jesus turned to the lawyers and Pharisees, saying, *"Does our Law allow healing on the Sabbath or not?" But they would not say a thing.* There was no immediate objection to that question. Beyond the Jordan, the Pharisees were much more open to dialogue. Jesus took the sick man by the hand, *healed him, and sent him away. Then he said to them, "If any one of you had a child or an ox that happened to fall in a well on a Sabbath, would you not pull it out at once on the Sabbath itself?"*

But they were not able to answer him about this. They remained silent, thinking about what they had heard and, above all, about what they had just witnessed. That man's legs and feet had become normal. Before leaving the house, he had thanked the Teacher, more with his eyes overflowing with gratitude than with his mouth.

Jesus began to teach again. And he spoke once again about the reversal of human logic ushered in by the kingdom of God. Without saying anything, he had observed how the invited guests tried to take the places of honor, the best places, when they arrived in the house. So he said to them, *"When someone invites you to a wedding feast, do not sit down in the best place. It could happen that someone more important than you has been invited, and your host, who invited both of you, would have to come and say to you, 'Let him have this place.' Then you would be embarrassed and have to sit in the lowest place. Instead, when you are invited, go and sit in the lowest place, so that your host will come to you and say, 'Come on up, my friend, to a better place.' This will bring you honor in the presence of all the other guests. For those who make themselves great will be humbled, and those who humble themselves will be made great."*

He was inviting them to not show off, not run ahead demanding the best places, and not to look for public recognition. Peter and Andrew, who were there that day at the Pharisee's house, looked at each other. The former reminded the latter of the words they had heard on the mountain in front of the Sea of Galilee, during the Sermon on the Mount.

"Humility is the way that leads to Heaven. As we know, the word 'humility' comes from the Latin word humus, *which means 'earth.' It is paradoxical—to arrive on high, in Heaven, what is needed is to stay low, like the earth! . . . God does not exalt us because of our gifts, because of our wealth, or because of our bravura, but because of humility. God loves humility. God lifts up those who humble themselves, those who serve."* [80]

Jesus then spoke directly to the person who had invited him to dinner. *"When you give a lunch or a dinner, do not invite your friends or your brothers or your relatives or your rich neighbors—for they will invite you back, and in this way you will be paid for what you did. When you give a feast, invite the poor, the crippled, the lame, and the blind; and you will be blessed, because they are not able to pay you back. God will repay you on the day the good people rise from death."*

When one of the guests sitting at the table who was seated farther away from Jesus heard these words, he exclaimed, "How happy are those who will sit down at the feast in the Kingdom of God!"

Jesus looked at him, smiled, and responded with a parable. *"There was once a man who was giving a great feast to which he invited many people. When it was time for the feast, he sent his servant to tell his guests, 'Come, everything is ready!' But they all began, one after another, to make excuses. The first one told the servant, 'I have bought a field and must go and look at it; please accept my apologies.' Another one said, 'I have bought five pairs of oxen and am on my way to try them out; please accept my apologies.' Another one said, 'I have just gotten married, and for that reason I cannot come.' The servant went back and told all this to his master. The master was furious and said to his servant, 'Hurry out to the streets and alleys of the town, and bring back the poor, the crippled, the blind, and the lame.' Soon the servant said, 'Your order has been carried out, sir, but there is room for more.' So the master said to the servant, 'Go out to the country roads and lanes and make people come in, so that my house will be full. I tell you all that none of those who were invited will taste my dinner!'"*

---

80. Angelus, August 15, 2021.

No one was predestined to sit down at table in the kingdom of God, or better, those people would be there whom human logic and the upper echelons would have excluded. There would be many surprises at the heavenly banquet!

Dinner ended without any verbal clashes or contentions. The Pharisee who had hosted Jesus, as well as the other guests, were impressed by his preaching, by the compassion he had demonstrated toward the man with dropsy, and by the teaching they had received regarding the Sabbath rest being for people and not vice versa. For those whose hearts were open, watching him and listening to him was a liberating experience.

The next day, *when large crowds of people were going along with Jesus, he turned and said to them, "Those who come to me cannot be my disciples unless they love me more than they love father and mother, wife and children, brothers and sisters, and themselves as well. Those who do not carry their own cross and come after me cannot be my disciples."*

The people were amazed at these words. His friends who had left everything to follow him were much less amazed, although they still did not understand what to "carry his own cross" meant. They would remember this, too, in the weeks to come when their Teacher would be forced to carry a heavy piece of wood on his shoulders.

Jesus continued to speak, using an example he drew from Joseph's words, from the man who had protected and guarded him, agreeing to be his father. When he was a child, he would visit the building site at Sepphoris with his father. As he grew older, he had learned from Joseph that before beginning any construction project, everything needed to be well calculated so as not to be forced to leave a project half-finished. Joseph had been a man of few words but of many examples and testimonies.

Jesus said, *"If one of you is planning to build a tower, you sit down first and figure out what it will cost, to see if you have enough money to finish the job. If you don't, you will not be able to finish the tower after laying the foundation; and all who see what happened will make fun of you. 'You began to build but can't finish the job!' they will say. If a king goes out with ten thousand men to fight another king who comes against him with twenty thousand men, he will sit down first and decide if he is strong enough to face that other king. If he isn't, he will send messengers to meet the other king to ask for terms of peace while he is still a long way off. In the same way,"* concluded Jesus, *"none of you can be my disciple unless you give up everything you have."*

To follow him meant being willing to surrender one's own existence into his hands, holding nothing back. It meant being free and detached from the possession of any earthly things, so as to gain everything. The goal of this radicality was directed toward bearing witness. *"Salt is good,"* Jesus added, *"but if it loses its saltiness, there is no way to make it salty again. It is no good for the soil or for the manure pile; it is thrown away. Listen, then, if you have ears!"*

He had described his followers' assignment—to be like salt.

"Salt is good when it is used to flavor things. . . . Salt loses its strength if it is kept in a bottle with humidity. It is useless. The salt that we have received is to be given; it is meant to give flavor, to be offered. Otherwise, it becomes insipid and is useless. But salt also has another feature—when it is used well, the flavor of the salt is not tasted. Salt does not change what things taste like. Rather, the flavor of every dish is savored, it becomes better and more savory. And this is Christian originality—when we proclaim the faith with this salt, all those who receive it do so with their uniqueness."[81]

They left the village and headed toward the city of Livias. Here, soon after they entered it on a sunny but cold afternoon, *tax collectors and other outcasts came to listen to Jesus.* Seeing all this, a group of scribes and Pharisees began to murmur, expressing their indignation as had happened on other occasions. *"This man welcomes outcasts and even eats with them!"*

This was true. Jesus would go to the houses of dignitaries, but also to those whose appearance in public was unacceptable. He would eat with the Pharisee and with the publican. He went to the house of the synagogue leader and the tax collector. He also showed a predilection for those who did not feel that they fit in, for those who begged, for those who were wounded in spirit or in body, for those who were waiting.

Here, far away from both Jerusalem and his own Galilee, he chose to narrate the parable that, more than any other, describes the faithful and infinite love of God for his children—for his children who were unfaithful, for his children who had fallen into sin, of that Good Shepherd God, always seeking the lost sheep, always waiting for a sign, a foothold, or at least a desire for repentance that would permit him to inundate with forgiveness and grace those who had strayed and were homesick.

It was just before dusk, but the city streets were still filled with people, and the crowd around Jesus kept growing. The Nazarene began to tell the story.

---

81. Homily, Santa Marta, May 23, 2013.

"There was once a man who had two sons. The younger one said to him, 'Father, give me my share of the property now.' So the man divided his property between his two sons."

Two sons—the eldest was his father's right hand, the youngest had a rebellious soul longing for freedom, captivated by the tales that exalted the beauty and pleasures that could be had in distant cities. So his father did what he asked; that is, he set him free, giving him everything he asked.

"After a few days," Jesus continued, *"the younger son sold his part of the property and left home with the money. He went to a country far away, where he wasted his money in reckless living."*

He deserted his father's land and farms, abandoned his brother. He took his money and went far away. He squandered the money he had received.

"He spent everything he had. Then a severe famine spread over that country, and he was left without a thing. So he went to work for one of the citizens of that country, who sent him out to his farm to take care of the pigs. He wished he could fill himself with the bean pods the pigs ate, but no one gave him anything to eat. At last he came to his senses and said, 'All my father's hired workers have more than they can eat, and here I am about to starve! I will get up and go to my father and say, "Father, I have sinned against God and against you. I am no longer fit to be called your son; treat me as one of your hired workers."' So he got up and started back to his father."

He had reached rock bottom, the depths of despair, the abyss of sin. When he had been at home with his father, he would never have exchanged his condition as son for one of the workers or servants who lived with them. But now, in his loneliness, misery, and desperation, even the role of an employee in his father's house seemed like a dream to him. He made the decision to leave, despite his shame, despite his fear of being rejected or reproached.

Jesus continued narrating the parable while the people strained their ears and those farthest away tried to get closer to better hear how the story ended. How would his father react? Would he severely punish his son as he deserved?

Jesus said, *"He was still a long way from home when his father saw him; his heart was filled with pity, and he ran, threw his arms around his son, and kissed him."* He saw his son because he was waiting for him. He saw him because he was scanning the horizon every day hoping to catch a glimpse of his figure. He saw him because he loved him. He did not wait for him to arrive but ran to meet him. He did not wait for him to apologize, to accuse himself, to humble himself. The first thing he did was to embrace him.

The Nazarene continued his story. *"'Father,' the son said, 'I have sinned against God and against you. I am no longer fit to be called your son.' But the father called to his servants. 'Hurry!' he said. 'Bring the best robe and put it on him. Put a ring on his finger and shoes on his feet. Then go and get the prize calf and kill it, and let us celebrate with a feast! For this son of mine was dead, but now he is alive; he was lost, but now he has been found.' And so the feasting began."*

He had hoped to have a job among his father's employees, but had found out he was a beloved, awaited, desired, welcomed, forgiven, celebrated son! He did not have time to humble himself, to apologize. It was enough that he had returned home to discover his father's love and embrace. The people around Jesus were dumbfounded before this demonstration of love and mercy.

Jesus continued the story because he still needed to describe another scene, an attitude of the heart, that of the elder son who had always stayed at home, faithful to his father.

"In the meantime the older son was out in the field. On his way back, when he came close to the house, he heard the music and dancing. So he called one of the servants and asked him, 'What's going on?' 'Your brother has come back home,' the servant answered, 'and your father has killed the prize calf, because he got him back safe and sound.' The older brother was so angry that he would not go into the house; so his father came out and begged him to come in. But he spoke back to his father, 'Look, all these years I have worked for you like a slave, and I have never disobeyed your orders. What have you given me? Not even a goat for me to have a feast with my friends! But this son of yours wasted all your property on prostitutes, and when he comes back home, you kill the prize calf for him!'

"'My son,' the father answered, 'you are always here with me, and everything I have is yours. But we had to celebrate and be happy, because your brother was dead, but now he is alive; he was lost, but now he has been found.'"

The older son, reasoning according to human logic, felt that the mercy his father showed was unjust. The father had not only welcomed back his second-born son who had been found again, but he had also restored him as a brother to his eldest son.

"Jesus is total mercy, Jesus is total love—he is God made man. Each of us, every one of us, is that little lost lamb, the coin that was lost. Each one of us is that son who has squandered his own freedom following false idols, illusions of happiness, and has lost everything. But God does not forget us, the Father never abandons us. He is a patient father, always waiting for us! He respects our freedom, but he always remains faithful. And when we return to him, he welcomes us into his house like children, for he never ceases, not even for one instant, to wait for us with love. And

his heart rejoices over every child who returns. He celebrates because he is joy. God has this joy when one of us sinners goes to him and asks his forgiveness. What is the danger? It is that we presume we are righteous and judge others. We also judge God, because we think he should punish sinners, condemn them to death, instead of forgiving. So yes, we risk staying outside the Father's house! Like the older brother in the parable who, rather than being content that his brother has returned, gets angry with his father who has welcomed him and celebrates. If there is no mercy in our heart, no joy of forgiveness, we are not in communion with God, even if we observe all his precepts, because it is love that saves, not the practice of precepts alone." [82]

That late afternoon in the city of Livias beyond the Jordan, this remained impressed on the minds and hearts of many. The disciples continued to talk about it during supper. Truly, God's logic eluded human calculations.

~

They remained in Perea a few more days, continuing to move from one village to another. During a dialogue with his friends, Jesus continued to teach them about detachment from earthly goods. He said, *"Whoever is faithful in small matters will be faithful in large ones; whoever is dishonest in small matters will be dishonest in large ones. . . . No servant can be the slave of two masters; such a slave will hate one and love the other or will be loyal to one and despise the other. You cannot serve both God and money."*

Some Pharisees, who were attached to money and had heard this from a distance began to make fun of him for these remarks. The Teacher turned toward them, saying, *"You are the ones who make yourselves look right in other people's sight, but God knows your hearts. For the things that are considered of great value by people are worth nothing in God's sight. The Law of Moses and the writings of the prophets were in effect up to the time of John the Baptist; since then the Good News about the Kingdom of God is being told, and everyone forces their way in. But it is easier for heaven and earth to disappear than for the smallest detail of the Law to be done away with."*

He was challenging not the law but human incrustations and formalism. This is why Jesus was asking his followers to adhere with their hearts, not exteriorly. Adhering with the heart generated free men on a journey toward God. The risk of hypocrisy always came with external adherence and formalism.

---

82. Angelus, September 15, 2013.

~

That evening, the Nazarene and his friends were in the house of one of Matthew's acquaintances who hosted them. Jesus told a parable.

"*There was once a rich man who dressed in the most expensive clothes and lived in great luxury every day. There was also a poor man named Lazarus, covered with sores, who used to be brought to the rich man's door, hoping to eat the bits of food that fell from the rich man's table. Even the dogs would come and lick his sores. The poor man died and was carried by the angels to sit beside Abraham at the feast in heaven. The rich man died and was buried, and in Hades, where he was in great pain, he looked up and saw Abraham, far away, with Lazarus at his side. So he called out, 'Father Abraham! Take pity on me, and send Lazarus to dip his finger in some water and cool off my tongue, because I am in great pain in this fire!'*

"*But Abraham said, 'Remember, my son, that in your lifetime you were given all the good things, while Lazarus got all the bad things. But now he is enjoying himself here, while you are in pain. Besides all that, there is a deep pit lying between us, so that those who want to cross over from here to you cannot do so, nor can anyone cross over to us from where you are.'*

"*The rich man said, 'Then I beg you, father Abraham, send Lazarus to my father's house, where I have five brothers. Let him go and warn them so that they, at least, will not come to this place of pain.'*

"*Abraham said, 'Your brothers have Moses and the prophets to warn them; your brothers should listen to what they say.' The rich man answered, 'That is not enough, father Abraham! But if someone were to rise from death and go to them, then they would turn from their sins.'*

"*But Abraham said, 'If they will not listen to Moses and the prophets, they will not be convinced even if someone were to rise from death.'*"

Jesus's story was so real. While he was speaking, it seemed as if he were there at the scene, listening to that dialogue. Some of his disciples had the sensation that this story was more than a parable, almost a snippet of news from the hereafter that only the Son of Man could have reported.

"*There are two things that are striking—the fact that the rich man knew the poor man was there, and knew his name, Lazarus. But he didn't care about him, it seemed normal to him. The rich man probably even carried out his business, which in the end was against the poor. He knew very clearly, he was informed of this fact. And the second thing that touches me greatly is the phrase 'great chasm,' which Abraham says to the rich man. 'Between us and you a great chasm has been fixed, in order that those who would pass from here to you may not be able.' It is the same chasm present during his life between the rich man and Lazarus—the chasm did not begin there, the abyss began here. I have thought about what this man's tragedy was—the tragedy of being extremely informed, but with a closed heart. This rich man's information did not reach his heart, he did not know how to feel for others, he was not moved by the tragedy of others. . . . Here, we know the name of the poor man—Lazarus. . . . But we do not know the name of the rich man. The Gospel does not tell us what the rich man's name was. He had no name. He had lost his name. He had only the adjectives of his life—rich, powerful . . . lots of adjectives. This is what selfishness does to us—it makes us lose our real identity, our name, and leads us to evaluate only in terms of adjectives."*[83]

Listening to Jesus that evening, his friends learned that the lack of compassion and indifference toward the needs of others were attitudes that carried consequences both in life and after death. Every day since they had been together with him, they had seen the Teacher become moved by those who were sick, by those who were in need, by sinners who were conscious of being such. Now he had revealed to them the "great chasm" that would divide those who had everything, blessed by their wealth, and unconcerned about the poor at their door, those poor people—bereft of goods and poor in spirit—whom Jesus had defined as "blessed" by promising that they would find consolation.

---

83. Homily, Santa Marta, March 12, 2020.

18

"Unless You Turn and Become like Children, You Will Never Enter . . . "

Year AD 30, February—March.

The Healing of the Ten Lepers. The Pharisee and the Publican.
Questions Regarding Marriage.
The Encounter with the Rich Young Man.

After spending two weeks in Perea, the Teacher decided to return to Galilee the first few days of February. This would be the last time. On the first day of their trip, while they were walking together along the road, Philip and Bartholomew said to Jesus, *"Make our faith greater."*

The Lord answered, "If you had faith as big as a mustard seed, you could say to this mulberry tree, 'Pull yourself up by the roots and plant yourself in the sea!' and it would obey you."

As he said these words, Jesus had turned his eyes toward the right. Not too far off in the distance stood a centuries-old mulberry tree. They stopped briefly to look at the tree. It was majestic with its thick, evergreen foliage. It had flourished in arid ground and had deep roots. The wind and chill seemed not to have affected it. Would faith allow that tree to be uprooted, and transported to the sea once its roots had been pulled up? They remained silent.

Two years ago, they would all have considered that strong and vivid statement to be impossible. Now it could not leave them indifferent, nor could they dismiss it as a paradox. They had seen him raise the dead, heal the sick, make paralytics walk, restore sight to the blind and hearing to the deaf and speech to the mute. They had seen him walk on water and divide five loaves and two fish into infinite pieces, thus feeding thousands of people. During their own brief experience as missionaries sent by Jesus, they had experienced that they were capable of working wonders because of their faith in him and his companionship with them.

"Suppose one of you," the Teacher continued, *"has a servant who is plowing or looking after the sheep. When he comes in from the field, do you tell him to hurry along and eat his meal? Of course not! Instead, you say to him, 'Get my supper ready, then put on your apron and wait on me while I eat and drink; after that you may have your meal.' The servant does not deserve thanks for obeying orders, does he? It is the same with you; when you have done all you have been told to do, say, 'We are ordinary servants; we have only done our duty.'"*

Being with him, being his friends, becoming his witnesses, were not titles they had merited so as to consider themselves protagonists. Through their lives and witness, it was Jesus who was giving growth to the kingdom of God little by little. He had even said as much to Peter, calling him "Satan," and telling him to get behind him, to follow him, to walk in his footsteps. Jesus was asking them to make room for him as he was making room for the Father. He was asking them to consider themselves "useless," for only this way, in humility, could they truly be useful for the kingdom of God.

They reached the vicinity of Capernaum. It was lovely returning home, to see the faces of family and friends again. There was a swarm of noisy children who welcomed Jesus. Some of them had noticed the group arriving and had immediately headed in that direction. Others were being brought to the Teacher because their parents wanted him to impose hands on them and pray over them. Jesus sat down to rest a bit. In no time, he was besieged by children.

Benjamin was the name of one of the smallest. He had two mischievous eyes and was dressed in a dove-colored tunic. The lad jumped onto Jesus's shoulders, putting his arms around Jesus. They began to talk. But the disciples who were there *scolded the people. Jesus said, "Let the children come to me and do not stop them, because the Kingdom of heaven belongs to such as these."* He placed his hands on them and then went away.

As he was going away, Jesus explained the meaning of those words to his friends. Children have simple and pure hearts. They depend on their parents for everything; they need to know their parents are watching them to feel safe; they need their parents in order to feel free. This is how we depend on God. The disciples were reminded what had happened a few months earlier when they had asked Jesus who would be the greatest in the kingdom of heaven and had heard him respond, *"Unless you change and become like children, you will never enter the Kingdom of heaven. The greatest in the Kingdom of heaven is the one who humbles himself and becomes like this child."*

Jesus knew that those days in Galilee were his last. He saw his mother Mary again and the places he had visited together with Joseph as a child. The Feast of Passover was drawing near, and they began preparations for the caravans that would slowly begin to move toward Jerusalem.

~

One morning near Ephraim, as Jesus and his disciples were just about to enter the city, ten lepers approached them. The law prescribed that they stay far away from inhabited centers, keeping their distance from everyone. It was almost as if they carried a curse along with their illness. The ten advanced as a group. They were from different areas, but sharing the same fate, they would help one another out. They *stood at a distance and shouted, "Jesus! Master! Have pity on us!"* They knew who he was since they had heard about him.

Jesus saw them and said to them, "Go and let the priests examine you."

They went off immediately. *On the way they were made clean.* Healed before they arrived at their destination, they looked at one another in surprise, looking at each other's faces, arms, legs. Skin and nerves had returned where they had been before they had gotten sick.

When one of them saw that he was healed, he came back, praising God in a loud voice. He threw himself to the ground at Jesus's feet and thanked him. The man was a Samaritan.

Jesus spoke up, "There were ten who were healed; where are the other nine? Why is this foreigner the only one who came back to give thanks to God?" And Jesus said to him, "Get up and go; your faith has made you well."

Once again, a witness of faith had come not from those who were near but from those who were far off; not from those who shared the same faith, but from the "foreigners." One, only one of the ten had returned to give thanks, prostrating himself at the feet of the Nazarene for the healing received. Jesus accompanied his words with a look filled with compassion. And that Samaritan was healed not only in body.

"Naturally, they were all happy about having recovered their health, thus being allowed to emerge from that unending, forced quarantine that excluded them from the community. But among them, there was one who experienced an additional joy—in addition to being healed, he rejoices at the encounter with Jesus. He is not only freed from evil, but he now possesses the certainty of being loved. This is the crux—when you thank someone, you express the certainty that you are loved. And

this is a huge step—to have the certainty that you are loved. It is the discovery of love as the force that governs the world."[84]

They were still in the city the next day. Some Pharisees approached and asked Jesus when the Kingdom of God would come. His answer was, *"The Kingdom of God does not come in such a way as to be seen. No one will say, 'Look, here it is!' or, 'There it is!'; because the Kingdom of God is within you."*

The kingdom of God did not advance accompanied by armies. It was like a seed that needed to be discovered and watered so it would grow. Jesus had always fled from the crowds that wanted to crown him king, who dreamed of him as the leader of a revolt against the Romans. He had not come for this.

As they were leaving Ephraim, the Nazarene turned and addressed his friends. *"The time will come when you will wish you could see one of the days of the Son of Man, but you will not see it. There will be those who will say to you, 'Look, over there!' or, 'Look, over here!' But don't go out looking for it. As the lightning flashes across the sky and lights it up from one side to the other, so will the Son of Man be in his day. But first he must suffer much and be rejected by the people of this day.*

"As it was in the time of Noah so shall it be in the days of the Son of Man. Everybody kept on eating and drinking, and men and women married, up to the very day Noah went into the boat and the flood came and killed them all. It will be as it was in the time of Lot. Everybody kept on eating and drinking, buying and selling, planting and building. On the day Lot left Sodom, fire and sulfur rained down from heaven and killed them all. That is how it will be on the day the Son of Man is revealed.

"On that day someone who is on the roof of a house must not go down into the house to get any belongings; in the same way anyone who is out in the field must not go back to the house. Remember Lot's wife! Those who try to save their own life will lose it; those who lose their life will save it."

Yet another prophecy of what was about to happen—his suffering, his passion. Yet another invitation to learn and always live vigilantly.

❦

They continued their journey in the direction of Jerusalem. One evening, after his disciples asked him again about prayer, Jesus told this parable. *"In a certain town there was a judge who neither feared God nor respected people. And there was a widow in that same town who kept coming to him and pleading for her rights,*

---

saying, 'Help me against my opponent!' For a long time the judge refused to act, but at last he said to himself, 'Even though I don't fear God or respect people, yet because of all the trouble this widow is giving me, I will see to it that she gets her rights. If I don't, she will keep on coming and finally wear me out!'"

And the Lord continued, "Listen to what that corrupt judge said. Now, will God not judge in favor of his own people who cry to him day and night for help? Will he be slow to help them? I tell you, he will judge in their favor and do it quickly. But will the Son of Man find faith on earth when he comes?"

No one should ever tire of asking, but with a humble attitude, that of a beggar who knows he or she is in need. The final question left his disciples speechless.

Then Jesus recounted another parable for those who presumed to be just and despised others.

"Once there were two men who went up to the Temple to pray: one was a Pharisee, the other a tax collector. The Pharisee stood apart by himself and prayed, 'I thank you, God, that I am not greedy, dishonest, or an adulterer, like everybody else. I thank you that I am not like that tax collector over there. I fast two days a week, and I give you one tenth of all my income.' But the tax collector stood at a distance and would not even raise his face to heaven, but beat on his breast and said, 'God, have pity on me, a sinner!' I tell you," said Jesus, "the tax collector, and not the Pharisee, was in the right with God when he went home. For those who make themselves great will be humbled, and those who humble themselves will be made great."

They understood it from his words and from his example. "Our Teacher wants our hearts to be involved," Bartholomew commented. "And he's inviting us not to feel better than others, not to judge, not to despise."

"O God, be merciful to me, a sinner." That night, Jesus's friends repeated this quietly a few times.

"That Pharisee prays to God, but in truth he is looking at himself. He is praying to himself! Instead of having the Lord before his eyes, he has a mirror. Although he is standing in the Temple, he does not feel the need to prostrate himself before the majesty of God. He stays on his feet, he feels secure, as if he were the lord of the Temple! He lists all the good works he has done—he is beyond reproach, observant of the law beyond what was due. . . . More than praying, he is pleased with his own observance of the precepts. Yet, his attitude and his words are far from the way God speaks and acts, the God who loves everyone and does not despise sinners. . . .

"The parable teaches that someone is just or sinful not because of social class, but because of their way of relating to God and their way of relating to their brothers and sisters. The gestures of repentance, and the tax collector's few and simple words, testify that he is aware of his own miserable condition. His prayer is essential. He acts out of humility, certain of one thing—that he is a sinner in need of mercy. If the Pharisee did not ask for anything because he already had everything, the tax collector could only beg for God's mercy."[85]

～

The month of March had begun. Jesus and his disciples were in Judea once again. There were always a lot of people following them, asking, begging for healing.

They continued meeting people and disputing with the doctors of the law—both those who asked questions out of curiosity and those whose only intention was to create trouble for Jesus. A group of Pharisees had gathered in one of the village squares where they had just arrived. Jesus did not avoid them and walked right up to them. They asked him, *"Does our Law allow a man to divorce his wife for whatever reason he wishes?"*

Jesus answered, *"Haven't you read the scripture that says that in the beginning the Creator made people male and female? And God said, 'For this reason a man will leave his father and mother and unite with his wife, and the two will become one.' So they are no longer two, but one. No human being must separate, then, what God has joined together."*

The Pharisees asked him, *"Why, then, did Moses give the law for a man to hand his wife a divorce notice and send her away?"*

Jesus answered, *"Moses gave you permission to divorce your wives because you are so hard to teach. But it was not like that at the time of creation. I tell you, then, that any man who divorces his wife for any cause other than her unfaithfulness, commits adultery if he marries some other woman."*

He had not responded whether divorce was lawful or not, nor had he followed the logic of those who had interrogated him and who thought of faith only in terms of "how far can I go—or not go." He had responded with a question regarding the Mosaic law and had unveiled their hearts, telling the truth.

Jesus looked directly into the eyes of his questioners, knowing full well that the Mosaic law regarding divorce was abused. The decree of divorce lay within the competence of the priests, and cost a lot of money. With his words, the

85. General Audience, June 1, 2016.

Teacher had recalled what was essential regarding God's will, distancing himself from the Hebrew legislation, which in the case of "illegitimate unions," that is, adultery, did not stipulate divorce, but stoning. The adulteress woman, whom Jesus had saved a few months earlier in Jerusalem, knew this well. And he had called anyone who remarried, after having divorced his wife, an adulterer. Their tradition, instead, permitted this.

These statements regarding marriage disturbed his friends, who said to him, *"If this is how it is between a man and his wife, it is better not to marry."*

Jesus answered, "This teaching does not apply to everyone, but only to those to whom God has given it. For there are different reasons why men cannot marry: some, because they were born that way; others, because men made them that way; and others do not marry for the sake of the Kingdom of heaven. Let him who can accept this teaching do so."

The discussion over, the pressure of the people on Jesus began easing, and the Pharisees had something to think about. The Teacher was just about to set out again when a well-dressed young man accompanied by two servants approached him. He, too, had a question. *"Teacher,"* he asked, *"what good thing must I do to receive eternal life?"*

"Why do you ask me concerning what is good?" answered Jesus. *"There is only One who is good. Keep the commandments if you want to enter life."*

"What commandments?" he asked.

Jesus answered, "Do not commit murder; do not commit adultery; do not steal; do not accuse anyone falsely; respect your father and your mother; and love your neighbor as you love yourself."

"I have obeyed all these commandments," the young man replied. *"What else do I need to do?"*

Jesus said to him, "If you want to be perfect, go and sell all you have and give the money to the poor, and you will have riches in heaven; then come and follow me."

When the young man heard this, he went away sad, because he was very rich.

He had not expected such a demanding response, accompanied by an invitation to follow Jesus, to stay with him. It was the same invitation his apostles had received. He was a good man, observant, intrigued by Jesus. He had approached without saying his name, now he remounted his horse, his face downcast due to his incapability of accepting the proposal he had received to liberate himself from his possessions. *"His restless heart, directly due to the Holy Spirit prompting him to approach Jesus and follow him, was a full heart, and he did not have the courage to empty it. And he made his choice—money. A heart filled with money. . . . But he was not a thief, a criminal, no, no, no! He was a good man—he never stole, never! Never cheated—his money was honest. But his heart was imprisoned there, he was attached to money, and he did not have the freedom to choose. Money chose for him."* [86]

For Jesus, it was an opportunity to add an image destined to embed itself into their minds. *"I assure you: it will be very hard for rich people to enter the Kingdom of heaven. I repeat: it is much harder for a rich person to enter the Kingdom of God than for a camel to go through the eye of a needle."*

When the disciples heard this, they were completely amazed. "Who, then, can be saved?" they asked.

Jesus looked straight at them and answered, "This is impossible for human beings, but for God everything is possible."

Then Peter spoke up. "Look," he said, "we have left everything and followed you. What will we have?"

Jesus said to them, "You can be sure that when the Son of Man sits on his glorious throne in the New Age, then you twelve followers of mine will also sit on thrones, to rule the twelve tribes of Israel."

Then he said to his friends that anyone who renounced their home, fields, relatives, father, mother, and children for his sake, would already receive on this earth a hundred times more and would inherit eternal life. *"But many who now are first will be last, and many who now are last will be first."*

Before dismissing the people to go to bed, the Nazarene looked at Peter, a smile on his lips. Immediately the apostle tried to escape his gaze. He had sincerely asked what the disciples would obtain for following him. Peter had become enveloped by Jesus's silent but eloquent gaze. Getting up quickly, Peter remained on his feet, thinking—they possessed much more than the hundredfold—every day they walked and spoke face-to-face with the Son of God, who was one with the Almighty—and at the end of the day, they even sat down to eat with him.

$$\sim$$

The following morning, as they prepared to continue on their journey toward Jerusalem, eating some bread together, Jesus wanted to pick up Peter's question again. The apostles, who had already thrown their knapsacks over their shoulders, deposited them at their feet and huddled around the Teacher. He told a new parable.

---

86. Homily, Santa Marta, March 3, 2014.

"The Kingdom of heaven is like this. Once there was a man who went out early in the morning to hire some men to work in his vineyard. He agreed to pay them the regular wage, a silver coin a day, and sent them to work in his vineyard. He went out again to the marketplace at nine o'clock and saw some men standing there doing nothing, so he told them, 'You also go and work in the vineyard, and I will pay you a fair wage.' So they went. Then at twelve o'clock and again at three o'clock he did the same thing. It was nearly five o'clock when he went to the marketplace and saw some other men still standing there. 'Why are you wasting the whole day here doing nothing?' he asked them. 'No one hired us,' they answered. 'Well, then, you go and work in the vineyard,' he told them.

"When evening came, the owner told his foreman, 'Call the workers and pay them their wages, starting with those who were hired last and ending with those who were hired first.' The men who had begun to work at five o'clock were paid a silver coin each. So when the men who were the first to be hired came to be paid, they thought they would get more; but they too were given a silver coin each. They took their money and started grumbling against the employer. 'These men who were hired last worked only one hour,' they said, 'while we put up with a whole day's work in the hot sun—yet you paid them the same as you paid us!' 'Listen, friend,' the owner answered one of them, 'I have not cheated you. After all, you agreed to do a day's work for one silver coin. Now take your pay and go home. I want to give this man who was hired last as much as I gave you. Don't I have the right to do as I wish with my own money? Or are you jealous because I am generous?'"

And Jesus concluded, "So those who are last will be first, and those who are first will be last."

It was a narrative that highlighted God's goodness, the superabundance of his mercy, the impossibility of reducing his heart to human calculations, to the logic of "giving to receive." It immediately reminded Jesus's friends about the parable of the second-born son who squandered his inheritance and had been welcomed back with open arms by his father, provoking the envious reaction of the firstborn son. It was the same complaint of the workers in the vineyard who, even after receiving the agreed upon wage, had something to say about the generosity of the landowner, who was magnanimous even with those who had worked much less than they had.

"The image of this owner, who goes out numerous times to the marketplace to look for day laborers for his vineyard, is touching. That owner represents God who calls everyone, who calls always, at any hour. God acts this way even today. He continues to call anyone, at whatever hour, to invite them to work in his kingdom. . . . The owner's second attitude, representing God's, is his way of compensating the

workers. How does God pay? . . .God always pays the highest amount. . . . God behaves like this—he does not look at the time and results, but at our availability. He looks at the generosity with which we put ourselves at his service. His way of acting is more than just, in the sense that it goes beyond justice and is manifested in Grace. Everything is Grace. Our salvation is Grace."[87]

Jesus finished speaking. His friends got up; each picked up their own knapsack and set out again on their journey. The apostles felt as though they were lighter walking at the Teacher's side. Little by little they were understanding. God's heart, and his logic, so different from that of humans, was making room in their hearts.

---

87. Angelus, September 20, 2020.

19

Making Yourself Little to Be Truly Great

Year AD 30, March.

Another Prophecy of the Passion. The Raising of His Friend Lazarus.
The Healing of Bartimaeus. Meeting with Zacchaeus.
Mary Anoints Jesus's Feet with Perfume.

It was a bright, sunny day. They were walking all together in silence. Suddenly, Jesus *took the twelve disciples aside and spoke to them privately, as they walked along. "Listen," he told them, "we are going up to Jerusalem, where the Son of Man will be handed over to the chief priests and the teachers of the Law. They will condemn him to death and then hand him over to the Gentiles, who will make fun of him, whip him, and crucify him; but three days later he will be raised to life."*

Another prophecy of his imminent suffering. His words were welcomed with a bit of embarrassment. It was not the first time he had said something similar regarding his future. But only one of the Twelve, in addition to feeling embarrassed, had a dark look on his face.

That was Judas Iscariot. The more time went by, the more he could not tolerate these prophecies and the exaltation of humility and meekness. He clearly understood that the Teacher had come to teach a new way of living the law and religious traditions—a more authentic way, more in harmony with God's heart. However, he was not able to comprehend why Jesus always fled the slightest proposition from the crowd who wanted him to lead the revolt against the Romans. Each day it became harder for Judas to bear that Jesus was not exploiting the huge popularity he had acquired in the public eye. He could not understand why he even refused to be a political messiah. He would have liked to see the Nazarene lead the rebellion. . . . It was a personal dream he had cultivated for quite some time. Since he held the common purse, he had secretly begun to designate part of the money for this purpose, subtracting it from the available funds. He was stealing. But in his heart, he was convinced he was not stealing.

After a few minutes of silence following those words regarding Jesus's approaching passion, *the wife of Zebedee came to Jesus,* Salome, with her sons James (who was older) and John (who was younger). She *bowed before him, and asked him for a favor.* "*What do you want?*" *Jesus asked her.*

She answered, "Promise me that these two sons of mine will sit at your right and your left when you are King." The woman admired the Teacher. She had no political aspirations like Judas. She loved her two sons and asked for the best for them.

"*You don't know what you are asking for,*" *Jesus answered the sons.* "*Can you drink the cup of suffering that I am about to drink?*"

"*We can,*" *they answered.*

"*You will indeed drink from my cup,*" *Jesus told them,* "*but I do not have the right to choose who will sit at my right and my left. These places belong to those for whom my Father has prepared them.*"

Salome's initiative and James's and John's response did not pass unnoticed.

When the other ten disciples heard about this, they became angry with the two brothers. So Jesus called them all together and said, "You know that the rulers of the heathen have power over them, and the leaders have complete authority. This, however, is not the way it shall be among you. If one of you wants to be great, you must be the servant of the rest; and if one of you wants to be first, you must be the slave of the others—like the Son of Man, who did not come to be served, but to serve and to give his life to redeem many people."

Lowering oneself to be truly great, humbling oneself to enter God's heart. Wasn't this what he was teaching every day and every hour as he walked from village to village, as he healed and accepted invitations to eat at the tables of sinners?

"*While we are on the way to Jerusalem, the Lord walks ahead of us to keep reminding us that the only credible form of authority comes from putting ourselves at the feet of others to serve Christ. It is the authority that comes from never forgetting that Jesus, before bowing his head on the cross, was not afraid of bowing before his disciples and washing their feet. This is the highest honor we can attain, the greatest promotion that can be awarded us—to serve Christ in God's faithful people, in those who are hungry, forgotten, imprisoned, sick. . . . None of us should look down on others from above. The only time we should look at a person in this way is when we help them get up.*"[88]

---

88. Homily for the Consistory for the Creation of New Cardinals, June 28, 2018.

～

Going up to Judea from Galilee was not a direct route. The disciples convinced Jesus to pass once again through Perea beyond the Jordan. The growing hostility of the Nazarene's enemies was perceptible more and more each day. Spending a few days in that area waiting for the Passover would allow the group to have a few tranquil days. Jesus's friends, despite the always more specific prophecies he gave them, had no clue what was about to happen. The only one who knew what he was about to encounter was Jesus. The Teacher knew his hour had not yet come, even if it was only a matter of days at that point. So he agreed to cross over the Jordan where he had been a few weeks earlier.

～

Meanwhile in Bethany, in his friends' house, Lazarus's life was coming to an end. His sisters, Martha and Mary, were assisting him. The man had gotten an infection that left him bedridden after just a few days with a high fever. He was also in tremendous pain. His sisters had ordered from Jerusalem the remedies his neighbors and doctors recommended. These remedies were of no avail, neither curing nor alleviating his illness. "If only Jesus were here!" the two young women repeated frequently, as they took turns at the bedside of their brother, who was getting worse day by day and was now unable to eat anything.

"Tell Jesus that I loved him," Lazarus repeated frequently to his sisters. Thanks to a caravan of merchants going up to Jerusalem, Martha and Mary learned that the Teacher was beyond the Jordan, a day's journey away from Bethany. Two neighboring friends offered to leave immediately to go in search of him. So the sisters sent word to him through their friends, *"Lord, your dear friend is sick."*

When Jesus heard it, he said, "The final result of this sickness will not be the death of Lazarus; this has happened in order to bring glory to God, and it will be the means by which the Son of God will receive glory."

Jesus loved Martha and her sister and Lazarus. Yet when he received the news that Lazarus was sick, he stayed where he was for two more days.

Jesus's response to the messengers from Bethany calmed his disciples. They thought Lazarus would be healed thanks to Jesus's prayers. Only Peter and Thomas, the most impulsive in the group, wondered in their hearts why the Teacher was not leaving immediately. They said nothing, knowing well the dangers that loomed over them as they neared Jerusalem.

Two days went by. In the meantime, back in the home of his friends in Bethany, Lazarus died and was buried the same day in a tomb hewn out of a rock not far from the village. On the morning of the third day, the Nazarene *said to the disciples, "Let us go back to Judea."*

"Teacher," the disciples answered, "just a short time ago the people there wanted to stone you; and are you planning to go back?"

Jesus said, "A day has twelve hours, doesn't it? So those who walk in broad day-light do not stumble, for they see the light of this world. But if they walk during the night they stumble, because they have no light." The twelve hours of Jesus's day were not yet over, even if evening was already drawing nigh. With these words, the Teacher wanted to tell his friends not to be afraid. His hour was near but had not yet struck.

Jesus said this and then added, "Our friend Lazarus has fallen asleep, but I will go and wake him up."

The disciples answered, "If he is asleep, Lord, he will get well."

Jesus meant that Lazarus had died, but they thought he meant natural sleep.

So Jesus told them plainly, "Lazarus is dead, but for your sake I am glad that I was not with him, so that you will believe. Let us go to him."

He had been explicit and, finally, understood. Lazarus was no longer alive. Some of the apostles observed that this would be useless and dangerous. True, they had witnessed miracles wrought by Jesus that brought people who had just died back to life—like the daughter of Jairus or the son of the widow of Nain. But these wondrous deeds had happened immediately, or a few hours at the most, after the two had passed away. This time it was evident that the tomb would already have been sealed by the time they arrived. Why expose himself like this, with the risk of being captured by his enemies?

Peter was just about to speak when someone from the back of the room raised his voice. One of them had already put his sandals on and had grabbed his knapsack. *Thomas (called the Twin) said to his fellow disciples, "Let us all go along with the Teacher, so that we may die with him!"*

~

So they started out on their journey. The atmosphere was thick with sadness over Lazarus's death. *When Jesus arrived, he found that Lazarus had been buried four days before. Bethany was less than two miles from Jerusalem, and many Judeans had come to see Martha and Mary to comfort them about their brother's death. When Martha heard that Jesus was coming, she went out to meet him, but Mary stayed in the house.*

Martha met him when he was already at the village gates. Her face was streaked with tears.

Martha said to Jesus, "If you had been here, Lord, my brother would not have died! But I know that even now God will give you whatever you ask him for."

"Your brother will rise to life," Jesus told her.

"I know," she replied, "that he will rise to life on the last day."

Jesus said to her, "I am the resurrection and the life. Those who believe in me will live, even though they die; and those who live and believe in me will never die. Do you believe this?"

"Yes, Lord!" she answered. "I do believe that you are the Messiah, the Son of God, who was to come into the world."

Martha's response had come impulsively from her heart. She had not completely understood Jesus's words about the resurrection. But his presence alone had shed a ray of light in the darkness of her sorrow and grief.

After Martha said this, she went back and called her sister Mary privately. "The Teacher is here," she told her, "and is asking for you."

When Mary heard this, she got up and hurried out to meet him. (Jesus had not yet arrived in the village, but was still in the place where Martha had met him.) The people who were in the house with Mary comforting her followed her when they saw her get up and hurry out. They thought that she was going to the grave to weep there.

Wrapped in her funeral garb, Mary got up quickly, and many people followed her. When she reached Jesus, *as soon as she saw him, she fell at his feet. "Lord," she said, "if you had been here, my brother would not have died!"*

Jesus saw her weeping, and he saw how the people with her were weeping also; his heart was touched, and he was deeply moved.

"Where have you buried him?" he asked them.

"Come and see, Lord."

Jesus wept.

The apostles approached him. They had seen him get moved many times, a few times they had seen him cry, but never had they seen him burst into tears.

"Jesus, too, knows what it means to weep for the loss of a loved one. . . . Jesus's tears have unsettled many theologians over the centuries. But even more, they have bathed so many souls and have been a balm for so many wounds. Jesus also personally experienced the fear of suffering and death, the disappointment and discouragement of betrayal . . . grief for the death of his friend Lazarus. . . . If God wept, then I too can weep, knowing that I am understood. Jesus's tears are an antidote to

my indifference toward the suffering of my brothers and sisters. His tears teach me to make the suffering of others my own."[89]

The group of people that had followed Mary thinking she was going to the tomb had stopped a little way off out of respect for the two sisters' grief and for Jesus. *"See how much he loved him!" the people said.*

But some of them said, "He gave sight to the blind man, didn't he? Could he not have kept Lazarus from dying?"

Deeply moved once more, Jesus went to the tomb, which was a cave with a stone placed at the entrance. All of them had moved silently toward the tomb. The Teacher's face was still streaked with tears. *"Take the stone away!" Jesus ordered.*

Martha, the dead man's sister, answered, "There will be a bad smell, Lord. He has been buried four days!"

Jesus said to her, "Didn't I tell you that you would see God's glory if you believed?" They took the stone away.

They obeyed even though they did not understand why they were doing it, knowing they would smell the putrid odor of death. It took a lot of effort on the part of four strong men, friends of Lazarus, to roll away the stone.

Jesus looked up and said, "I thank you, Father, that you listen to me. I know that you always listen to me, but I say this for the sake of the people here, so that they will believe that you sent me." After he had said this, he called out in a loud voice, "Lazarus, come out!"

He came out, his hands and feet wrapped in grave cloths, and with a cloth around his face.

"Untie him," Jesus told them, "and let him go."

Everyone's astonished faces turned toward the figure struggling to emerge from the darkness of the tomb. According to common belief, the soul of the deceased would wander around the body for three days before definitively abandoning it when the decaying process began. It had been four days since he had died. Out from the bandages that the sisters hastily removed came Lazarus smiling, his eyes fixed on Jesus. Rather than the stench of death, there was the scent of life. After having recovered from this surprise, some of those present broke into shouts of joy, still incapable of believing their own eyes.

∼

89. Meditation for the Prayer Vigil of the Extraordinary Jubilee of Misericordia, May 5, 2016.

Many of the people who had come to visit Mary saw what Jesus did, and they believed in him. Others instead left Bethany quickly, heading to the temple to give their eyewitness testimony regarding what Jesus had done. It was not the healing of a blind person or a cripple this time. They could not question the good faith of the person who was healed this time. They could not dismiss the event, insinuating it was a fraud. They had seen Lazarus's corpse; they had seen it buried. They had seen the tomb sealed, and they had seen him come out alive four days later.

So the Pharisees and the chief priests met with the Council and said, "What shall we do? Look at all the miracles this man is performing! If we let him go on in this way, everyone will believe in him, and the Roman authorities will take action and destroy our Temple and our nation!"

Jesus's presence and his signs that corroborated his preaching were in evidence. These men who clung to power and were distant from the people were worried only about self-preservation.

One of them, named Caiaphas, who was High Priest that year, said, "What fools you are! Don't you realize that it is better for you to have one man die for the people, instead of having the whole nation destroyed?"

Actually, he did not say this of his own accord; rather, as he was High Priest that year, he was prophesying that Jesus was going to die for the Jewish people, and not only for them, but also to bring together into one body all the scattered people of God. From that day on the Jewish authorities made plans to kill Jesus.

The Passover was drawing near. Jesus's fate had been sealed. Only exile could have saved him now. But he knew what would happen, and he had tried to prepare his friends, not without meeting with difficulty.

Jesus did not travel openly in Judea, but left and went to a place near the desert, to a town named Ephraim, where he stayed with the disciples. So they left Bethany and, instead of heading to Jerusalem, took the road toward Ephraim, turning toward the border between Judea and Galilee.

They remained in Ephraim a week, then set out again on the road, once more toward Jerusalem. They reached the city of Jericho, constructed by Herod the Great and his son Archelaus not far from the ancient Canaanite city that bore the same name that had been destroyed centuries before. In addition to an amphitheater and a stadium, it boasted a huge, luxurious royal palace. Numerous pools collected water flowing around the city. Jericho was an important commercial center in ancient Judea. The arrival of caravans never went unnoticed. News of the miracles the Teacher performed had long since reached even here. Thus, the disciples were joined by a large crowd at the entrance to the city.

A short distance ahead, they passed by a beggar dressed in rags. His name was Bartimaeus, the son of Timaeus. He was blind and spent his days in the open. His skin was dark and wrinkled, dried out from the wind. He was not yet forty years old, but he looked twenty years older. *When he heard that it was Jesus of Nazareth, he began to shout, "Jesus! Son of David! Have mercy on me!" Many of the people scolded him and told him to be quiet. But he shouted even more loudly, "Son of David, have mercy on me!"*

Even a few of the disciples asked the blind man to keep quiet, not to bother the Teacher. Bartimaeus, however, heedless of these rebukes, continued to cry out in Jesus's direction. He could not see, but he could make out very well the commotion coming from his left where the small procession was passing by.

Jesus stopped and said, "Call him."

So they called the blind man. "Cheer up!" they said. "Get up, he is calling you."

So he threw off his cloak, jumped up, and came to Jesus.

"What do you want me to do for you?" Jesus asked him.

"Teacher," the blind man answered, "I want to see again."

"Go," Jesus told him, "your faith has made you well."

At once he was able to see and followed Jesus on the road.

Everything had happened in a few seconds. As soon as they had called him, Bartimaeus got up immediately. He almost seemed propelled by a force not his own. He did not see Jesus—Jesus had seen him. In a split second, Bartimaeus could see again. He squinted his eyes, filled with astonishment, and picked up his cloak again from the ground. How beautiful every corner of the city, every sight in the heavens, appeared to him. How penetrating had been those eyes of the One who, even prior to healing his eyes and restoring his sight, had healed his heart and restored his dignity. It came naturally to Bartimaeus to set out on the road to follow Jesus.

"Many of those who were with Jesus rebuked Bartimaeus so he would be quiet. For those disciples, a person in need was a nuisance along the way, something unexpected on the agenda. They preferred their own schedule instead of the Teacher's, their own words instead of listening to others. They were following Jesus, but they had their own plans in mind. . . .

"For Jesus, instead, the cry of those pleading for help is not a nuisance that gets in his way on the road, but a vital question. Let us look at Jesus. He does not delegate someone from the 'large crowd' following him, but goes personally to meet

Bartimaeus. He asks him, 'What do you want me to do for you?' 'What do you want . . . (Jesus empathizes with Bartimaeus, he does not disregard him), me to do . . . (to do, not only to say), for you . . .' (not according to preconceived ideas about anyone, but for you, in your situation). That is how God works. He gets personally involved with preferential love for every person. Through his way of acting, his message is already transmitted. Faith thus blossoms in life."[90]

About one hundred yards away, a rather short young man dressed in expensive clothing left his house and went out into the street. One of his servants had just told him that Jesus of Nazareth had entered the city and that he would soon be passing nearby together with his disciples and a large crowd. The man's name was Zacchaeus. He was a chief tax collector, that is, he was one of the people who collected taxes on behalf of the Romans. He was considered a sinner, hated by just about everyone in the city—hated, but feared at the same time. He had gotten rich because of his profession and because he did it dishonestly, asking more than what he had to and keeping a lot of money for himself. All his friends were wealthy and collaborated with the Romans. Everyone avoided his luxurious home built next to the main tax-collecting post of the city and protected by security.

This man could never have explained why he desired to see this itinerant prophet so many people were talking about. Out of pure curiosity, it could' be said. Zacchaeus feared the crowd, knowing that due to his short stature it would not be easy to see anything from a distance. And he was aware that people would not take it well at all if his approach were intrusive. So as the procession came nearer, he decided to watch without being seen.

So he ran ahead of the crowd and climbed a sycamore tree to see Jesus, who was going to pass that way. The tree was not that tall, its trunk was formed in such a way that it was very easy to climb up. He settled himself among the branches, thinking he would not be seen.

But what he did had not gone unnoticed. A few of the bystanders on the side of the road noticed what he had done and began to snicker. One of them approached the apostle Philip, who was coming ahead of the rest of the crowd surrounding Jesus, and said to him, "See him up there in the branches of that sycamore? He's the chief publican, Zacchaeus. Be careful of him!" He said it with a sarcastic smile, certain that nobody would deign to look up at him. Instead, exactly the opposite occurred. The man who did not want to be seen was seen. The man whom everyone hated was loved.

---

90. Homily for the conclusion of the Synod of Bishops, October 28, 2018.

When Jesus came to that place, he looked up and said to Zacchaeus, "Hurry down, Zacchaeus, because I must stay in your house today."

It had taken only an instant. The Nazarene's eyes had rested on that tax collector clumsily clinging to the tree's green foliage. It was like the wall of Jericho had come tumbling down once again. Blown down were the walls he had built to protect his corruption. That loving and merciful look invaded him. Not only had Jesus stopped for him, looked squarely at him, but he also had invited himself to Zacchaeus's home—to that house everyone shunned, at that table that everyone scorned, in that company with whom none of his neighbors would have associated since they were sinners, thieves, collaborationists.

Zacchaeus hurried down and welcomed him with great joy. All the people who saw it started grumbling, "This man has gone as a guest to the home of a sinner!"

He did not even have time to think, so great was the joy that filled his heart. He approached the Teacher and showed him the way to his house just a few dozen yards away. Jesus went in and sat down to table with him. Peter, Andrew, and Bartholomew went in with him. The crowd remained outside, murmuring from a distance. They were all enraged at Jesus's decision.

During the meal, Zacchaeus stood up and said to the Lord, "Listen, sir! I will give half my belongings to the poor, and if I have cheated anyone, I will pay back four times as much."

Only two hours previously, Jesus of Nazareth was only the name of a person. Two hours after having been seen by him, Zacchaeus felt forgiven. Feeling loved, welcomed, and forgiven, he discovered he was a sinner and a corrupt man. His decision to divide his possessions with the poor and to make restitution fourfold for what he had stolen was the concrete consequence of the welcome he had received from the Nazarene.

Jesus said to him, "Salvation has come to this house today, for this man, also, is a descendant of Abraham. The Son of Man came to seek and to save the lost."

Zacchaeus was another lost sheep; indeed, it could be said of him that he had been away from the sheepfold for a very long time.

"The man of small stature, rejected by everyone and far away from Jesus, is lost in anonymity. But Jesus calls him. And the name 'Zacchaeus,' in the language of the time, has a beautiful meaning, full of allusions. 'Zacchaeus,' in fact, means 'God remembers.' So Jesus goes to Zacchaeus's house, drawing criticism from all the people of Jericho . . . who said, 'How come? With all the good people in the city, he's going to be with that tax collector?'"

"Yes, because he was lost. . . . From that day on, joy entered Zacchaeus's house, peace entered, salvation entered, Jesus entered. There is no profession or social condition, there is no sin or crime of any kind, that can erase even one of God's children from his memory and heart. . . . He is a Father who waits vigilantly and lovingly to perceive in the hearts of his children the desire to return home, to be reborn. And when he sees that desire, even a simple hint of it, so often almost unconscious, he is there immediately, and by his forgiveness he lightens the path of conversion and return. Let us behold Zacchaeus in the tree—what he does is ridiculous, but it is an act of salvation."[91]

Before everyone got up from table, Jesus *told them a parable. He was now almost at Jerusalem, and they supposed that the Kingdom of God was just about to appear. So he said, "There was once a man of high rank who was going to a country far away to be made king, after which he planned to come back home. Before he left, he called his ten servants and gave them each a gold coin and told them, 'See what you can earn with this while I am gone.' Now, his own people hated him, and so they sent messengers after him to say, 'We don't want this man to be our king.'*

"The man was made king and came back. At once he ordered his servants to appear before him, in order to find out how much they had earned. The first one came and said, 'Sir, I have earned ten gold coins with the one you gave me.'

"'Well done,' he said; 'you are a good servant! Since you were faithful in small matters, I will put you in charge of ten cities.'

"The second servant came and said, 'Sir, I have earned five gold coins with the one you gave me.' To this one he said, 'You will be in charge of five cities.'

"Another servant came and said, 'Sir, here is your gold coin; I kept it hidden in a handkerchief. I was afraid of you, because you are a hard man. You take what is not yours and reap what you did not plant.'

"He said to him, 'You bad servant! I will use your own words to condemn you! You know that I am a hard man, taking what is not mine and reaping what I have not planted. Well, then, why didn't you put my money in the bank? Then I would have received it back with interest when I returned.' Then he said to those who were standing there, 'Take the gold coin away from him and give it to the servant who has ten coins.'

"But they said to him, 'Sir, he already has ten coins!'

---

91. Angelus, November 3, 2013.

'I tell you,' he replied, *'that to those who have something, even more will be given; but those who have nothing, even the little that they have will be taken away from them. Now, as for those enemies of mine who did not want me to be their king, bring them here and kill them in my presence!'"*

The money should have been invested; gifts received should bear fruit; things needed to be done to develop the capacity to love and to be loved. A final judgment awaits everyone, and the triumph of the kingdom of God would arrive after the departure and absence of the claimant, who would appear acting truly as king only on his return. Yet again, the expectation of his listeners for a political messiah was scaled back. The Son of Man's horizon was set on something completely different.

The parable had a historical background, which the eldest among those present at table would have understood. Thirty years previously, King Herod Archelaus had traveled to Rome to receive his investiture from Caesar Octavian Augustus. A delegation of about fifty Jews were sent to oppose the claimant to the throne and to ask the Roman Emperor to put an end to the Herodian dynasty. From the windows of the house in which they were gathered to eat, they could still see Archelaus's luxurious royal palace.

It was late afternoon when they left Zacchaeus's house. He could not stop thanking Jesus for the gift he had received. That day, the chief tax collector began to look on those around him in the same way in which he had been looked on. He was finally aware of the poor people who stood not far from his front door.

Jesus and his apostles stayed in the city a few more days. One morning they left Jericho for what would be their last journey together. *The time for the Passover Festival was near, and many people went up from the country to Jerusalem to perform the ritual of purification before the festival. They were looking for Jesus, and as they gathered in the Temple, they asked one another, "What do you think? Surely he will not come to the festival, will he?" The chief priests and the Pharisees had given orders that if anyone knew where Jesus was, he must report it, so that they could arrest him.*

The decision about the life and death of the Nazarene had already been made. It was just a matter of time. If he showed up in Jerusalem, he would have no means of escape.

Six days before the Passover, Jesus went to Bethany, the home of Lazarus, the man he had raised from death. They prepared a dinner for him there, which Martha helped serve; Lazarus was one of those who were sitting at the table with Jesus. Then Mary took a whole pint of a very expensive perfume made of pure nard,

poured it on Jesus's feet, and wiped them with her hair. The sweet smell of the per-
fume filled the whole house.

One of Jesus's disciples, Judas Iscariot—the one who was going to betray
him—said, "Why wasn't this perfume sold for three hundred silver coins and the
money given to the poor?" He said this, not because he cared about the poor, but
because he was a thief. He carried the money bag and would help himself from it.

But Jesus said, "Leave her alone! Let her keep what she has for the day of my
burial. You will always have poor people with you, but you will not always have
me."

He had taught Judas a lesson, speaking once again of his impending death.
Once again, Mary had chosen the better part for that perfumed ointment was
only apparently wasted.

A large number of people heard that Jesus was in Bethany, so they went there,
not only because of Jesus but also to see Lazarus, whom Jesus had raised from death.
So the chief priests made plans to kill Lazarus too, because on his account many
Jews were rejecting them and believing in Jesus.

20

"Hosanna to the Son of David!"

Year AD 30, Sunday, April 2–Tuesday morning, April 4.

The Triumphal Entry into the Holy City. Jesus Weeps over Jerusalem.
The Withered Fig Tree. The Parable of the Wicked Tenants.
Tax Collectors and Prostitutes Enter the Kingdom of God First.
Paying the Tax to Caesar. The Sadducees and the Resurrection.
The First Commandment. The Widow's Mite.

Many people in Jerusalem were talking about the raising of Lazarus. Martha and Mary's brother, Jesus's friend, had come back to life on the Teacher's command after he had already been in the tomb for four days. The story of his miraculous and stupendous "reawakening" flew from one mouth to the next. Many who did not believe the hearsay traveled to Bethany to see the risen dead man. Among them were also friends who had gone the same day Lazarus had died and had seen his body placed in the tomb. A crowd of people had gathered in front of the house where the three siblings lived and where Jesus had been a guest.

The same thing had happened countless other times. After every miracle, after each healing . . . the people would bless the Nazarene, wanting to proclaim him king and messiah. Jesus had always fled, finding every possible way of escape to evade the enthusiasm of the crowds. He had not come for that purpose. He did not intend to be "crowned." The kingdom he proclaimed was not political—the freedom he preached had nothing to do with the Roman oppressors.

At the beginning of the week, however, what had happened all the other times was not repeated. The crowd was looking for him, was crying out, "Hosanna" to him, was asking for him, they wanted to worship him, crown him . . . and this time it did not seem he was escaping.

He went out and mingled with the people who were waiting for him. On Judas Iscariot's face you could notice growing satisfaction. Had the reconquest begun? Would the Teacher finally use his immense power as leader of the people? Was the hour drawing near when the collaborationists and corrupt rulers would be overthrown by the liberating messiah of the people of Israel? It did not seem true to the apostle that Jesus was agreeing to be acclaimed. . . . It was as if Judas's plans, his grandiose dreams, were taking shape.

～

The distance between Bethany to Jerusalem was short, not even two miles, with a stream to cross, the Cedron. On other occasions, the Nazarene had preferred a more winding, but less travelled, route. The morning of Sunday, April 2, he chose the more direct route instead, that went from the village of Martha, Mary, and Lazarus up through the Mount of Olives, then descended along the western slope, where it finally reached the city, ending at one of the corners of the monumental temple constructed by Herod the Great. This route included passing by the ancient village of Bethphage. As they were walking, Jesus called two of his disciples and *said to them,*

"Go into the village in front of you, and immediately as you enter it you will find tied there a colt that has never been ridden. Untie it and bring it. If anyone says to you, 'Why are you doing this?' just say this, 'The Lord needs it and will send it back here immediately.'"

They went away and found a colt tied near a door outside in the street. The Teacher had described ahead of time every detail of the scene they would encounter. *As they were untying it, some of the bystanders said to them, "What are you doing untying the colt?" And they told them what Jesus had said; and they allowed them to take it.*

The bystanders, who had also heard talk of the prophet of Nazareth, offered the two disciples no resistance. *Then they brought the colt to Jesus and threw their cloaks on it, and he sat on it.* The Son of Man was not used to riding horses. He had always journeyed on foot throughout Galilee from one city to the other throughout Samaria and Perea. The beasts of burden, when they were to be had, were always used to carry provisions, not human beings. Yet that first day of the week that already smelled of spring air, Jesus chose to mount the animal, allowing the people singing hosanna to precede and follow.

From Bethphage to Jerusalem, *many people spread their cloaks on the road, and others spread leafy branches that they had cut in the fields. Then those who went before and those who followed were shouting,*

"Hosanna!
  Blessed is he who comes in the name of the Lord!
  Blessed is the coming kingdom of our ancestor David!
  Hosanna in the highest heaven!"

These were spontaneous acclamations coming from their hearts. They were messianic acclamations, even though this Messiah had not arrived riding on a steed accompanied by soldiers armed to the teeth. He had arrived riding the back of a colt, surrounded by friends, welcomed by the waving of palm and olive branches. Jesus passed through the two sides of the crowd, smiling. A swarm of noisy children surrounded him on the way. They were scampering around everywhere, darting back and forth among the people. The Teacher followed them with his eyes. He knew the names and destinies of each one, and he prayed to the Father for each of them.

Along the way, the festive parade came upon a small group of Pharisees who had heard the noise and the "hosannas."

They said to him, *"Teacher, order your disciples to stop."*

They were annoyed by the over-the-top enthusiasm, by that messianic-like reception. . . .

He answered, *"I tell you, if these were silent, the stones would shout out."*

Jesus's days were coming to completion. These "hosannas" would soon be followed by "crucify him."

"Jesus enters the city surrounded by his people, surrounded by a cacophony of singing and shouting. We can imagine that resounding loudly all together in this entry are the voices of the forgiven son, the healed leper, or the bleating of the lost sheep. There is the song of the publican and the unclean man, the cry of those living on the margins of the city, and the cry of those men and women who had followed Jesus because they had experienced his compassion for their pain and misery. . . . It is the song and spontaneous joy of all the marginalized people, who, having been touched by Jesus, can shout, "Blessed is he who comes in the name of the Lord." How could they not acclaim the One who had restored their dignity and hope? It is the joy of so many forgiven sinners who had regained trust and hope. And they cry out. They rejoice. This is joy.

"This 'hosannic' joy is a source of discomfort and becomes absurd and scandalous for those who consider themselves righteous and 'faithful' to the law and its ritual precepts. This joy is unbearable for those who had blocked their sensitivity when faced with pain, suffering and misery. Many of them think, 'Look at these ill-mannered people!' This joy is intolerable for those who have lost their memory

and have forgotten the many opportunities received. How hard it is to comprehend the joy and celebration of God's mercy for those who try to justify themselves and make it on their own! How hard it is for those who trust only in their own power, and feel superior to others, to share in this joy!" [92]

⁓

The walls surrounding the temple that seemed distant on the horizon were drawing closer and closer. *As he came near and saw the city, he wept over it, saying, "If you, even you, had only recognized on this day the things that make for peace! But now they are hidden from your eyes. Indeed, the days will come upon you, when your enemies will set up ramparts around you and surround you, and hem you in on every side. They will crush you to the ground, you and your children within you, and they will not leave within you one stone upon another; because you did not recognize the time of your visitation from God."*

The crowd cheering "hosanna" was not aware of what had happened. Not many people had heard what Jesus's soft voice had uttered, not being able to be heard over the festive outcries of the people and, in particular, of the littlest ones. Jesus's face was streaked with tears. But even those who noticed thought them to be tears of joy, tears welling up from an unexpected emotion caused by this unexpected and spontaneous celebration. Only Andrew and John had distinctly heard those words of the Nazarene and his prophesy regarding the destruction of Jerusalem, which some among that generation would in fact live to see fulfilled with the siege of Titus in the year 70.

And he entered Jerusalem and went into the temple.

Now among those who went up to worship at the festival were some Greeks.

These were the so-called devout who, although they did not belong to the chosen nation of Israel and were not circumcised, observed the Sabbath rest, prayed, and gave alms. They remained in the outer court of the temple. They had been impressed by the affection of the cheering crowd, and they wanted to see the Nazarene up close.

They came to Philip, who was from Bethsaida in Galilee, and said to him, "Sir, we wish to see Jesus." Philip went and told Andrew; then Andrew and Philip went and told Jesus.

The two were not expecting a response like this.

---

92. Palm Sunday homily, March 25, 2018.

Jesus answered them, "The hour has come for the Son of Man to be glorified. Very truly, I tell you, unless a grain of wheat falls into the earth and dies, it remains just a single grain; but if it dies, it bears much fruit. Those who love their life lose it, and those who hate their life in this world will keep it for eternal life. Whoever serves me must follow me and where I am, there will my servant be also. Whoever serves me, the Father will honor. Now is my soul troubled. And what shall I say—'Father, save me from this hour'? No, it is for this reason that I have come to this hour. Father, glorify your name."

The condition for serving him was to follow him, and the disciples knew this well. Those who served Jesus by following him honored the Father. The Teacher had concluded his words by lifting his eyes to heaven, just like when he prayed, thus demonstrating that intimate relationship he had with God the Father, woven into every one of his words and actions.

That invocation uttered almost under his breath did not fall on deaf ears.

Then a voice came from heaven, "I have glorified it, and I will glorify it again."

The Father's name would be "glorified" with the epilogue of his Son's mission.

Those words that had come from on high were not distinctly picked up by everyone.

The crowd standing there heard it and said that it was thunder. Others said, "An angel has spoken to him."

Jesus answered, "This voice has come for your sake, not for mine. Now is the judgment of this world; now the ruler of this world will be driven out. And I, when I am lifted up from the earth, will draw all people to myself." He said this to indicate the kind of death he was to die.

The people did not understand. Even his followers, notwithstanding his repeated prophecies, found it hard to understand.

A man, a scribe, came forward through the crowd. He had been listening very attentively all along to Jesus's words. And he said, *"We have heard from the Law that the Messiah remains forever. How can you say that the Son of Man must be lifted up? Who is this Son of Man?"*

Jesus said to them, "The light is with you for a little longer. Walk while you have the light, so that the darkness may not overtake you. If you walk in the darkness you do not know where you are going. While you have the light, believe in the light, so that you may become children of light."

He was speaking of himself; he is the light of the world. The Son of Man had to be lifted up, but to suffer and then to die for the salvation of all, hanging on the most infamous of gallows.

After Jesus had said this, he departed and hid from them.

Jesus and the disciples slipped into the throng lining the narrow lanes surrounding the temple.

And when he had looked around at everything, as it was already late, he went out to Bethany with the twelve.

As dark was falling and a cold wind picked up and was hissing through the ancient stones, Jesus left Jerusalem. The Holy City was safe during the day because while the crowd surrounded him, protecting him, the Pharisees and members of the Sanhedrin could not order his arrest. The people would have revolted against them and would have prevented it. But after sunset fell, when even the caravans from elsewhere sought shelter in the inns, those streets could become treacherous.

～

April 3, Monday morning, they got up early. Jesus invited them to take the road leading back to the city. There were still groups of people waiting for him outside the house.

When they came from Bethany, he was hungry.

The apostles had eaten something as soon as they had awakened. Jesus had not. He had spent a good part of the night alone in prayer.

Seeing in the distance a fig tree in leaf, he went to see whether perhaps he would find anything on it. When he came to it, he found nothing but leaves, for it was not the season for figs.

The tree was lush, but it was April. It was not the season for fruit. With unusual harshness, Jesus turned to the tree and *said to it, "May no one ever eat fruit from you again." And his disciples heard it.* That curse seemed strange to them. Why had he become so angry with a tree for not finding fruit on it at a time when no other fig tree would have had any either? They did not say anything but turned that question over in their minds the entire day. His action and those words had to mean something. . . .

Then they came to Jerusalem. And he entered the temple. As he had done another time, Jesus overturned the money changers' tables and the dove sellers' chairs, repeating his condemnation for those who transformed the house of God into a den of thieves.

Many more people approached him and his disciples, while the chief priests, summoned by the uproar, murmured among themselves, seeking a way to put him to death. He remained in the temple, continuing to teach until late afternoon.

And when evening came they went out of the city.

~

The next morning, Tuesday, they left Bethany even earlier, going the same way they had the day before. *In the morning as they passed by, they saw the fig tree withered away to its roots. Then Peter remembered and said to him, "Rabbi, look! The fig tree that you cursed has withered."*

They stopped, impressed. Overnight, the tree had lost all its foliage and was completely withered. It had taken on a ghastly appearance.

And Jesus answered them, "Have faith in God. Truly, I tell you, if you say to this mountain, 'Be taken up and thrown into the sea,' and if you do not doubt in your heart, but believe that what you say will come to pass, it will be done for you. So I tell you, whatever you ask for in prayer, believe that you have received it, and it will be yours. Whenever you stand praying, forgive, if you have anything against anyone, so that your Father in heaven may also forgive you your trespasses."

That tree, full of leaves but bearing no fruit, had become the symbol of those men and women who had received many gifts but had not brought them to fruition.

"The fig tree represents infertility, that is to say, a barren life, incapable of giving anything, a life that does not bear fruit, incapable of doing good because that type of person lives for him or herself, tranquil, selfish, not wanting problems. . . . Jesus curses the fig tree for being sterile because it made no effort to bear fruit, thus becoming a symbol of the person who does nothing to help, who lives only for him or herself, so as not to lack anything."[93]

Jesus took the opportunity to reaffirm the power of prayer uttered in faith, with a humble heart, but only after being reconciled with a brother or sister.

There were many people waiting to greet Jesus when he reached the temple. This morning appointment had by now become a daily appointment for many people. The Nazarene attracted people to himself with his words and deeds, and the crowd followed his speeches attentively, always ready to observe the reactions of the authorities who were listening off in the distance,

---

93. Homily, Santa Marta, May 29, 2015.

murmuring among themselves, more and more certain of how dangerous this prophet was.

⁓

Again they came to Jerusalem. As he was walking in the temple, the chief priests, the scribes, and the elders came to him and said, "By what authority are you doing these things? Who gave you this authority to do them?"

They had come up with this question to create trouble for him. He had, in fact, said many times where his authority came from. The miraculous signs that accompanied his ministry were exactly that—"signs"—signs that pointed to someone else. This time, too, those who had come to create problems and to find pretexts were themselves put on the spot.

Jesus said to them, "I will ask you one question; answer me, and I will tell you by what authority I do these things. Did the baptism of John come from heaven or was it of human origin? Answer me."

The chief priests, the elders, and the scribes remained silent for a few moments, then they went away from him to whisper together under their breaths and to decide on a common response. Meanwhile, Jesus stared at their faces.

They argued with one another, "If we say, 'From heaven,' he will say, 'Why then did you not believe him?' But shall we say, 'Of human origin?'"—they were afraid of the crowd, for all regarded John as truly a prophet.

In the first case, they would have immediately gone over to the wrong side. In the second case, they would have provoked a reaction from the people who loved John. Thus, they chose not to respond, and *so they answered Jesus, "We do not know."*

And Jesus said to them, "Neither will I tell you by what authority I do these things."

Having silenced the priests and scribes, the Teacher addressed the crowd. But above all, he wanted to make them understand, the ones who were plotting to kill him.

Then he began to speak to them in parables. "A man planted a vineyard, put a fence around it, dug a pit for the winepress, and built a watchtower; then he leased it to tenants and went to another country. When the season came, he sent another slave to the tenants to collect from them his share of the produce of the vineyard. But they seized him, and beat him, and sent him away empty-handed. Again he sent to slave to them; this one they beat over the head and insulted. Then he sent another, and that one they killed. And so it was with many others: some they beat, and others they killed. He had still one other, a beloved son. Finally he sent him to them, saying, 'They will respect my son.' But those tenants said to one another, 'This is the heir. Come, let us kill him, and the inheritance will be ours.' So they seized him, killed him, and threw him out of the vineyard. What then will the owner of the vineyard do? He will come and destroy the tenants and give the vineyard to others. Have you not read this Scripture:

> *"'The stone that the builders rejected*
> *has become the cornerstone; this was the Lord's doing,*
> *and it is amazing in our eyes'?"*

God the Father had sent the prophets, and they had neither been accepted nor heeded. He had sent his Son, but he, too, was about to be rejected and killed.

"The prophets, the men of God who spoke to the people, who were not listened to, who were rejected, would be his glory. His Son, the last one to be sent, who was truly cast out, judged, not heeded and killed, became the cornerstone. This story, that begins with a dream of love and seems to be a love-story, but then seems to end as a story of failures, ends with the tremendous love of God, who draws forth salvation from rejection. Through his outcast Son, he saves us all."[94]

They understood all too well that he was speaking about them. Jesus then told them another parable.

"What do you think? A man had two sons. He went to the first and said, 'Son, go and work in the vineyard today.' And he answered, 'I will not'; but later he changed his mind and went. The father went to the second and said the same; and he answered, 'I go, sir'; but he did not go. Which of the two did the will of his father?"

They said, "The first."

Jesus said to them, "Truly, I tell you, the tax collectors and the prostitutes are going into the kingdom of God ahead of you. For John came to you in the way of righteousness, and you did not believe him, but the tax collectors and the prostitutes believed him. And even after you saw it, you did not change your minds and believe him."

Publicans and prostitutes, public sinners would precede priests, men of the law who were orthodox, into the kingdom of heaven? The apostles looked at one another. Peter turned to his brother, Andrew, and said, "After all, he always did this . . . he called Matthew, he went to eat in the house of the chief tax collectors, he saved the adulteress woman, he allowed the sinful woman to pour

---

perfume on his feet and dry them. . . ." These words illuminated the actions he had been performing over the last three years, since they had known him and had begun to follow him. Jesus read the depths of people's souls; he captivated those who were seeking and who surrendered to the evidence represented by his words coupled with his deeds. He could not stand the hypocrisy and formalistic application of the norms by those who felt they were perfect and judged others without being aware of their own hardness of heart.

As they murmured, the chief priests and elders thought, there for a moment, that they would be able to arrest him. But in the end, they were afraid of how the people might react. *So they left him and went away.*

⁓

The pitfalls, however, were not over. After withdrawing, the chief priests asked others to come forward so as to trap him. *They sent to him some Pharisees and some Herodians, to trap him in what he said. And they came and said to him, "Teacher, we know that you are sincere, and show deference to no one; for you do not regard people with partiality, but the way of God in accordance with truth. Is it lawful to pay taxes to the emperor, or not?"*

Apparently, these other higher-ups presented themselves as if they had nothing to do with the previous group. They had begun speaking in a laudatory way, recognizing Jesus's authority so as to trap him. So they presented another question that would not be easy to answer and could have immediate political consequences. This was their thinking—if Jesus responded that it was lawful to pay the tax, he would lose the esteem of the crowd, who would consider him a collaborationist of the Roman oppressors; if instead, he responded that it was not lawful, he could easily be reported to the Roman procurator as a seditious rebel.

Jesus had always stayed far away from this type of politics. *But knowing their hypocrisy, he said to them, "Why are you putting me to the test? Bring me a denarius and let me see it." And they brought one.*

It was a silver Roman coin, forged outside the country, bearing the emperor's image, and was used as common currency for the payment of taxes. Money forged on Jewish territory was made of bronze and did not bear a human image, in adherence to the religious prescriptions.

So Jesus *said to them, "Whose head is this, and whose title?"*

They answered, "The emperor's."

Their response was arrogant and showed their annoyance—everyone, absolutely everyone, knew that the emperor's face was depicted on every Roman coin. For this very reason, it could not be used as alms in the temple. Yet as he held the coin in his hands, the Nazarene wanted them to be the ones to say it. He had provoked the response out of them. *Jesus said to them, "Give to the emperor the things that are the emperor's, and to God the things that are God's."*

His response was rooted in the reality they themselves recognized—they, too, were using those coins, thus demonstrating that they recognized the authority of the one who had issued those coins. He thus rendered vain the trap that the Pharisees and the Herodians had construed for him, teaching them that God should be given what was his due.

"On the one hand, suggesting they give back to the emperor what belongs to him, Jesus declares that paying the tax is not an act of idolatry, but a legal obligation to the earthly authority. On the other hand—and it is here that Jesus 'strikes his blow'—recalling the primacy of God—he asks them to render to God what is his due as the Lord of the life and history. The reference to Caesar's image engraved on the coin means that it is acceptable that they consider themselves—with rights and duties—rightful citizens of the state. But symbolically it makes them think about the other image imprinted on every man and woman—the image of God. He is the Lord of all. And we, who were created 'in his image,' belong to him first and foremost. From the question posed to him by the Pharisees, Jesus draws a more radical and vital question for each of us, a question we can ask ourselves: Who do I belong to? . . . First and foremost—Jesus reminds us—you belong to God."[95]

The Herodians and Pharisees went away, some pensive, others admiring Jesus.

~

The long day was not yet over, however. Pleased with the fact that the Pharisees had been sent back defeated, some Sadducees came forward. These were the aristocrats who held the majority in the Sanhedrin. They had a keen interest in politics and collaborated with the Romans, who considered them their greatest allies. They did not believe in the resurrection. They came to Jesus *and asked him a question, saying, "Teacher, Moses wrote for us that if a man's brother dies, leaving a wife but no child, the man shall marry the widow and raise up children for his brother. There were seven brothers; the first married and, when he died,*

---

95. Angelus, October 22, 2017.

left no children; and the second married the widow and died, leaving no children; and the third likewise; none of the seven left children. Last of all the woman herself died. In the resurrection whose wife will she be? For the seven had married her."

They had not dared to pose to the Nazarene a direct question regarding the resurrection. They had beat around the bush, citing an abstract and fictitious case study that had evidently already been the subject of their debates. Their example was supposed to demonstrate the impossibility of the resurrection since, once raised from the dead, the woman in question would have simultaneously been the wife of seven husbands. Jesus did not flinch or back off from their territory. It was evident that they considered the resurrection—which the Pharisees believed in—as a reawakening, a return to life as it was before death, under the same previous conditions.

The Teacher, after looking at them, said to them, *"Is this not the reason you are wrong, that you know neither the Scriptures nor the power of God? For when they rise from the dead, they neither marry nor are given in marriage, but are like angels in heaven. And as for the dead being raised, have you not read in the book of Moses, in the story about the bush, how God said to him, 'I am the God of Abraham, the God of Isaac, and the God of Jacob'? He is God not of the dead, but of the living; you are quite wrong."*

He had cited a passage from the Torah, the only part of the Scriptures the Sadducees accepted. It was there that he was able to refute their argument, based on the Word of God.

"What will happen is quite the opposite of what the Sadducees expected. This life is not a reference point for eternity, for the other life, the life that awaits us. Rather, it is eternity—that life—that illuminates and gives hope to the earthly life of each one of us! If we look at things from only a human perspective, we tend to say that the human journey moves from life toward death. . . . But this is only so if we look at things from a human perspective. Jesus turns this perspective upside down and states that our pilgrimage moves from death toward life—the fullness of life! We are on a journey, on a pilgrimage toward the fullness of life."[96]

Leaning against a pillar on the sidelines, a scribe had witnessed this discussion. His name was Seth. He was forty years old and had already heard Jesus. Till now, he had not yet found the courage to become his disciple and follow him, but he was fascinated by Jesus. He now got up his courage and, after the Sadducees had left the scene, he approached the Nazarene. His question was

---

96. Angelus, November 10, 2013.

not designed to make things difficult for Jesus. It was a question that welled up from his heart. He *asked him, "Which commandment is the first of all?"*

Jesus answered, "The first is, 'Hear, O Israel: The Lord our God, the Lord is one; you shall love the Lord your God with all your heart, and with all your soul, and with all your mind, and with all your strength.' The second is this, 'You shall love your neighbor as yourself.' There is no other commandment greater than these."

Jesus had fixed his eyes on Seth and approached him. The scribe had asked which of the commandments was the greatest because the Torah contained 613 of them. The Teacher had recited the beginning of the prayer *Shema Israel*, but he had not stopped at only one commandment. He had indicated two of them as indissolubly connected—love toward God and love toward neighbor.

Seth appreciated Jesus's response, but even more the authority with which Jesus had pronounced it. *Then the scribe said to him, "You are right, Teacher; you have truly said that 'he is one, and besides him there is no other'; and to love him with all the heart, and with all the understanding, and with all the strength, and 'to love one's neighbor as oneself,'—this is much more important than all whole burnt offerings and sacrifices."*

The scribe had understood—to love God with one's heart and mind, and one's neighbor, was worth more than any burnt offering. *When Jesus saw that he answered wisely, he said to him, "You are not far from the kingdom of God." And after that no one dared to ask him any questions.*

Seth stayed on with Jesus and the other disciples—from that day on he became Jesus's disciple.

～

Addressing the people who were still surrounding him and who had followed the discussions that had taken place that day, Jesus said, *"Beware of the scribes, who like to walk around in long robes and to be greeted with respect in the market-places, and to have the best seats in the synagogues and places of honor at banquets! They devour widows' houses and for the sake of appearance make long prayers. They will receive the greater condemnation."* Seeking the front seats and showing off were not what was pleasing to God.

At that moment, *he sat down opposite the treasury, and watched the crowd putting money into the treasury.* At the entrance to the temple treasury stood thirteen chests called "trumpets" due to the elongated shape of their openings. *Many rich people put in large sums.* And many times, they did so ostentatiously, certain of gaining the esteem of the priests who kept guard over the offering boxes.

A poor widow came and put in two small copper coins, which are worth a penny.

Jesus had been moved seeing her arrive, hunched over under the weight of her years and sorrows. *Then he called his disciples and said to them, "Truly I tell you, this poor widow has put in more than all those who are contributing to the treasury. For all of them have contributed out of their abundance; but she out of her poverty has put in everything she had, all she had to live on."*

∽

They finally left the temple. It was late afternoon. *As he came out of the temple, one of his disciples said to him, "Look, Teacher, what large stones and what large buildings!" Then Jesus asked him, "Do you see these great buildings? Not one stone will be left here upon another; all will be thrown down."*

They took the way they were used to, and when they reached the Mount of Olives, Jesus sat down, looking at the temple in the distance. Peter, James, John, and Andrew approached him to ask him a question without the other disciples hearing. They *asked him privately, "Tell us, when will this be, and what will be the sign that all these things are about to be accomplished?"*

Then Jesus began to say to them, "Beware that no one leads you astray. Many will come in my name and say, 'I am he!' and they will lead many astray. When you hear of wars and rumors of wars, do not be alarmed. This must take place; but the end is still to come. For nation will rise against nation, and kingdom against kingdom. There will be earthquakes in various places; there will be famines. This is but the beginning of the birth pangs.

"As for yourselves, beware; for they will hand you over to councils, and you will be beaten in synagogues; and you will stand before governors and kings because of me, as a testimony to them. And the good news must first be proclaimed to all nations. When they bring you to trial and hand you over, do not worry beforehand about what you are to say, but say whatever is given you at that time, for it is not you who speak, but the Holy Spirit. Brother will betray brother to death, and a father his child, and children will rise against parents and have them put to death. And you will be hated by all because of my name. But the one who endures to the end will be saved."

They were shaken by what he was predicting. He spoke of days of tribulation, saying that false christs and prophets would come displaying deceptive signs. He spoke of the sun that would be eclipsed. *"Then they will see 'the Son of Man coming in clouds' with great power and glory. Then he will send out the angels and gather his elect from the four winds, from the ends of the earth to the ends of heaven."*

"Keep awake," he added, *"for you do not know when the master of the house will come . . . in the evening, or at midnight, or cockcrow, or at dawn, or else he may find you asleep when he comes suddenly. And what I say to you I say to all: Keep awake."*

By that time, the sun was setting over Jerusalem. Peter, James, John, and Andrew, pensive over what they had heard, joined the others who were preparing something to eat. They all stayed to eat something on the Mount of Olives. The air was clear, and the Holy City was lit by many small lights as dusk fell. Many torches surrounded the walls of the temple. Jesus stayed there contemplating them, thinking about what was soon to happen.

21

Thirty Pieces of Silver and the Last Supper

Year AD 30, Tuesday evening, April 4–Thursday, April 6.

The Parable of the Ten Virgins.
The "Criteria" for Admittance into Heaven.
Judas's Betrayal. Preparations for the Passover.
The Washing of the Feet.
Jesus's Prayer: "That They May All Be One."

That Tuesday evening, April 4, Peter, James, John, and Andrew did not feel like going to sleep after eating dinner. They were still disturbed by the words they had heard Jesus say. Rather, they joined Jesus as he was praying, seated on the ground, the sight of Jerusalem by night before him. The Teacher seemed to be expecting them. He smiled, made them sit beside him, and began to tell a new parable to his friends.

"The kingdom of heaven will be like this. Ten bridesmaids took their lamps and went to meet the bridegroom. Five of them were foolish, and five were wise. When the foolish took their lamps, they took no oil with them; but the wise took flasks of oil with their lamps."

It was a Jewish bridal custom that the friends of the bride would await the arrival of the groom with her. That scene was not a new image for the apostles.

"As the bridegroom was delayed," Jesus continued, *"all of them became drowsy and slept. But at midnight there was a shout, 'Look! Here is the bridegroom! Come out to meet him.'*

"Then all those bridesmaids got up and trimmed their lamps. The foolish said to the wise, 'Give us some of your oil, for our lamps are going out.'

"But the wise replied, 'No! There will not be enough for you and for us; you had better go to the dealers and buy some for yourselves.' And while they went to buy it, the bridegroom came, and those who were ready went with him into the wedding banquet; and the door was shut.

"Later the other bridesmaids came also, saying, 'Lord, lord, open to us.'

"But he answered, 'Truly, I tell you, I do not know you.' Keep awake therefore, for you know neither the day nor the hour."

Neither the day nor the hour. . . . The prolonged period of waiting could cause people to neglect taking care of the necessary preparations and remain on the alert. The Teacher did not stop speaking. He told another parable to remind them yet again that gifts received must be put into play, "invested," brought to fruition. Only those who have thus spent their lives can expect to receive a recompense, not those who have stayed put, who considered the gift received as something to be safeguarded, thus burying it in the ground.

James asked Jesus to speak again about his return. So he began to speak again.

"When the Son of Man comes in his glory, and all the angels with him, then he will sit on the throne of his glory. All the nations will be gathered before him, and he will separate people one from another as a shepherd separates the sheep from the goats, and he will put the sheep at his right and the goats at the left. Then the king will say to those at his right hand, 'Come, you that are blessed by my Father, inherit the kingdom prepared for you from the foundation of the world; for I was hungry and you gave me food, I was thirsty and you gave me something to drink, I was a stranger and you welcomed me, I was naked and you clothed me, I was sick and you took care of me, I was in prison and you visited me.'

"Then the righteous will answer him, 'Lord, when was it that we saw you hungry and gave you food, or thirsty and gave you something to drink? And when was it that we saw you a stranger and welcomed you, or naked and gave you clothing? And when was it that we saw you sick or in prison and visited you?'

"And the king will answer them, 'Truly, I tell you, just as you did it to one of the least of these who are members of my family, you did it to me.'

"Then he will say to those at his left hand, 'You that are accursed, depart from me into the eternal fire prepared for the devil and his angels; for I was hungry and you gave me no food, I was thirsty and you gave me nothing to drink, I was a stranger and you did not welcome me, naked and you did not give me clothing, sick and in prison and you did not visit me.'

"Then they also will answer, 'Lord, when was it that we saw you hungry or thirsty or a stranger or naked or sick or in prison, and did not take care of you?'

"Then he will answer them, 'Truly, I tell you, just as you did not do it to one of the least of these, you did not do it to me.' And these will go away into eternal punishment, but the righteous into eternal life."

Keeping quiet, the four apostles looked at one another, while Jesus looked up to heaven for a few moments. They had understood the meaning of the commandment of love. Peter said under his breath, "So is this what we'll be judged on? Is this the door to enter his kingdom?"

Jesus stared the apostle in the eye. "Yes, Peter . . . anything you have done to even one of the least of my brothers or sisters, you have done it to me."

"The lesson of Jesus that we have heard does not allow escape routes. . . . We are, therefore, asked to remain vigilant like sentinels, so that it will not happen that the gaze of the Christian might weaken when faced with the poverty produced by the culture of well-being, and become incapable of focusing on what is essential. To focus on what is essential. What does this mean? To focus on Jesus, to see Jesus in the hungry, in the imprisoned, in the sick, in the naked, in those who have no work and must provide for their family. To see Jesus in these our brothers and sisters, to see Jesus in those who are lonely, sad, in those who have made mistakes and need advice, in those who need to make their way with him in silence so that they feel companionship. These are the works that Jesus asks of us! To see Jesus in them, in these people. Why? Because this is the way Jesus sees me, sees all of us."[97]

The chill was getting bitter. Only embers remained of the fire they had lit. Jesus rose to his feet and, looking at his friends, said, *"You know that after two days the Passover is coming, and the Son of Man will be handed over to be crucified."* None of them had the courage to add anything else. They hugged each other before parting. The apostles went to lie down with the other disciples who were already sleeping. Jesus continued to keep vigil.

∽

Meanwhile, in Jerusalem, *the chief priests and the elders of the people gathered in the palace of the high priest, whose name was Caiaphas, and they conspired to arrest Jesus by stealth and kill him. But they said, "Not during the festival, or there may be a riot among the people."* It had to be done in secret. It had to be done under the cover of night. It had to be done before Passover.

Caiaphas was a well-built man in the prime of life. He was authoritarian and often rude in how he expressed himself. He had married the daughter of Annas, the powerful high priest who had led the temple rituals from the years 6 to 15. He had then been deposed by the Roman prefect Valerius Gratus. The elder Annas had succeeded in perpetuating his power, influencing the

---

97. Jubilee Audience, June 30, 2016.

Sanhedrin, and making sure that the highest position, that of high priest, was held not only by his son-in-law, but also by five of his six sons.

Caiaphas was completely united with Annas, who tightly controlled the reins of command. They lived together in the same palace. Son-in-law and father-in-law had spoken many times about Jesus in the last few months. They had interrogated those priests and elders who had heard his teachings and who, in some cases, had also witnessed the miracles he had performed. Even if Caiaphas possessed both religious and civil authority, his authority actually depended ultimately on the Roman prefect. Neither the high priest nor his father-in-law had a high approval rating because of their association with the occupiers.

As the hours went by, as the air of excitement that had accompanied Jesus's entry into Jerusalem on Sunday waned, there was an apostle who was becoming increasingly restless. He had imagined seeing the Son of Man finally crowned king; he had hoped that the messiah would use his power to sway the crowds and to put an end to Roman domination. He had put aside some money, stealing it from the common purse, so there would be an initial sum of money with which to support these actions.

But after having rejoiced for the festive welcome, Judas Iscariot became aware that the Nazarene was never taking the decisive step. It was like Jesus kept putting off till the last moment the inevitable confrontation with his enemies, avoiding the ultimate showdown. The apostle had not assimilated the words and deeds regarding service, regarding the least, regarding the poor. . . . Yes, he wanted them to be redeemed, but through manifestations of power, of grandeur. Instead of being converted by the Teacher, he still hoped to convert Jesus to the political and messianic ideal of the liberator who would finally drive out the Romans and the corrupt ruling class who were religiously and civilly oppressing the people of Israel.

On Sunday evening, something had already broken in Judas's heart when the group returned to the small house in Bethany at dusk. A strange frenzy took possession of him. Jesus had ignited enormous hopes. He had to force things to happen, force Jesus to reveal himself in all the splendor of his greatness and power. He had to be cornered. This is why he decided to betray him, facilitating his arrest.

With the break of dawn on Wednesday morning, April 5, 30, Judas Iscariot snuck through the door of the high priest's palace *and said, "What will you give me if I betray him to you?" They paid him thirty pieces of silver. And from that moment he began to look for an opportunity to betray him.*

He left, clutching the leather pouch containing thirty shekels, or staters. Each one was worth four silver denarii. According to Jewish law, this was the amount that had to be paid by the person who owned an ox in the event that it ran over and killed someone's slave. It was, therefore, the average worth of a slave. This was the price paid for the Son of Man who was about to sacrifice himself as a servant, as a victim, for the sins of all.

In the hours that followed, Judas was waiting for the most opportune moment to hand Jesus over to those who wanted to arrest and prosecute him. He joined the other disciples once again, not wanting to open that pouch that day to count the money the priests had given him.

Wednesday evening went by in apparent tranquility. Hanging in the air, however, was an aura of expectation well beyond the usual expectation preceding the celebration of the upcoming feast.

~

With Thursday, April 6, *came the day of Unleavened Bread, on which the Passover lamb had to be sacrificed.* To celebrate the solemn feast, they would need to stay in the Holy City without returning to Bethany on the Mount of Olives.

So Jesus sent Peter and John, saying, "Go and prepare the Passover meal for us, that we may eat it."

They asked him, "Where do you want us to make preparations for it?"

He said to them, "When you have entered the city, a man carrying a jar of water will meet you; follow him into the house he enters and say to the owner of the house, 'The teacher asks you, Where is the guest room, where I may eat the Passover with my disciples?' He will show you a large room upstairs, already furnished. Make preparations for us there."

The two apostles entered Jerusalem through the gate near the pool of Siloam. There they met a man holding a jug of considerable size in his hand. They were once again astonished at the accuracy with which Jesus had described the scene, which seemed a bit odd to them since it was generally women who went to the springs to fetch water.

Dan was the man's name. He was the father of a young man named Mark and had met Jesus the year before, becoming his friend. He owned a two-story house near the city's ancient walls, on Mount Zion, near the palace of the high priests Annas and Caiaphas. On the second floor of the house was a spacious room furnished with carpets and colorful drapes. About fifteen people could seat themselves comfortably, reclining on the carpet, around the low horseshoe-shaped table. The temple could be seen through a large window that could be opened. Jesus knew the place and had already stayed there.

So Peter and John prepared the Passover, surprised by the fact that Judas was not with them since their funds were in his hands. Mary, Dan's wife, helped them, along with his son, Mark.

That dinner was the meal in which they celebrated the Passover, the memorial of the flight of the Hebrews from the slavery of Egypt. They ate bitter uncooked herbs, roasted lamb, and a sauce made of apples, pomegranates, figs, dates, almonds, walnuts, and cinnamon. This sauce symbolized the mud with which the Hebrew slaves used to make bricks. Everything was prepared with utmost care, just as the occasion demanded.

In the afternoon, Jesus and the other apostles went down into the city from the Mount of Olives.

When the hour came, he took his place at the table, and the apostles with him. He said to them, "I have eagerly desired to eat this Passover with you before I suffer; for I tell you, I will not eat it until it is fulfilled in the kingdom of God."

Before sitting down to table, they had performed the ritual purifications. But suddenly, Jesus *got up from the table, took off his outer robe, and tied a towel around himself. Then he poured water into a basin and began to wash the disciples' feet and to wipe them with the towel that was tied around him.* He washed everyone's feet, even Judas's.

He came to Simon Peter, who said to him, "Lord, are you going to wash my feet?"

Jesus answered, "You do not know now what I am doing, but later you will understand."

Peter said to him, "You shall never wash my feet."

Jesus answered, "Unless I wash you, you have no share with me."

Simon Peter said to him, "Lord, not my feet only but also my hands and my head!"

Jesus said to him, "One who has bathed does not need to wash, except for the feet, but is entirely clean. And you are clean, though not all of you." For he knew who was to betray him; for that reason he said, "Not all of you are clean."

After he had washed their feet, had put on his robe, and had returned to the table, he said to them, "Do you know what I have done to you? You call me Teacher and Lord—and you are right, for that is what I am. So if I, your Lord and Teacher, have washed your feet, you also ought to wash one another's feet. For I have set you an example, that you also should do as I have done to you. Very truly, I tell you, servants are not greater than their master, nor are messengers greater than the one who sent them."

By now they were used to Jesus acting in ways that left them speechless. This time they were moved. The Nazarene wanted to demonstrate with a concrete example that service he had just spoken to them about. This was the service, the only activity, that was worth trying to be the best at.

Jesus *"does something the disciples do not understand—wash their feet. At that time, this was usual, it was customary, because when people went into a home, their feet were dirty with the dust of the road. . . . And they would wash their feet at the entrance to the house. But this was not done by the master of the house, but by the slaves. That was the task of a slave. And like a slave, Jesus washes our feet, the feet of his disciples. . . . Jesus's love is so great that he became a slave to serve us, to heal us, to cleanse us."*[98]

~

They sat back down around the table. As they were eating, something extraordinary happened. Jesus *took a loaf of bread, and when he had given thanks, he broke it and gave it to them, saying, "This is my body, which is given for you."*

This is exactly what he said: "This is my body."

And then he added, *"Do this in remembrance of me."*

The Twelve sitting at table with him looked at him with questioning glances. What did it mean to eat his "body"? After he had blessed the bread, broken it, and given it to them, Jesus seemed troubled.

He said, *"Very truly, I tell you, one of you will betray me."*

The disciples looked at one another, uncertain of whom he spoke. One of his disciples—the one whom Jesus loved, was reclining next to him. Simon Peter therefore motioned to him to ask Jesus of whom he was speaking. So while reclining next to Jesus, he asked him, "Lord, who is it?"

Jesus answered, "It is the one to whom I give this piece of bread when I have dipped it in the dish."

So when he had dipped the piece of bread, he gave it to Judas, son of Simon Iscariot, who was seated near John. *After he received the piece of bread, Satan entered* the traitor apostle.

---

98. Homily during the Mass of the Lord's Supper, "Our Father" Church, Rebibbia New Complex District Prison, April 2, 2015.

"*The Son of Man,*" the Teacher added, "*goes as it is written of him, but woe to that one by whom the Son of Man is betrayed! It would have been better for that one not to have been born.*"

Judas, who betrayed him, said, "Surely not I, Rabbi?"

He replied, "You have said so."

He continued to speak softly to Judas. "*Do quickly what you are going to do.*"

Now no one at the table knew why he said this to him. Some thought that, because Judas had the common purse, Jesus was telling him, "Buy what we need for the festival"; or that he should give something to the poor. So, after receiving the piece of bread, he immediately went out. And it was night.

At the end of the supper, Jesus took the final cup, the cup of blessing. *And after giving thanks, he gave it to them, saying, "Drink from it, all of you; for this is my blood of the covenant, which is poured out for many for the forgiveness of sins. I tell you, I will never again drink of this fruit of the vine until that day when I drink it new with you in my Father's kingdom."*

After his body, his blood. They drank from the cup together. Even this act was impressed on their minds and hearts. This act would also be repeated in his memory. At that moment some of them remembered something from the year before. They had been in Gennesaret, just before they went up to Jerusalem to celebrate the Passover, when the Teacher had said some things that had seemed incomprehensible to them. "*Unless you eat the flesh of the Son of Man and drink his blood, you have no life in you. Those who eat my flesh and drink my blood have eternal life, and I will raise them up on the last day.*" He had called himself the "bread come down from heaven." And behold, a year later, those words were repeated, first in the breaking of the bread, and then in the blessing of the wine. . . . What a unique way to remain present among them, through the command to repeat his words and his actions so they could always remain united to him.

~

A dispute also arose among them as to which of them was to be regarded as the greatest. Everything about the Teacher's words and actions pointed in another direction, overturning designs of greatness and the desire of being first. Yet again, he bore witness to them regarding the primacy of service. *He said to them, "The kings of the Gentiles exercise lordship over them; and those in authority over them are called benefactors. But not so with you; rather the greatest among you must become like the youngest, and the leader like one who serves. For who is greater, the one who is at the table or the one who serves? Is it not the one at table? But I am among you as one who serves. You are those who have stood by me in my trials; and I confer on you, just as my Father has conferred on me, a kingdom, so that you may eat and drink at my table in my kingdom, and you will sit on thrones judging the twelve tribes of Israel."*

They ended the dinner singing the Hallel psalms, psalms of joy. After, they remained seated at table while Jesus continued speaking.

"I give you a new commandment, that you love one another. Just as I have loved you, you also should love one another. By this everyone will know that you are my disciples, if you have love for one another."

He spoke of his imminent departure. *Simon Peter said to him, "Lord, where are you going?"*

Jesus answered, "Where I am going, you cannot follow me now; but you will follow afterward."

Peter said to him, "Lord, why can I not follow you now? I will lay down my life for you."

Jesus answered, "Will you lay down your life for me? Very truly, I tell you, before the cock crows, you will have denied me three times."

The apostle was disturbed. He would deny Jesus? "Impossible," he thought to himself.

Reading the look of bewilderment on their faces, Jesus added,

"Do not let your hearts be troubled. Believe in God, believe also in me. In my Father's house there are many dwelling places. If it were not so, would I have told you that I go to prepare a place for you? And if I go and prepare a place for you, I will come again and will take you to myself, so that where I am, there you may be also. And you know the way to the place where I am going."

Thomas said to him, "Lord, we do not know where you are going. How can we know the way?"

Jesus said to him, "I am the way, and the truth, and the life. No one comes to the Father except through me. If you know me, you will know my Father also. From now on you do know him and have seen him."

Andrew was struck by the fact that Jesus had said he was the "way" even before being the "truth."

Philip then intervened, *"Lord, show us the Father, and we will be satisfied."*

Jesus said to him, "Have I been with you all this time, Philip, and you still do not know me? Whoever has seen me has seen the Father. How can you say, 'Show us the Father'? Do you not believe that I am in the Father and the Father is in me? The words that I say to you I do not speak on my own; but the Father who dwells in me does his works. Believe me that I am in the Father and the Father is in me; but if you do not, then believe me because of the works themselves. Very truly, I tell you, the one who believes in me will also do the works that I do and, in fact, will do greater works than these, because I am going to the Father. I will do whatever you ask in my name, so that the Father may be glorified in the Son. If in my name you ask me for anything, I will do it. If you love me, you will keep my commandments. And I will ask the Father, and he will give you another Advocate, to be with you forever." He had promised them the companionship of the Holy Spirit.

Then he asked that they remain united with him and in him.

"I am the true vine, and my Father is the vinegrower. He removes every branch in me that bears no fruit. Every branch that bears fruit he prunes to make it bear more fruit. You have already been cleansed by the word that I have spoken to you. Abide in me as I abide in you. Just as the branch cannot bear fruit by itself unless it abides in the vine, neither can you unless you abide in me. I am the vine, you are the branches. Those who abide in me and I in them bear much fruit, because apart from me you can do nothing. Whoever does not abide in me is thrown away like a branch and withers; such branches are gathered, thrown into the fire, and burned. If you abide in me, and my words abide in you, ask for whatever you wish, and it will be done for you. My Father is glorified by this, that you bear much fruit and become my disciples."

He also gave them a clear indication regarding what would become their distinctive characteristic.

"This is my commandment, that you love one another as I have loved you. No one has greater love than this, to lay down one's life for one's friends. You are my friends if you do what I command you. I do not call you servants any longer, because the servant does not know what the master is doing; but I have called you friends, because I have made known to you everything that I have heard from my Father. You did not choose me but I chose you. And I appointed you to go and bear fruit, fruit that will last, so that the Father will give you whatever you ask him in my name. I am giving you these commands so that you may love one another."

He then added that they, his followers, would be hated just as he had been hated, and that their words would be believed and observed, just as his had been.

Then Jesus lifted his eyes to heaven and said, *"Father, the hour has come; glorify your Son so that the Son may glorify you, since you have given him authority over all people, to give eternal life to all whom you have given him. And this is eternal life, that they may know you, the only true God, and Jesus Christ whom you have sent. I glorified you on earth by finishing the work that you gave me to do. So now, Father, glorify me in your own presence with the glory that I had in your presence before the world existed.*

"I have made your name known to those whom you gave me from the world. They were yours, and you gave them to me, and they have kept your word. Now they know that everything you have given me is from you; for the words that you gave to me I have given to them, and they have received them and know in truth that I came from you; and they have believed that you sent me. I am asking on their behalf; I am not asking on behalf of the world, but on behalf of those whom you gave me, because they are yours. . . . I ask not only on behalf of these, but also on behalf of those who will believe in me through their word, that they may all be one. As you, Father, are in me and I am in you, may they also be in us, so that the world may believe that you have sent me. The glory that you have given me I have given them, so that they may be one, as we are one, I in them and you in me, that they may become completely one, so that the world may know that you have sent me and have loved them even as you have loved me."

To be perfectly one with him, one with each other—from this unity their testimony would flow, the proclamation of the kingdom of God.

"This is what we are called to: unity, communion, the fraternity born from the experience of being embraced by the one love of God—all of us, without distinction."[99]

They got up from the table in silence. No one had the courage to add a word to those extraordinary words they had just heard. They understood they were on the verge of a great event, for they had never heard Jesus pray that way, nor had he ever been so explicit about their own role and what lay ahead.

After thanking Dan, his wife, Mary, and young Mark, they left the house. Mark followed them, accompanying them to his family's olive grove, where the small group was going to find shelter. They went down from the upper city, taking the ancient step street, and passed through the Siloam area. Despite how late it was, the streets of Jerusalem were filled with people leaving the houses where they had celebrated the Passover meal. They left Jerusalem through Zion Gate.

Jesus *went out with his disciples across the Kidron valley to a place where there was a garden, which he and his disciples entered.*

---

99. Address for the Opening of the Synod, October 9, 2021.

They went to the Mount of Olives, to the garden called Gethsemane, which means "oil press." It was an area protected by a low stone wall. The "oil press" was stored in the lowest part, inside a small wooden shack.

Now Judas, who betrayed him, also knew the place, because Jesus often met there with his disciples.

22

Gethsemane

Year AD 30, Thursday night, April 6–Friday morning, April 7.

Prayer in the Garden of Olives. Jesus's Arrest.
The Nazarene before Annas.
Peter's Denial. Jesus before the Sanhedrin.
The Repentant Judas Hangs Himself.

The temperature had dropped. That night an unusual mist descended upon the olive trees, making the atmosphere in Gethsemane almost ghostly. The eleven apostles and the young Mark were so sleepy that they struggled to stay on their feet. Jesus *said to his disciples, "Sit here while I pray."*

He took with him Peter and James and John, and began to be distressed and agitated. And he said to them, "I am deeply grieved, even to death; remain here, and keep awake."

He then went off a few feet from them and knelt down on the grass in front of a cavern that opened in the rock, an ideal refuge for an animal in search of shelter. Jesus did not go in but stayed there staring at that dark entrance to the cavern. A terrifying reality began to take shape before his eyes—a maelstrom of evil and sin. He saw the sins of humanity, past sins and future sins. He saw it all. The vision was horrific. Who could have sustained it? He was not only asked to sustain it, but to take it on himself—all the dark magma of evil.

"Jesus 'made himself to be sin,' and took upon himself all of humanity's filth, all the filth of sin. And 'he made himself to be sin.' He let himself be lifted up so that all people could look on him, the people wounded by sin—us. This is the mystery of the Cross." [100]

The cavern's fissure in front of him expanded till it enveloped him.

---

100. Homily, Santa Marta, April 4, 2017.

And he said, "Abba, Father, for you all things are possible; remove this cup from me; yet not what I want, but what you want."

The sins of the world were being shown to him in all their horror—massacres, murders, betrayals. . . . It became an unbearable burden. Jesus was crushed, broken. *Then an angel from heaven appeared to him and gave him strength. In his anguish he prayed more earnestly, and his sweat became like great drops of blood falling down on the ground.* The emotion was so strong that he began to sweat blood. He was so distraught that his features became unrecognizable. It was as if an ocean of evil had imprinted itself on his body.

He retraced his steps to seek solace from his friends *and found them sleeping; and he said to Peter, "Simon, are you asleep? Could you not keep awake one hour? Keep awake and pray that you may not come into the time of trial; the spirit indeed is willing, but the flesh is weak." And again he went away and prayed, saying the same words.*

Still more dark visions. From the depths of the abyss that had burst open before him, he saw a figure coming toward him. He recognized him immediately. His appearance had not changed since he had approached him in the desert to tempt him. He wore the same white turban. Whispering, he said, "All this evil . . . all this evil cannot be placed on the shoulders of only one man. . . ." Jesus drove Satan away with a stifling cry, invoking his Father. Then he prostrated himself on the ground in prayer.

When he got up from prayer, he came to the disciples and found them sleeping because of grief, and he said to them, "Why are you sleeping? Get up and pray that you may not come into the time of trial."

He began to pray again. He physically sensed the enormous weight of the evil he was bearing on his shoulders. An immense weight. When he got up again, the bloody sweat had stopped. He approached the slumbering apostles *a third time and said to them, "Are you still sleeping and taking your rest?"*

The Teacher, too, collapsed but a few moments, leaning against an old olive tree whose roots formed a welcoming hollow.

"While the disciples are unable to stay awake and Judas is approaching with the soldiers, Jesus begins to feel 'distressed and troubled.' He feels all the anguish of what awaits him: betrayal, contempt, suffering, failure. He is 'sorrowful' and there in the abyss, in that desolation, he addresses the Father with the tenderest and sweetest word, 'Abba,' that is, Father. Jesus teaches us to embrace the Father in our trials because, in praying to him, we find the strength to go forward in suffering. In hardship, prayer is relief, reliance, comfort. Having been abandoned by everyone, in his inner desolation, Jesus is not alone. He is with the Father.

"In our own Gethsemanes, we, on the other hand, often choose to remain alone rather than saying, 'Father,' and entrusting ourselves to him like Jesus did, entrusting ourselves to his will which is our true good." [101]

~

Jesus rested just for a few minutes. Then the silence of that late night in Gethsemane was broken by the voices of the temple guard. Fully armed and led by Judas, they had come looking for Jesus to arrest him. Because of the darkness and the fog, they would never have found that isolated place unless someone familiar with it had led them there.

The Nazarene got up. He looked affectionately at his apostles who had spent three years of their lives with him, always on the move, from one side of the Sea of Galilee to the other, from one city to another, from one village to another. They were all fast asleep, unaware of what was about to unfold and the oppressing weight their Teacher was bearing. The Nazarene's eyes lingered on the faces of each one of them. He had met them, he had chosen them, he had loved them, he had prepared them.

Under his breath, Jesus repeated some of the words he had addressed to his Father just a few hours before while they were sitting at table during the Passover dinner.

"I pray for those whom you have given me, for they are yours. And I pray for all those who will believe in me through their word, that they may all be one, just as you, Father, are in me, and I in you, that they also may be in us, so that the world may believe that you sent me."

The sound of footsteps, the murmuring of the soldiers, and the glow of torches made it clear that the troop was quite near.

Jesus called out to his friends and said in a loud voice, *"See, the hour is at hand, and the Son of Man is betrayed into the hands of sinners. Get up, let us be going. See, my betrayer is at hand."*

He was still speaking when they arrived. Judas was guiding them. There were temple guards armed with swords, and other servants with clubs. They had been sent by the chief priests, the scribes, and the elders to arrest Jesus and bring him before the Sanhedrin. *Now the betrayer had given them a sign, saying,* "The one I will kiss is the man; arrest him and lead him away under guard."

Then Jesus, knowing all that was to happen to him, came forward and asked them, "Whom are you looking for?"

---

101. General Audience, April 17, 2019.

They answered, "Jesus of Nazareth."

Jesus replied, "I am he."

Judas, who betrayed him, was standing with them. When Jesus said to them, "I am he," they stepped back and fell to the ground.

Again he asked them, "Whom are you looking for?"

And they said, "Jesus of Nazareth."

Jesus answered, "I told you that I am he. So if you are looking for me, let these men go."

Judas approached the Teacher and kissed him, calling him "Rabbi." That was the signal they had set up.

Jesus said to him, "Friend, do what you are here to do." Judas had come to betray him, and he heard himself called "friend."

The temple guard immediately encircled Jesus.

As always, Peter reacted impetuously. He grabbed the knapsack he had set down next to him beneath an olive tree and drew a small sword from its scabbard. Then he pounced on a tall, robust man named Malchus, who was the servant of the high priest. He took a quick swing at him, cutting off his right ear. The man fell to the ground, clutching his head, trying to stop the blood with his hand. Jesus screamed at Peter to stop.

Then Jesus said to him, "Put your sword back into its place; for all who take the sword will perish by the sword. Do you think that I cannot appeal to my Father, and he will at once send me more than twelve legions of angels? But how then would the Scriptures be fulfilled, which say it must happen in this way?"

Then Jesus approached Malchus, who continued to sob with pain. Jesus picked up the ear that had been cut off and reattached it, healing the wound. The servant of the high priest remained kneeling on the ground as though paralyzed. He could not get up after having been miraculously healed.

At that hour Jesus said to the crowds, "Have you come out with swords and clubs to arrest me as though I were a bandit? Day after day I sat in the temple teaching, and you did not arrest me. But all this has taken place, so that the Scriptures of the prophets may be fulfilled."

The guards were all over him. They bound his hands behind his back with a strong rope. Then they put a chain around his neck and led him out of the Garden of Olives. *Then all the disciples deserted him and fled.* Mark, the son of the man who owned the estate, fled too. He was crouched in the shack where the oil press was kept, wrapped in a sheet. A soldier tried to take hold of him, but was left with only the sheet in his hands as the boy escaped naked. The temple guards did not pursue the apostles. Their mandate was to arrest Jesus of Nazareth, not his followers.

They headed toward Jerusalem, walking at a quick pace, tugging their prisoner along and taunting him. Every now and then, they would give him a few punches. Jesus endured it in silence.

Meanwhile, after having run about twelve minutes among the olive trees, and having assured themselves that no one had continued chasing them, Peter and John retraced their steps and began to follow the small procession of guards, maintaining their distance. They saw them enter the city and move in the direction of the high priest's palace, which that evening was illuminated with torches all along its perimeter.

～

The Nazarene was first led to Ananiah, called Annas, *who was the father-in-law of Caiaphas, the high priest that year. Caiaphas was the one who had advised the Jews that it was better to have one person die for the people.*

There were a few elders in the small hall. The elderly Annas was seated on a small throne. The look on the faces of his collaborators said they wanted to get it over with quickly, using a script already written.

Then the high priest questioned Jesus about his disciples and about his teaching.

Jesus answered, "I have spoken openly to the world; I have always taught in synagogues and in the temple, where all the Jews come together. I have said nothing in secret. Why do you ask me? Ask those who heard what I said to them; they know what I said."

When he had said this, one of the police standing nearby struck Jesus on the face, saying, "Is that how you answer the high priest?" Jesus answered, "If I have spoken wrongly, testify to the wrong. But if I have spoken rightly, why do you strike me?"

～

Meanwhile, the two apostles who had been following the cohort at a distance neared the palace. John was known to the high priest, and he *went with Jesus into the courtyard of the high priest.* Peter, instead, remained *outside at the gate.*

So the other disciple, who was known to the high priest, went out and spoke to the servant girl who kept watch at the door, and brought Peter in.

The servant girl at the door said to Peter, "You also are not one of this man's disciples, are you?"

He said, "I am not."

Now the servants and officers had made a charcoal fire, because it was cold, and they were standing and warming themselves. Peter also was with them, standing and warming himself. So they said to him, "You also are not one of his disciples, are you?"

He denied it and said, "I am not."

One of the servants of the high priest, a relative of the man whose ear Peter had cut off, asked, "Did I not see you in the garden with him?"

Peter again denied it, and at once a rooster crowed.

At that moment, the procession of guards was coming out, leading Jesus through the courtyard to Caiaphas. The prisoner's hands were stilled bound behind his back. Peter saw him from a distance. Jesus, turning around, recognized him and looked at him. The apostle recalled the word the Nazarene had said to him just a few hours earlier as they were beginning supper, "Today, before the cock crows, you will deny me three times."

Peter jumped up, ran outside the courtyard and, when he was in the street, threw himself to the ground, weeping bitterly. He had denied Jesus, left Jesus alone. And yet, when Jesus turned toward him for those few seconds, his eyes were overflowing with mercy. It was because of that gratuitous love that Simon Peter, the "rock," felt undeservedly accepted, despite his sin. He was weeping with remorse because he had denied Jesus. He was weeping because of that look from his Teacher who, bound like an evildoer, had forgiven him.

"How beautiful was Jesus's look! And Peter weeps . . . he is a great man, this Peter. A sinner, a sinner. But the Lord makes him feel, him and all of us as well, that we are all sinners, and that the problem is not being sinners, but not repenting of the sin, not feeling ashamed of what we have done. That is the problem. Peter feels this shame, this humility. . . . Peter had a great heart and this brings him to a new experience with Jesus that evening, to the joy of forgiveness when he wept."[102]

~

It was a short distance from Annas's house to Caiaphas's, who was high priest that year. They lived in two separate wings of the same palace. All they had to do was cross the courtyard. While Annas had been interrogating Jesus, Caiaphas had been busy convoking a session of the Sanhedrin at dawn's early light. Some members of the elders did not approve of the high priest's behavior and did not present themselves for the reunion. Among them were

---

102. Homily, Santa Marta, May 17, 2013.

Nicodemus, the Pharisee who had met with Jesus secretly at night two years previously; Joseph of Arimathea; and Gamaliel. For days, Caiaphas had already been seeking testimony against Jesus.

It was now five o'clock in the morning. Daylight was breaking through, reducing the darkness. The hall facing the courtyard was the largest in the palace, but many seats remained vacant during the session. The chief priests had sought testimony with which to accuse Jesus, but it was not easy to find credible testimony. *For many gave false testimony against him, and their testimony did not agree.*

The chief of the temple guards, a man in Caiaphas's confidence, had found two witnesses who got up and stated falsely, *"We heard him say, 'I will destroy this temple that is made with hands, and in three days I will build another, not made with hands.'"*

But even on this point their testimony did not agree. The details did not coincide. Their statements were not truthful. They were referring to the words Jesus had pronounced more than two years before when he had cast the merchants out of the temple. When he was asked for a sign, he had stated, "Destroy this temple, and in three days I will raise it up." He was speaking of the temple of his body. But even if his words could be attributed to the temple made of stone, he had never said he would destroy it. In any case, that false testimony was not that serious after all, nor was it useful for those who wanted to condemn the Nazarene. For even if he had truly said what the false witnesses had just repeated, he would have been judged a braggart, a loudmouth, pretending to be capable of doing in three days what it had taken years of hard labor for the Jewish people to accomplish, and which Herod the Great had luxuriously reconstructed and decorated by mobilizing considerable resources. But this certainly did not prove that he was impious or a blasphemer.

Jesus listened to the testimony silently, without getting upset.

With badly concealed irritation, Caiaphas got up in the midst of the assembly. Speaking loudly so even those outside the hall could hear, he *asked Jesus, "Have you no answer? What is it that they testify against you?"*

But he was silent and did not answer.

Again the high priest asked him, "Are you the Messiah, the Son of the Blessed One?"

Caiaphas had used two terms synonymously which in reality were not synonyms. "The Christ" was the Messiah of Israel. "The Son of the Blessed," meaning blessed by God, would have taken on quite another meaning. The high priest, therefore, wanted to provoke Jesus to make a messianic statement.

This would have been serious, since severe punishments were connected with it, but it would not have been blasphemous and, therefore, would not have led to the death penalty.

For the Jews at that time, the messiah was supposed to have embodied all the hopes of Israel—he was supposed to reestablish David's kingdom; he was supposed to purify and renew the worship of God; and he was supposed to finally put an end to the pain and humiliation of the oppressed people who had suffered slavery and who were now forced to support Roman domination. The Jews had recognized various messiahs among their kings and prophets who, in the past, had received that title reminiscent of the consecration through anointing.

Faced with Jesus's silence, Caiaphas repeated the question with an even more powerful voice, *"Are you the Messiah, the Son of the Blessed One?"*

Jesus lifted up his eyes, and staring into the high priest's face, responded, *"I am, and*

> *'you will see the Son of Man*
> *seated at the right hand of Power,'*
> *and 'coming with the clouds of heaven.'"*

A few seconds of shocked silence greeted these words. The priests, elders, and scribes opened wide their eyes. They all turned to look at the person sitting next to them, questioning looks on their faces. Had they understood well?

The words Jesus said combined two biblical texts: Psalm 110 that speaks of a human messiah awaited by Israel; the other was a passage taken from chapter 7 of the prophet Daniel where the messianic "Son of man" is presented as coming on the clouds and, therefore, participating in God's own life. How many times during the last three years had the Nazarene avoided declaring himself publicly as the Messiah. How many times had he retreated before the crowds marveling over the miraculous deeds he was performing. The moment had come for the final revelation. He was the Messiah; he was the Son of Man, he was the Son of God. To say this, and to say it in front of that Sanhedrin where his primary enemies were sitting, had catastrophic consequences.

Several members of the assembly rose to their feet, murmuring, and asking, almost in unison, the same and yet even more explicit question, *"Are you, then, the Son of God?"*

He said to them, "You say that I am." The Nazarene's fate was definitively sealed by these unambiguous words.

His face seething with anger, Caiaphas performed a ritual gesture to express his deepest sadness and outrage at what Jesus had said. He *tore his clothes and said, "Why do we still need witnesses? You have heard his blasphemy. What is your decision?"* He had torn the upper part of his tunic, but in his heart, he was pleased that he had succeeded in "making Jesus blaspheme," thus having a reason to condemn him.

All of them condemned him as deserving death. Some began to spit on him, to blindfold him, and to strike him, saying to him, "Prophesy!" The guards also took over and beat him.

They put him in chains and sent him away so he might be handed over to the Roman governor, Pontius Pilate.

~

Meanwhile, there was a man whose head was covered with a hood, pacing restlessly in the courtyard. It was Judas Iscariot. Several times he had approached the hall where the Sanhedrin was gathered and had looked inside. He had been trying to distinguish the voices, the comments, the questions, the responses. Leaning against the doorpost, he had witnessed the last exchange between Jesus and Caiaphas. What then happened right after, when the Nazarene was made the object of taunts and spitting, and the priests were in turmoil, had hit him deeply. "Rabbi, you said you're the Messiah, why aren't you showing your power? Why aren't you kicking out this corrupt Sanhedrin whom the people hate? Why aren't you doing anything? Why?" As he was thinking this, anger and unease over what he had done were growing inside of him.

When Judas, his betrayer, saw that Jesus was condemned, he repented and brought back the thirty pieces of silver to the chief priests and the elders. He said, "I have sinned by betraying innocent blood."

Annas and Caiaphas greeted him coldly and with obvious disdain *said, "What is that to us? See to it yourself." And throwing down the pieces of silver into the temple, he departed.*

But the chief priests, taking the pieces of silver, said, "It is not lawful to put them into the treasury, since they are blood money." After conferring together, they used them to buy the potter's field as a place to bury foreigners. For this reason that field has been called the Field of Blood to this day.

In the meantime, on leaving the palace, Judas obtained a strong rope and went out of the Essene Gate. He reached Gehenna, used as a garbage dump, where gaseous fumes from the putrefying material caused fires from time to time. He found a fig tree that seemed to hang over a cliff. There, he hanged himself. The tree branch could not support his weight and his convulsions. It snapped, and the Iscariot's body fell, splattering all over the stones. He had repented, but, unlike Peter, he had not seen Jesus's merciful gaze. He had been crushed under the unbearable weight of his guilt.

"What a poor man! What a poor man, this brother Judas, as Father Mazzolari called him, in that very beautiful sermon—'Brother Judas, what happened in your heart?'... The Lord is good even with these sheep and never stops going to search for them. In the Bible there is a word that says that Judas hung himself, he hung himself and was 'remorseful.'... What does that word mean? That till the end, God's love was working on his soul, even till the moment of despair."[103]

---

103. Homily, Santa Marta, December 6, 2016.

Pontius Pilate and the "King of the Jews"

Year AD 30, Friday morning, April 7.

Jesus Appears the First Time before Pontius Pilate.
The Nazarene before Herod Antipas.
The Roman Governor's Final Decision.
Scourging and Crowning with Thorns.

She had slept badly that night, spending it in the clutches of nightmares. Claudia Procula, Pontius Pilate's wife, was a Roman noblewoman who spoke little. Her incredible intelligence and deep humanity had made her an irreplaceable counselor for her husband, who had become the highest representative of Caesar's rule in this remote and riotous province of the Roman Empire. She was a petite woman with elegant features who neither liked appearances nor places of honor. Gladly did she live in the palace in Caesarea Maritima, and only reluctantly would she accompany Pontius Pilate to Jerusalem, having witnessed the many negative consequences of certain shows of force and attempts to "tame" the people who were proud of their own independence and religious traditions that were so unique from the peoples in the surrounding areas.

Pontius Pilate, the Roman governor, was a stocky man, brusque, a capable organizer, inflexible. He could also be ruthless. He loved to read and study and was a recognized strategist. It was not easy to decipher his emotions or thoughts by looking at his face. His look instilled fear. For years, the emperor had trusted him and his capacity to subjugate the people of Israel, even though Pilate had been forced to deal with the growing influence of the Galilean tetrarch, Herod Antipas, son of Herod the Great, who had gained in importance little by little with the imperial family. Pilate, therefore, felt he was under observation since Emperor Tiberius could always count on an alternative source of information, even though less reliable, and Herod was much more interested in flattering him than in describing the reality of the situation.

⟿

The night between Thursday and Friday, Claudia had dreamt of Jesus of Nazareth. She had "seen" the evil about to be unleashed against him. Claudia had never personally met him but had heard about him, remaining impressed by what the witnesses had recounted. She whispered a few words into her husband's ear as he quit their bedroom, already wearing the insignia of his role.

The Roman governor's workday always began at dawn. Pilate and his wife were residing in the Antonia Fortress during those days. It was a massive building constructed of light-colored stone located on a height on the side of the temple where it dominated the entire area. This was also where the garrison of Roman soldiers was housed.

With the arrival of so many pilgrims in the city, the Passover celebration was always kept under close observation by the Roman governor. That morning of Friday, April 7, just before seven, the centurion Petronius came and knocked on the wooden door of the governor's quarters, a fairly spartan dwelling. Having already been awake for quite some time, Pilate was intent on reviewing some documents. "The priests are here and want to bring a man to trial, Jesus of Nazareth," the official said.

The Roman governor knew there were three other trials to process that day: one against Barabbas, a zealot guilty of homicide who had led a group of rioters; and the trials against two thieves. News of this latest accused man who had been brought by the priests greatly annoyed him.

It could hardly be said that he enjoyed a good relationship with the religious leaders. Distrust, and more often antipathy, were readily reciprocated. During the first years of his administration, Pilate had provoked the Sanhedrin when he had the emperor's image on the army's flag placed within the temple. This gesture, which was considered to be sacrilegious, had sparked a revolt that was brutally suppressed by the Romans. Eventually, however, the governor had been forced to withdraw the image.

Then they took Jesus from Caiaphas to Pilate's headquarters. It was early in the morning. They themselves did not enter the headquarters, so as to avoid ritual defilement and to be able to eat the Passover. So Pilate went out to them and said, "What accusation do you bring against this man?"

They answered, "If this man were not a criminal, we would not have handed him over to you."

It was the chief priests who spoke: *"We found this man perverting our nation, forbidding us to pay taxes to the emperor, and saying that he himself is the Messiah, a king."*

They understood immediately that the governor found it difficult to believe their accusations and was not well disposed toward the religious dignitaries and the small crowd of their supporters who had accompanied them. Pilate said, *"I find no basis for an accusation against this man."*

But they were insistent and said, *"He stirs up the people by teaching throughout all Judea, from Galilee where he began even to this place."*

〜

Having ascertained that Jesus was a Galilean and therefore fell under the authority of the tetrarch of Galilee and Perea, the governor *sent him off to Herod, who was himself in Jerusalem at that time.* The tetrarch was also in the city during the days of Passover, staying in his palace, which was halfway between Antonia Fortress and the high priest's house. His court was slowly awakening at that time of day since it followed neither the military rhythm of the Roman garrison nor the intense priestly activities during those days. Having been informed by one of Pilate's messengers, Herod Antipas was sitting in the most luxurious hall of the palace, awaiting the arrival of the Nazarene. *When Herod saw Jesus, he was very glad, for he had been wanting to see him for a long time, because he had heard about him, and was hoping to see him perform some sign.*

He got up from his throne and headed to the center of the room adorned with mosaics and precious material. He wanted to look into Jesus's eyes, but Jesus continued to keep his eyes lowered.

He questioned him at some length, but Jesus gave him no answer. He tried several times to get Jesus to speak. First, he tried coaxing him, then he assumed an increasingly inquisitorial tone. It was all in vain. Jesus the Galilean gave no response to the tetrarch.

Tension heightened because *the chief priests and the scribes stood by, vehemently accusing him. Even Herod with his soldiers treated him with contempt and mocked him; then he put an elegant robe on him, and sent him back to Pilate.* After dressing him in splendid clothing, as the Nazarene was leaving the room, Herod approached him and, filled with anger because of his silence during the interrogation, hissed, "You don't seem to be a king to me! I see only a madman!" He burst into haughty laughter, which only annoyed the chief priests, since they feared the accusations against Jesus might be dropped.

So the entourage under the escort of the temple guard left the tetrarch's palace to return to the praetorium, to Pilate.

Seeing Jesus coming back again, the governor reacted impatiently, *"Take him yourselves and judge him according to your law."*

They responded, *"We are not permitted to put anyone to death."* The priests, the scribes, and the small crowd of their supporters were determined to finish what they had begun.

Then Pilate entered the headquarters again, summoned Jesus, and asked him, "Are you the King of the Jews?"

Jesus answered, "Do you ask this on your own, or did others tell you about me?"

Pilate replied, "I am not a Jew, am I? Your own nation and the chief priests have handed you over to me. What have you done?"

Jesus answered, "My kingdom is not from this world. If my kingdom were from this world, my followers would be fighting to keep me from being handed over to the Jews. But as it is, my kingdom is not from here."

Pilate asked him, "So you are a king?"

Jesus answered, "You say that I am a king. For this I was born, and for this I came into the world, to testify to the truth. Everyone who belongs to the truth listens to my voice."

Pilate asked him, "What is truth?"

Jesus did not let the Roman governor hear his response to this last question, but barely moving his lips, he said, "Not what, but who. . . . It is he who stands before you."

Just like Herod, Pilate found no grounds to apply the death penalty to the Nazarene. He alone could decide this because only Caesar had power over life and death. Not wanting to give the religious leaders what they wanted, he did not want to acquiesce to the Sanhedrin's request. He feared that if he did not condemn Jesus, Caiaphas would start a revolt. But he also feared that should he condemn Jesus, then Jesus's disciples and the crowds that had greeted him with hosannas on his arrival in Jerusalem would also stir up a revolt.

He went out once again before them and said, *"I find no case against him."*

He then recalled the tradition of freeing a prisoner during the days of the feast. So he added, *"But you have a custom that I release someone for you at the Passover. Do you want me to release for you the King of the Jews?"*

The small crowd witnessing the scene cried out, *"Not this man, but Barabbas!"*

Yeshua bar Abbas, or Barabbas, was a zealot who had committed homicide. He was a giant of a man who was dressed in rags, and had a thick, long beard. He had endured imprisonment well. The crowd preferred him over Jesus. This response was obvious—after all, they had done everything to bring the Nazarene before the Roman governor so that he might be put to death. What sense would it make now to ask if they wanted him to release Jesus? They chose Barabbas, even though almost none of those present nurtured any sympathy whatsoever or admiration for him. The soldiers, receiving Pilate's order, freed the prisoner Barabbas from his chains and pushed him toward the crowd. He disappeared in no time, swallowed up by the hustle and bustle surrounding the temple.

~

Then Pilate took Jesus and had him flogged.

The governor decided to punish the Teacher, hoping that would be enough to appease the agitated tempers in the crowd.

Jesus was handed over to the Roman soldiers, who led him to a secluded area of the internal courtyard of the fortress where they would inflict corporal punishment. Up till then, Jesus had been bound in chains, being yanked and slapped about. Now the hostility against him was about to reach its climax.

In the meantime, Peter, John, Mary the mother of Jesus, and Mary of Magdala, were following step by step from a distance the drama that was unfolding that morning. Mary seemed to have aged ten years all of a sudden. She knew for a long time that a sword would transfix her soul, as the elderly Simeon had predicted right near there, in the temple of Jerusalem, when she had come, together with Joseph, to present the child. They kept their distance, mingling among the crowd so as not to be seen. Mary was hoping to catch her son's eyes so he would know she was there suffering with him. Terror and sadness were visible in her own eyes. Jesus knew she was near.

They took off his robe and bound his wrists to a short marble post. There were four torturers. The first two beat him with rods made from the nerves of ox. Jesus's body writhed and jolted with every blow. Muffled cries came out of his mouth. When they had finished, their exhausted victim slumped over the post. Armed with whips, two others came forward. These wooden-handled whips were made of strips of leather that had fragments of bone and metal balls on the ends. Each time they hit their target, shreds of flesh would go flying and blood splattered all over the place. It was a cruel form of torture, from which not every victim survived.

Jesus had not slept the night before. Not having eaten or had anything to drink, Jesus began to die under the blows. After they had whipped his back, they turned him so they could also whip him in the front as well. Every inch of his flesh bore wounds. They finished their work and freed his wrists. Jesus collapsed to the ground, slumped on the large white stones, now stained with his blood, with which the courtyard was paved. It took two soldiers to pull him back up to his feet.

As is if this were not enough, *the soldiers wove a crown of thorns and put it on his head, and they dressed him in a purple robe. They kept coming up to him, saying, "Hail, King of the Jews!" and striking him on the face.*

This was one of their customs, a cruel "game" called *basileus*, or "the king," which was typically played during the Festival of Saturn in December when a prisoner, selected by drawing lots, would be made a mock king for a week before he was executed. He would be "crowned" and, after having been beaten and mocked for days, would be taken to the gallows. The "crown" was a helmet woven of branches bristling with thorns that was pressed onto the prisoner's head. The thorns would penetrate the scalp, thus causing further bleeding. Even though it was not that time of year, these merciless men could not pass up the opportunity to satiate their ferocious appetite on someone who called himself a king.

They then brought him back to Pilate who, seeing the condition he was in, rebuked the centurion. Yes, he had wanted the Nazarene punished, but not brought to death's door.

The governor *went out again and said to them, "Look, I am bringing him out to you to let you know that I find no case against him."*

So Jesus came out, wearing the crown of thorns and the purple robe. Pilate said to them, "Here is the man!"

Jesus remained standing, staggering on his bare feet, with the royal purple robe sticking to the bleeding wounds that covered his entire body. His face was swollen, his head capped by that extremely painful, not-so-royal "crown." They had placed a reed in his hands bound by chains, as if it were a scepter. There was no more breath on the Nazarene's lips.

On seeing him, the chief priests and temple guard accompanying them were taken aback a few seconds by the vision of this unrecognizable man. Then right away *they cried out, "Crucify him, crucify him!"*

Pilate said to them, "Take him yourselves and crucify him; I find no case against him."

The Jews answered him, "We have a law, and according to that law he ought to die because he has claimed to be the Son of God."

Pilate grew afraid hearing those words. *He entered his headquarters again and said to Jesus, "Where are you from?"*

But Jesus gave him no answer.

So Pilate said to him, "You will not speak to me? Do you not know that I have power to release you and power to crucify you?"

Barely whispering, almost stuttering because of the pain, *Jesus answered him, "You would have no power over me unless it had been given you from above; therefore the one who handed me over to you is guilty of a greater sin."*

Pilate made one last attempt to avoid condemning Jesus to death. He felt tremendous resistance at the thought of giving in to the corrupt religious leaders who were not greatly loved by the people, whom he himself hated. He could not get out of his mind the words his wife, Claudia, had whispered to him that day at dawn when she was about to get out of bed: "Have nothing to do with the death of that Nazarene prophet. . . ." But he also feared how the Sanhedrin might react, and the possibility of a new revolt. Other "Barabbasses," always in search of pretexts to rebel against the Roman occupation, were not lacking in those hours in Jerusalem. For a few moments, Pilate scrutinized the small crowd asking that Jesus be killed. "Where are his disciples, his friends?" the governor asked himself.

The chief priests and the guard *cried out, "If you release this man, you are no friend of the emperor. Everyone who claims to be a king sets himself against the emperor."*

When Pilate heard these words, he brought Jesus outside and sat on the judge's bench at a place called The Stone Pavement, or in Hebrew Gabbatha. Now it was the Day of Preparation for the Passover, and it was about noon.

Once again, Pilate presented Jesus, still dressed in purple and crowned with thorns—not a king, but a sacrificial lamb who was facing the ultimate sacrifice without any cries of agony.

"His love led him to sacrifice himself for us, to take upon himself all of our evil. This astonishes us. God saved us by allowing our evil to be unleashed upon him—without reacting, only with the humility, patience and obedience of a servant, exclusively through the power of love. And the Father sustained Jesus's service. He did not obliterate the evil that was crushing him, but rather sustained his suffering so that our evil could be conquered solely by good, so that it might be completely transfixed by love—all the way through. The Lord served us to the point

of experiencing the most painful ordeals of those who love: betrayal and abandon-ment."[104]

Pilate drew near to Jesus for the last time, saying, *"Here is your King!"*
They cried out, "Away with him! Away with him! Crucify him!"
Pilate asked them, "Shall I crucify your King?"
The chief priests answered, "We have no king but the emperor."

Not giving consent, Pilate ran the risk of getting into trouble with the emperor. It was certain that wily Herod would have found a way to inform Tiberius all about it, thus putting Pilate in a bad light. So the Roman governor decided to decree the Nazarene's death, but not before performing a symbolic act, trying to assuage his conscience.

He took some water and washed his hands before the crowd, saying, "I am innocent of this man's blood; see to it yourselves."

But the deliberation had been his. The request for the death penalty that the Sanhedrin had insistently demanded needed the endorsement of the high-est Roman authority present in the city—his. That gesture of washing his hands, which did not come from Roman tradition, was the high point of his hypocrisy.

So he handed Jesus over to be crucified, together with the other two thieves who had been condemned to death. One was named Dismas, the other Gestas.

The soldiers took off the purple robe given to him by Herod and made him put on his own tunic again. Then they placed on his shoulders the *pati-bulum*, the horizontal beam of the cross, binding it to him with rope. Of the three, Jesus was the one who struggled the most to sustain the heavy beam because of the torture that had been inflicted on him, which the other two had not undergone. Each footstep, each jerk, caused excruciating pain.

Led by the centurion Petronius, who went ahead on horseback escorted by the soldiers, accompanied by a small crowd of acquaintances of the con-demned men, passersby and onlookers, the procession slowly left the Antonia Fortress and headed toward the place of execution, just outside the city walls.

Mary watched the cruel scene from a distance. She felt faint seeing what her son had been reduced to. John's arm supported her. He, too, was in tears.

Everything was about to be fulfilled as the hot sun in the cloudless sky reached its zenith that Friday, April 7, of the year 30, in Jerusalem.

---

104. Palm Sunday Homily, April 5, 2020.

24

Sacrifice on Golgotha

Year AD 30, Friday, early afternoon, April 7.

Jesus Is Helped to Carry His Cross. Jesus Is Nailed to the Cross.
Jesus Dies at Three in the Afternoon.
His Body Is Laid in Joseph of Arimathea's Tomb.

The city streets were filled to overflowing. It was difficult for the procession headed toward the place of execution to make its way along the narrow streets. The shortest and most direct route would have been less than a mile, but they were not always able to take it. Jesus was exhausted, dehydrated. It seemed he might fall with every step. He crumbled to the ground several times, overcome by the weight of the crossbeam strapped to his shoulders. Many who had seen him preaching in the temple did not recognize him because of the mask of blood and dust covering his face.

Aided by John and Mary of Magdala, Mary had taken a shortcut through the alleys, thus managing to get ahead of the procession a little. She wanted to see him up close, to embrace him. She braced herself . . . then after the centurion on horseback and the thieves had passed her, she approached him. The soldier was about to push her roughly away when John yelled, "That's his mother!" He shouted it so loudly that even Petronius the centurion, who was farther ahead, heard it, notwithstanding the clamor of the crowd. One look from the Roman official was enough to keep the soldier from harming Mary. She was allowed to approach and embrace him, his blood smearing all over her.

"How can you stand all this?" she asked him, staring at her son's disfigured body.

He responded gently, trying to smile at her and conceal the excruciating pangs ripping through his body. "Mamma, you know I must fulfill my Father's will. . . ." He said it in such a voice that Mary thought she was hearing the little boy when she found him again amid the doctors in the temple after having spent three days searching for him. It all took place in a matter of seconds. The soldier approached to pull her aside.

The march resumed, but Jesus fell.

They compelled a passer-by, who was coming in from the country, to carry his cross; it was Simon of Cyrene, the father of Alexander and Rufus. A tall, strong man, a peasant farmer, he was returning with his two sons after working in the fields, just in time to observe the Sabbath rest. He was carrying a bundle of wood to burn and did not flinch from the order received. After entrusting his two boys to one of the women on the side of the road, he approached Jesus, shouldered the crossbeam, and offered his arm to the Nazarene so that by leaning on him, he could reach Golgotha.

A great number of the people followed him, and among them were women who were beating their breasts and wailing for him. But Jesus turned to them and said, "Daughters of Jerusalem, do not weep for me, but weep for yourselves and for your children." His voice was hoarse, his words, slurred; it was difficult for him to speak.

Momentarily relieved from the weight of the cross, it seemed he had regained that minimum of strength necessary to keep going.

Along a bend in the road, when they were just about to leave behind the ancient city walls, a short woman came toward them. She was carrying a large terracotta cup of aromatic wine in one hand, and in the other, a square piece of white cloth about the size of a veil. Her name was Seraphia. She was the wife of one of the temple scribes and belonged to a group of noblewomen who tried to assist in some way those who were condemned to death, offering them wine mixed with incense, believing that this drink could relieve pain. The soldiers did not stop her. Jesus did not want to drink the wine but took the veil and wiped his face with it, leaving an imprint of his face on the bloodstained cloth.

In the meantime, Pilate had composed the inscription to be placed on the Nazarene's cross. It was inscribed on a wooden tablet, and *read, "Jesus of Nazareth, the King of the Jews." Many of the Jews read this inscription, because the place where Jesus was crucified was near the city; and it was written in Hebrew, in Latin, and in Greek.* The chief priests had tried to make Pilate change it, saying, *"Do not write, 'The King of the Jews' but 'This man said, I am King of the Jews.'"*

Incensed, the governor responded, *"What I have written, I have written."*

Thus they reached *the place that is called The Skull.* Just outside the city walls, on the northern side, stood a rock formation a few feet higher than the surrounding terrain. Both its color and shape made it look exactly like a human skull. This was the place of crucifixion—outside of Jerusalem so as not to "contaminate" the city—but extremely close to one of its main gates. A heavily trafficked area, the area served another function—that of displaying these gallows to the most people possible. There were sepulchers all around, tombs hewn out of rock. The stipes, the wide vertical beams of the three crosses, were already in place on Golgotha. Once they arrived, the soldiers took the beam from Simon of Cyrene's shoulders. Before going on his way, aching from the effort, the man who had helped Jesus turned one last glance his way. Jesus gave him a faint smile.

The soldiers offered the three condemned men some wine mixed with myrrh. Both thieves drank it; the Nazarene refused. Then they saw to Jesus. They stripped him of his tunic, laid him on the ground with his arms on the crossbeam. They then drew two heavy, long nails from a sack along with some heavy clubs to hammer them in. There were holes already drilled into the wood, but the length the carpenter had calculated did not correspond to the length of Jesus's arms. After having nailed the wrist of his left arm, the executioners realized that his right arm would not reach the hole. So they took a rope, tied it to Jesus's wrist, and then both of them pulled on it, dislocating Jesus's arm. They drove the nail through the palm of his right hand rather than through his wrist.

As they were ferociously handling him, *Jesus said: "Father, forgive them; for they do know not what they are doing."* After nailing him to the crossbeam, they then hoisted Jesus onto the vertical beam of the cross using ropes and a ladder. At a certain point on the vertical beam, a sort of seat protruded on which the condemned person could lean so as to relieve their arms from some of their weight. The Nazarene's feet were nailed on either side of the beam.

Once the executioner's grisly work was over, Jesus was exposed to the ridicule of the passersby. He was already gasping and struggling to breathe. Then Dismas was crucified on his right, and Gestas on his left.

When the soldiers had crucified Jesus, they took his clothes and divided them into four parts, one for each soldier. They also took his tunic; now the tunic was seamless, woven in one piece from the top. It was a valuable garment and would have been worthless if divided into four parts. *So they said to one another, "Let us not tear it, but cast lots for it to see who will get it."*

This was to fulfill what the Scripture says,

> *"They divided my clothes among themselves,*
> *and for my clothing they cast lots."*

And that is what the soldiers did.

Jesus's mother, together with Mary of Magdala and the other women, were standing a short distance away. John, too, the only apostle, was with them.

Standing, wrapped in a black cape, her tears were mixed with her son's blood left on her face from their meeting just moments before. More than any other, she was aware of Jesus's fate, of that will of the Father embraced to the point of total sacrifice. And yet she remained in suspense, hoping that something or someone would stay the executioners' hands and the heavy iron club nailing her son to that wooden beam. She felt each blow inflicted on the one being crucified, stabbing into her own flesh.

But there were not only friends or other people who were overcome with compassion by the heartbreaking scene. There were also people watching that macabre spectacle who were not shaken in the least. Rather, some of *those who passed by derided him, shaking their heads and saying, "Aha! You who would destroy the temple and build it in three days, save yourself, and come down from the cross!"*

Some of those who had been directly involved in his condemnation were also gathered on Golgotha to make sure the sentence was carried out hastily so that everything would be over before the Sabbath rest began. *The chief priests, along with the scribes, were also mocking him among themselves and saying, "He saved others; he cannot save himself. Let the Messiah, the King of Israel, come down from the cross now, so that we may see and believe."*

Jesus gave no response. No. He would not get down from the cross. He had to die on that scaffold that had become infinitely heavy with humanity's sins, the sin that he had willingly lifted to his shoulders for the salvation of all. What he was accomplishing on the cross was united with what had taken place the day before, Thursday evening, in that house where he had consumed his last supper with his friends. His body was offered, his blood poured out.

The two criminals crucified on either side were more talkative. They were responding to the people's taunts. Hanging to Jesus's left, one of them, Gestas, began to insult Jesus with the same arguments used just before by the chief priests, *"Are you not the Messiah? Save yourself and us!"*

But from the other side, on Jesus's right, the other thief, Dismas, *rebuked him, saying, "Do you not fear God, since you are under the same sentence of condemnation? And we indeed have been condemned justly, for we are getting what we deserve for our deeds, but this man has done nothing wrong."*

His mouth was dry; he, too, had begun to gasp for air. But he had cried out to silence his companion. *And he said, "Jesus, remember me when you come into your kingdom."*

Jesus moved his head slightly toward the right, succeeding for a few seconds to meet Dismas's gaze. And *he replied, "Truly I tell you, today you will be with me in Paradise."*

Today, not in the future. Today . . . A promise that would be kept shortly thereafter. Dismas managed to smile, and for a few moments he felt relieved. He had caught a glimpse of Jesus's merciful gaze. He had "stolen" paradise.

"The good thief declares Jesus's innocence and openly confesses his own guilt. . . . Therefore, Jesus is there on the cross to be with those who are guilty. Through this closeness, he offers them salvation. What was scandalous to the leaders and the first thief, to those who were there and those who mocked Jesus is, instead, the foundation of his faith. Thus, the good thief becomes a witness of Grace—the unthinkable happened—God loved me to the point of dying on the cross for me. This man's very faith is a fruit of Christ's grace. In the Crucified One, his eyes contemplate the love God has for him, a poor sinner. It is true he was a thief; he was a criminal; he had stolen things his whole life. But in the end, he repented for what he had done. Seeing Jesus, so good and merciful, he managed to steal heaven. This man is a great thief!" [105]

Two hours had passed since the Nazarene had been hoisted up on Golgotha. In no time at all, black clouds covered the skies over Jerusalem, transforming a sunny spring day into gloomy darkness.

Meanwhile, standing near the cross of Jesus were his mother, and his mother's sister, Mary the wife of Clopas, and Mary Magdalene. When Jesus saw his mother and the disciple whom he loved standing beside her, he said to his mother, "Woman, here is your son." Then he said to the disciple, "Here is your mother." And from that hour the disciple took her into his own home.

After this, when Jesus knew that all was now finished, he said (in order to fulfill the scripture), "I am thirsty." A jar full of sour wine was standing there. It was a Roman custom to travel with a good supply of vinegar, which was used to purify and disinfect water. *So they put a sponge full of the wine on a branch of hyssop and held it to his mouth.*

At three in the afternoon, *Jesus cried out with a loud voice, "Eloi, Eloi, lema sabachthani?" which means, "My God, my God, why have you forsaken me?" When some of the bystanders heard it, they said, "Listen, he is calling for Elijah."*

---

105. General Audience, September 28, 2016.

Then Jesus uttered a loud cry and breathed his last. His heart was broken. His head fell, leaning to the left.

"*Right here, at the height of his annihilation, Jesus reveals the true face of God, which is mercy. He forgives his crucifiers, opens the gates of paradise to the repentant thief, and touches the heart of the centurion. If the mystery of evil is unfathomable, then the reality of Love poured out through him is infinite, reaching even the tomb and hell, taking upon himself all our pain to redeem it, bringing light into the darkness, life into death, love into hatred. God's way of acting may seem very distant, that God who annihilated himself for our sake, while it seems difficult for us to even forget ourselves a little bit. He comes to save us; we are called to choose his way—the way of service, of giving, of forgetfulness of self. We can take up this way, pausing during these days to gaze upon the Crucifix, 'God's royal throne.'*"[106]

With Jesus's death, time seemed to stand still once again, just as had happened the moment of his birth in Bethlehem. *The curtain of the temple was torn in two, from top to bottom.*

Inside the sacred building hung two huge, embroidered curtains. The second one, the innermost one, was called the *paroketh* and veiled the Holy of holies, where God dwelled. This was the curtain that was torn in two, from top to bottom.

Tremors shook the earth all around. The crosses swayed. *And when the centurion, who stood facing him, saw that in this way he breathed his last, he said, "Truly this man was the Son of God!"*

Since it was the day of Preparation, the Jews did not want the bodies left on the cross during the sabbath, especially because that sabbath was a day of great solemnity. So they asked Pilate to have the legs of the crucified men broken and the bodies removed.

The death sentence needed to be completed prior to sunset. So *the soldiers came and broke the legs of the first and of the other who had been crucified with him.* Dismas and Gestas, who could no longer prop themselves up on the seat, quickly expired.

But when they came to Jesus and saw that he was already dead, they did not break his legs. Instead, one of the soldiers pierced his side with a spear, and at once blood and water came out. . . . These things occurred so that the Scripture might be fulfilled, "None of his bones shall be broken." And again another passage of Scripture says, "They will look on the one whom they have pierced."

---

106. Palm Sunday Homily, March 20, 2016.

Mary remained on her knees before the cross of her son, her gaze fixed on his tortured and motionless body. Many of those present had fled, terrorized by the earthquake. *When evening had come, and since it was the day of Preparation, that is, the day before the sabbath, Joseph of Arimathea, a respected member of the council, who was also himself waiting expectantly for the kingdom of God, went boldly to Pilate and asked for the body of Jesus.* Pilate granted it to him.

Joseph was a good and upright man who had not participated in the condemnation of the Nazarene. He had become a secret follower of Jesus and did not want his body to end up in the common grave where they would throw the corpses of the condemned, where Dismas's and Gestas's remains were about to end up. Joseph *came and removed his body.* He waited for them to lower Jesus's body from the cross, and for Mary, his mother, to hold him in her arms for the last time.

Nicodemus, who had at first come to Jesus by night, also came, bringing a mixture of myrrh and aloes, weighing about a hundred pounds. They took the body of Jesus and wrapped it with the spices in linen cloths, according to the burial custom of the Jews. They had brought a large linen cloth, woven with a herringbone pattern, large enough to completely wrap his body, a shroud to cover his face, and strips to wrap his neck, his hips, and his heels.

Now there was a garden in the place where he was crucified, and in the garden there was a new tomb in which no one had ever been laid. It was a noble sepulcher, consisting of a small antechamber and then the burial chamber, with a niche for the corpse. The two rooms were connected with a small low and narrow passage. They placed the corpse on the rock slab.

Everything was done with great haste, without being able to carry out the traditional preparation of the body of the deceased. There was no time. The Sabbath rest had to be observed. *The women who had come with him from Galilee followed Joseph, and they saw the tomb and how his body was laid.* Even the apostle John, who in the meantime had taken care of accompanying Mary back to the house where she was a guest, had come to the tomb and had followed the final phases of the preparation and deposition of Jesus's body. He threw one last glance inside before the large, millstone-like stone was rolled in place to close the tomb. The sight of the Teacher's body, wrapped in the sheet and lying motionless on the rock impressed itself in his mind. The women said they would return after having observed the Sabbath rest.

The next morning, the chief priests paid Pilate a visit. They said to him, *"Sir, we remember what that impostor said while he was still alive, 'After three days I will rise again.' Therefore command the tomb to be made secure until the third day; otherwise his disciples may go and steal him away, and tell the people, 'He has been raised from the dead,' and the last deception would be worse than the first."*

Pilate said to them, "You have a guard of soldiers; go, make it as secure as you can." So they went with the guard and made the tomb secure by sealing the stone.

25

The Empty Tomb and the Living Jesus

Year AD 30, Saturday, April 8–Sunday, April 9.

The Fright and Shock of the Disciples. The Women at the Tomb.
The Encounter of Jesus with Mary of Magdala.
Peter and John "See and Believe." The Disciples of Emmaus.
The Risen One Responds to Thomas.

The tragic events of that Friday afternoon had left the followers of Jesus stunned. Even if of the eleven remaining apostles, only John had been present on Golgotha and had participated in Jesus's burial, all the others knew almost in real time what had happened to their Teacher. In the hours following his death, some of them sought refuge in Gethsemane. Others had remained in Dan's house, where on Thursday they had eaten supper for the last time with Jesus. Mary, his mother, and Mary of Magdala were also staying there. Saturday evening, after sunset, Philip, James, and Matthew, who had spent a day on the Mount of Olives, returned to Jerusalem as well. Each of them went on his own, taking a different route. They all found themselves reunited together in the place where they had eaten the last supper.

One profound anguish gripped the apostles. What would happen to them now? Would the Sanhedrin try to condemn them? Or should they return to their homes and the occupations they had abandoned to follow Jesus? True, he had explained to them several times that he had come to serve, not to triumph, and that his kingdom was not of this world. But why had the Son of God allowed himself to be killed in that infamous way? Why had he allowed himself to be annihilated on the cross, on the worst of scaffolds? Why had he not lifted even a single finger? Why had he not manifested even one sign of his power?

They certainly remembered his words and those references to his resurrection. But that memory was not enough to fill the anguished void, the sense of abandonment in which they had sunk in those hours. Each moment was veiled with sadness. Aided by her son, Mark, Dan's wife did what she needed to do to secure food for them. No one, however, wanted to eat. Jesus had been dead one day, and they were missing him tremendously. They had lost their compass, their rock, their reason for living. They had staked everything and their entire selves. Afraid of their own shadows, they found themselves closed up in the house.

They tried to encourage one another, reminding themselves of what their Teacher had said in the last part of his life. Every discourse, every memory, however, ended bitterly, in dejection. During those hours, Jesus's death on the cross, the tragedy on Golgotha, was the only lens through which they reviewed their lives and their relationship with Jesus in the last three years. There were only two people in that house who preferred silence rather than words—Peter and Mary.

This apostle, a man who outwardly appeared tough, gave himself no peace for having left Jesus alone on Golgotha. It seemed to him that he had denied Jesus yet another time. For this reason, even though the others looked to him as a point of reference, and sought his comfort, "Cephas," Simon "the Rock," was evasive. He could not bear the lost looks of the other apostles without remembering that look that Jesus gave him in the courtyard of the high priest's home. He felt unworthy, the most unworthy of them all.

Mary's silence was different. The mother of the Nazarene comforted more than being comforted. After her tears on Friday and the immense pain she lived sharing moment by moment her son's passion, Mary's gaze had changed on Saturday. Mary of Magdala did not leave her alone even for an instant. She and the other women present under the cross and for Jesus's burial had all made arrangements to stay near Dan's house and would come to visit her. The apostles had not the courage to go to her to speak, imagining how profound her sorrow must be as a mother. And yet, her eyes indicated something. While the others, all the others, seemed inexorably taken by sadness over that death, looking back to the past, Mary of Nazareth was the only one living in expectation. She was waiting for something indefinable, but still the same, she was expecting something good, beautiful, grand. In the face of Jesus's mother that Sabbath, it was as if the death of her son had not been the last word. She was the only who had been given the presentiment of what was about to happen. It was a caress that God the Father wanted to give her through Jesus.

The night between Friday and Saturday, no one in that house had slept. The following night, everyone rested.

~

During the first hours on the day after the Sabbath, the women had prepared anointing spices. They wanted to go to the tomb to finish preparing Jesus's body which had remained incomplete due to the need to close the tomb hastily on Friday afternoon, in observance of the Sabbath rest.

After the Sabbath was over, Mary Magdalene, Mary the mother of James, and Salome bought spices to go and anoint the body of Jesus. Very early on Sunday morning, at sunrise, they went to the tomb. On the way they said to one another, "Who will roll away the stone for us from the entrance to the tomb?" (It was a very large stone.) Then they looked up and saw that the stone had already been rolled back.

It was still dark. The garden where he was buried was still shrouded in mist.

"We can imagine ourselves in what the women were feeling on that day. . . . In their eyes they still saw the drama of suffering, of an unexpected tragedy that happened all too suddenly. They had seen death and bore death in their hearts. Pain was mixed with fear—would they suffer the same fate as the Teacher? Then too there was fear about the future—everything needed to be rebuilt. A painful memory, a hope cut short. It was their darkest hour. . . .

"Yet in this situation the women did not allow themselves to be paralyzed. They did not give in to the gloom of lamentation and regret, they did not close themselves in pessimism, nor did they flee from reality. They accomplished something simple yet extraordinary, preparing in their homes the spices to anoint Jesus's body. They did not renounce love. In the darkness of their hearts, they lit mercy. Our Lady prays and hopes on that Sabbath, on the day that would come to be dedicated to her. In this sorrowful challenge, she trusts in the Lord.

"In the darkness of that Sabbath, without knowing it, these women were preparing for 'the dawn of the first day of the week,' the day that would change history."[107]

Mary of Magdala arrived at the tomb first and noticed that the stone had been rolled away. The temple guards were not there keeping watch. They had escaped after seeing the stone move itself as though pushed away from inside the tomb. At first, they thought they were dreaming. But then the men had to surrender before the evidence and had abandoned the tomb, fearing the punishment that awaited them.

---

107. Easter Vigil Homily, April 11, 2020.

Mary of Magdala was stunned by the vision. She remained *crying outside the tomb. While she was still crying, she bent over and looked in the tomb and saw two angels there dressed in white, sitting where the body of Jesus had been, one at the head and the other at the feet. "Woman, why are you crying?" they asked her.*

She answered, "They have taken my Lord away, and I do not know where they have put him!"

Having said this, she turned around and saw a man standing, watching her. She did not recognize him, and turned back toward the tomb again. *"Woman, why are you crying?" Jesus asked her. "Who is it that you are looking for?"*

She thought he was the gardener, so she said to him, "If you took him away, sir, tell me where you have put him, and I will go and get him."

Jesus said to her, "Mary!"

She turned toward him and said in Hebrew, "Rabboni!" (This means "Teacher.")

"Do not hold on to me," Jesus told her, "because I have not yet gone back up to the Father. But go to my brothers and tell them that I am returning to him who is my Father and their Father, my God and their God."

The Magdalene's face was radiant.

"Jesus calls her, 'Mary!'—the revolution of her life, the revolution destined to transform the existence of every man and woman, begins with a name that echoes in the garden of the empty tomb. The Gospels describe Mary's happiness. Jesus's resurrection is not a joy given with an eyedropper, but a waterfall that invades all of life. Christian existence is not woven of fluffy happiness, but of waves that engulf everything. You too, try to imagine, right now, with the baggage of disappointments and failures that each of us carries in our heart, that there is a God close to us who calls us by name and says to us, 'Get up, stop weeping, for I have come to free you!' This is beautiful." [108]

In the meantime, the other women arrived as well. They, too, remained shocked at seeing the stone that had been rolled away. *Suddenly Jesus met them and said, "Peace be with you." They came up to him, took hold of his feet, and worshiped him. "Do not be afraid," Jesus said to them. "Go and tell my brothers to go to Galilee, and there they will see me."*

They left the garden, running. An uncontainable happiness lightened their steps as they returned to the place where the apostles were gathered. They went quickly through the city streets, which were beginning to show signs of life.

---

108. General Audience, May 17, 2017.

With the first light of day, they arrived home. They knocked forcefully, crying out in joy. The apostles were already on their feet. They entered quickly, repeating, "The Lord is risen! He's alive! We've seen him!"

Peter approached Mary of Magdala. "What are you saying? What have you seen?"

"Jesus! The Teacher! The Lord!" the woman repeated. "The tomb was empty," she added, "and he spoke to me! It was he! It was he!"

The others confirmed her account.

But the apostles thought that what the women said was nonsense, and they did not believe them. They wanted to go personally, not trusting what they had just heard. Peter slipped his shoes on quickly, while John was already waiting for him at the door. "Let's go see!" Peter said.

The other apostles who remained in the room of the Last Supper continued to interrogate the women. Mary, Jesus's Mother, entered in the meantime, and everyone became silent. She was smiling. She headed toward Mary of Magdala. They hugged each other. Our Lady said to the Magdalene under her breath, "I know . . . I know. I have seen him. I encountered him as well." The two women wept with joy. Mary did not reveal out loud to the others the gift her son had given her, appearing to her as soon as he had risen.

∾

Peter and John ran like madmen through the streets of Jerusalem. Several times, wayfarers and merchants who had begun to crowd the streets at that hour, turned to each other asking, "Where are they running?" Others searched the horizon in the opposite direction to see if someone was chasing them.

Every now and then, John stopped to wait for Peter, who was less agile and slower than he. The apostle had strong fisherman's arms, but he had never been a runner. Both of their hearts were beating a mile a minute, and not only because they were running. Little by little as they approached the burial place, the women's "babbling" made them think more and more deeply, revealing a seed of imperishable hope that had been buried by the events of the past Friday but they had always preserved, even if unconsciously.

Both of them were running together, but the other disciple outran Peter and reached the tomb first. And stooping to look in, he saw the linen cloths lying there, but he did not go in. Then Simon Peter came, following him, and went into the tomb. He saw the linen cloths lying stretched out, and the face cloth, which had been on Jesus's head, not lying with the linen cloths stretched out but rolled up instead in a place by itself.[109] *Then the other disciple, who had reached the tomb first, also went in; he saw and believed.*

After Jesus's death, Peter had not gone near the tomb. He had not seen how his body had been deposed. John had, instead. After waiting for Peter, giving him priority so he could be the first to enter, he, too, went in. The young apostle was profoundly touched. The linen sheet that had been wrapped around the Nazarene's body was in the exact same position in which he had seen it before the tomb was closed, but it had completely sagged, as if the person that had been closed up in it had escaped through it, without opening it, without breaking it open at all. The face cloth, instead, had remained wrapped, raised, as if it still concealed the head of the deceased, perhaps due to the excessive amount of ointment. Nothing about what they saw made them think that someone had stolen the body. Everything had remained identical, exactly the way they had left it. Only that Jesus was no longer there.

John's heart had always been ready to cling to the Teacher, to his word, to his deeds. For this reason, he saw and immediately believed, even though *they still did not understand the scripture which said that he must rise from death.*

They returned home to bring the news right away and to confirm what Mary of Magdala and the others had told them. Peter *went back home amazed at what had happened.* But the other apostles still did not believe.

In the meantime, the temple guard who had been ordered to guard the tomb—they had been there only one night—went to the chief priests and told them what had happened. *The chief priests met with the elders and made their plan; they gave a large sum of money to the soldiers and said, "You are to say that his disciples came during the night and stole his body while you were asleep. And if the Governor should hear of this, we will convince him that you are innocent, and you will have nothing to worry about."*

The guards took the money and did what they were told to do. They were still really frightened by what they had seen, for the stone appeared to have moved by itself, pushed by a mysterious force. Then there was that shadow

---

109. The translation proposed here from the Gospel of John (20:7) is not the official translation. This translation was chosen based on an essay written by Father Antonio Persili in 1998, which, in my opinion, better renders the Greek expression *allà choris entetyligmenon* referring to the face cloth. The Good News Bible translation is as follows: "He saw the linen cloths lying there, and the cloth which had been around Jesus's head. It was not lying with the linen cloths but was rolled up by itself."

they seemed to have seen coming out of the tomb. Having been handsomely compensated, they would lie just as their employers bade them.

~

That same Sunday, April 9, two disciples *were going to a village named Emmaus, about seven miles from Jerusalem, and they were talking to each other about all the things that had happened. As they talked and discussed, Jesus himself drew near and walked along with them; they saw him, but somehow did not recognize him. Jesus said to them, "What are you talking about to each other, as you walk along?"*

They stood still, with sad faces. One of them, named Cleopas, asked him, "Are you the only visitor in Jerusalem who doesn't know the things that have been happening there these last few days?"

"What things?" he asked.

"The things that happened to Jesus of Nazareth," they answered. "This man was a prophet and was considered by God and by all the people to be powerful in everything he said and did. Our chief priests and rulers handed him over to be sentenced to death, and he was crucified. And we had hoped that he would be the one who was going to set Israel free! Besides all that, this is now the third day since it happened. Some of the women of our group surprised us; they went at dawn to the tomb, but could not find his body. They came back saying they had seen a vision of angels who told them that he is alive. Some of our group went to the tomb and found it exactly as the women had said, but they did not see him."

Then Jesus said to them, "How foolish you are, how slow you are to believe everything the prophets said! Was it not necessary for the Messiah to suffer these things and then to enter his glory?" And Jesus explained to them what was said about himself in all the Scriptures, beginning with the books of Moses and the writings of all the prophets.

He was walking alongside them, explaining the Scriptures to them. But they still did not recognize him. They had almost reached their destination. *As they came near the village to which they were going, Jesus acted as if he were going farther; but they held him back, saying, "Stay with us; the day is almost over and it is getting dark."*

It was really early afternoon. It was still not time for the sun to set, but it was a hospitable custom to invite someone to stop and share a meal and lodging with them. What that unknown wayfarer had said had fascinated them.

Jesus accepted their invitation. *So he went in to stay with them.*

He sat down to eat with them, took the bread, and said the blessing; then he broke the bread and gave it to them. They remembered that gesture, and, for the first time, his wrists appeared out from under his tunic, and they saw the nail marks. *Then their eyes were opened and they recognized him, but he disappeared from their sight. They said to each other, "Wasn't it like a fire burning in us when he talked to us on the road and explained the Scriptures to us?"*

Jesus had been at their side for hours. *They got up at once and went back to Jerusalem, where they found the eleven disciples gathered together with the others.*

"We are the two going to Emmaus, with many doubts, many sins. Many times we are cowards and want to distance ourselves from the cross, from trials. But let us make room to feel Jesus, who warms our hearts. And let us ask for the grace to be like them."[110]

It was almost night. While they were still telling the apostles about the encounter they had had, something extraordinary happened.

They were all together, seated around the same table. The doors and windows of the house were barred. *While the two were telling them this, suddenly the Lord himself stood among them and said to them, "Peace be with you."*

They were terrified, thinking that they were seeing a ghost. But he said to them, "Why are you alarmed? Why are these doubts coming up in your minds? Look at my hands and my feet, and see that it is I myself. Feel me, and you will know, for a ghost doesn't have flesh and bones, as you can see I have." He said this and showed them his hands and his feet.

They approached him to touch him and hug him. It was he! It was truly he, even though they did not understand how he could have entered when the doors were barred. His body was made of flesh and bones, but at the same time it appeared glorified to them, belonging to another dimension. He had not simply returned to a previous life, like Lazarus, like the son of the widow of Nain, like Jairus's daughter. He was real, and at the same time, he no longer belonged to this world. Their reaction was so laden with amazement that Jesus asked, *"Do you have anything here to eat?" They gave him a piece of cooked fish, which he took and ate in their presence.* They watched him eat, not believing their eyes.

As he ate, he reminded them of what he had said: *"These are the very things I told you about while I was still with you: everything written about me in the Law of Moses, the writings of the prophets, and the Psalms had to come true."*

---

110. Homily, Santa Marta, May 2, 2017.

Then he opened their minds to understand the Scriptures, and said to them, "This is what is written: the Messiah must suffer and must rise from death three days later, and in his name the message about repentance and the forgiveness of sins must be preached to all nations, beginning in Jerusalem. You are witnesses of these things."

Then, after eating, *Jesus said to them again, "Peace be with you. As the Father sent me, so I send you." Then he breathed on them and said, "Receive the Holy Spirit. If you forgive people's sins, they are forgiven; if you do not forgive them, they are not forgiven."*

One of the twelve disciples, Thomas (called the Twin), was not with them when Jesus came. He had gone out with Dan and Mark that afternoon to Gethsemane and still had not returned. When he returned in the middle of the night, *the other disciples told him, "We have seen the Lord!"*

But Thomas said to them, "Unless I see the scars of the nails in his hands and put my finger on those scars and my hand in his side, I will not believe." What Thomas heard his friends telling him was too much.

A week later the disciples were together again indoors, and Thomas was with them. The doors were locked, but Jesus came and stood among them and said, "Peace be with you." Then he said to Thomas, "Put your finger here, and look at my hands; then reach out your hand and put it in my side. Stop your doubting, and believe!"

Thomas answered him, "My Lord and my God!"

Jesus said to him, "Do you believe because you see me? How happy are those who believe without seeing me!"

He did not rebuke him for wanting to touch, to put his finger in the marks left by the nails, and his hand into the wound still open on his side, in that glorified body which still bore the distinctive characteristics of the wounds of crucifixion. Jesus reminded him that he should have trusted in the word and the looks on the faces of his friends, his witnesses.

"The Lord knows when and how to do things. He gives everyone the time he believes most opportune. He granted Thomas eight days. Precisely because the apostle had said he would not believe unless he put his finger into the Lord's wounds, Jesus wanted the wounds to still be visible on his own body, even though it was clean, extremely beautiful, and filled with light. Thomas was stubborn! But the Lord wanted a stubborn man to make us understand something greater. Thomas saw the Lord. He was invited to put his finger in the wounds made by the nail, to put his hand into his side. But he did not say, 'It's true, the Lord is risen.' No. He went further, saying, 'My Lord and my God.' He is the first of the disciples to

confess the divinity of Christ after the Resurrection. And he adored him. . . . But to adore, to find God, the Son of God, he had to put his finger into the wounds, put his hand into his side. This is the journey.[111]

After spending that week in Jerusalem and having seen Jesus in the upper room twice, the apostles did what they had been asked. They left the city and headed to Galilee, far away from the religious capital, from the men who had put their Teacher to death. They returned there where it had all begun, along the banks of that lake that had always been a sea for them, and where for the first time they had met the gaze of the Son of Man who had upset their lives forever.

---

111. Homily, Santa Marta, July 3, 2013.

26

From Galilee to the World

Year AD 30, April—May.

*Jesus Encounters His Disciples on the Banks of the Sea of Galilee.
"Simon, Do You Love Me?" Return to Jerusalem. The Ascension.*

A week after the Resurrection, when he had again appeared to the apostles gathered in the upper room to show Thomas his wounds, Jesus had found his friends intent on travel preparations. The Passover celebrations of AD 30 (which would forever remain unique in the history of humanity) had come to an end. So the disciples were preparing themselves to return to Galilee as he himself had asked through the women in front of the tomb the morning he had risen. To leave Jerusalem, to move away from the religious capital, meant removing themselves from the control of the chief priests who were wondering what had become of his followers, even though they were convinced they had resolved their problem with the Nazarene's death.

So they set out and arrived in Capernaum after five days of travel.

They embraced their families, relatives, and friends. They recounted what had happened, and many believed. Anyone who encountered the apostles, and even the other disciples during those days, expected to find themselves in the company of friends who were mourning and digesting complete failure. Instead, they discovered themselves in the company of men and women who possessed a certainty—the one they had seen tortured, hung high on a cross, and killed, had returned and had met with them, had spoken with them, had eaten with them. Their Teacher had died and had risen. This did not mean that they no longer had questions, or that they no longer encountered daily difficulties, or that there were no longer squabbles among them. But that certainty, that certainty regarding what they had seen and touched, pervaded everything.

Those who knew them well, knew that all of them were anything but visionaries. They were fishermen, tax collectors, handymen. . . . They were not priests or philosophers, even less were they hallucinating, or in the throes of some mystical crisis. The resurrection of the Lord was the only thing they proclaimed to anyone with whom they came into contact. The fact that he had surprised them and had filled them with amazement, the fact that he had conquered their resistances and their doubts, was the stamp of approval on the words that Jesus had said and on the deeds he had accomplished in their midst. No, whoever it was they had seen alive was certainly not a phantasm, even less a hallucination. It truly was he, their Teacher.

⌒

Days went by. By now, the group had no funds in their purse, and they had not yet found someone to replace Judas Iscariot. By day, they walked from city to city, and from village to village, proclaiming what they had seen. But they also partially went back to doing some of their previous activities.

One evening, *Simon Peter, Thomas (called the Twin), Nathanael (the one from Cana in Galilee), the sons of Zebedee, and two other disciples of Jesus were all together. Simon Peter said to the others, "I am going fishing."*

"We will come with you," they told him. So they went out in a boat, but all that night they did not catch a thing.

They turned back and were nearing the shore. *As the sun was rising, Jesus stood at the water's edge, but the disciples did not know that it was Jesus. Then he asked them, "Young men, haven't you caught anything?"*

"Not a thing," they answered.

They had not caught anything the entire night. *He said to them, "Throw your net out on the right side of the boat, and you will catch some." So they threw the net out and could not pull it back in, because they had caught so many fish. The disciple whom Jesus loved said to Peter, "It is the Lord!"*

John had seen him first. Every day they had been expecting that he would come, hoping they could encounter him once again. They would never have imagined that he would be awaiting them on the shore, seated on a rock that jutted out, with a fire burning beside him.

When Peter heard that it was the Lord, he wrapped his outer garment around him (for he had taken his clothes off) and jumped into the water. He was not wearing his tunic while fishing. He tightened his shirt well around his waist so it would not get in the way of swimming. The water was icy cold. The apostle used huge strokes. Every time his head emerged above the surface, his gaze was directed straight to the rock where Jesus was seated. His heart was in turmoil. As he swam, he kept picking up speed. Memories swam about in his mind—the memory of when they first met, right there, on that shore; the memory of that time he was about to sink and Jesus, who was walking on the water, had rescued him.

The other disciples came to shore in the boat, pulling the net full of fish. They were not very far from land, about a hundred yards away. When they stepped ashore, they saw a charcoal fire there with fish on it and some bread.

There was a wonderful aroma. Everyone was really hungry. *Then Jesus said to them, "Bring some of the fish you have just caught."*

Simon Peter went aboard and dragged the net ashore full of big fish, a hundred and fifty-three in all; even though there were so many, still the net did not tear. Jesus said to them, "Come and eat." None of the disciples dared ask him, "Who are you?" because they knew it was the Lord. So Jesus went over, took the bread, and gave it to them; he did the same with the fish. This, then, was the third time Jesus appeared to the disciples after he was raised from death.

They ate, enjoying each other's company. They ate, watching Jesus who was smiling, eating next to them, since he had prepared the fire and had cooked for them. Andrew thought to himself, "How beautiful it would be to live like this always, just like we are right now." . . .

Jesus asked them about the people they had encountered, about their families, their friends. But long moments of silence also went by.

Then, when they had finished that breakfast on the lakeshore, *Jesus said to Simon Peter, "Simon son of John, do you love me more than these others do?"*

"Yes, Lord," he answered, "you know that I love you."

Jesus said to him, "Take care of my lambs." A second time Jesus said to him, "Simon son of John, do you love me?"

"Yes, Lord," he answered, "you know that I love you."

Jesus said to him, "Take care of my sheep." A third time Jesus said, "Simon son of John, do you love me?"

He had asked him the same thing three times. Everyone else was watching, touched by that dialogue. Three times, just like the three times that he, "the rock," had denied him in the high priest's courtyard. *Peter became sad because Jesus asked him the third time, "Do you love me?" and so he said to him, "Lord, you know everything; you know that I love you!"*

Jesus said to him, "Take care of my sheep. I am telling you the truth: when you were young, you used to get ready and go anywhere you wanted to; but when you are old, you will stretch out your hands and someone else will tie you up and take you where you don't want to go." Thus he predicted the imprisonment and death Peter would suffer for remaining faithful to his Teacher.

Then Jesus said to him, "Follow me!"

He had established that it would be Peter who would help lead the flock, standing behind him. An authority founded on love. Simon Peter, the fisherman from Bethsaida, was becoming the leader of the others, not because he was the most educated, the most consistent, the most religious, or the best organizer. He was becoming their leader because, even despite his sin and his betrayal, he had continued loving Jesus and had allowed Jesus to look at him and to be forgiven by him.

"Jesus asks us just as he asked Peter, 'Who am I to you?' and 'Do you love me?' Let us allow these words to penetrate our hearts and ignite the desire to not remain content with the minimum, but to aim for the heights, so that we too can become living witnesses of Jesus."[112]

Before going away, leaving them all together on the shore with the immense catch of fish they had just caught because they had trusted in his word, Jesus invited them to return to Jerusalem for the last time, and added, *"I have been given all authority in heaven and on earth. Go, then, to all peoples everywhere and make them my disciples: baptize them in the name of the Father, the Son, and the Holy Spirit, and teach them to obey everything I have commanded you. And I will be with you always, to the end of the age."*

They had begun with a small catch of fish of the men and women in Capernaum and in the villages of Galilee, following him and living together with him. Now, the horizon he was indicating to them was the entire world. They looked at each other, speechless, and they embraced each other.

"All the nations. . . . How we will do it, Peter?" his brother, Andrew, asked.

Peter responded, "I don't know how we'll do it, my brother. We'll do it because he has promised to be with us each and every day, until the end. . . ."

⁓

So they returned to Jerusalem just as he had asked them. Forty days had gone by since his resurrection. They found themselves all together in Dan's house, around the same table where they had eaten with their Teacher. There were *Peter, John, James and Andrew, Philip and Thomas, Bartholomew and Matthew, James son of Alphaeus, Simon the Patriot, and Judas son of James. They gathered*

---

112. Homily for the Mass on the Solemnity of Saints Peter and Paul, June 29, 2019.

frequently to pray as a group, together with the women and with Mary the mother of Jesus and with his brothers.

All of a sudden, the Nazarene entered and sat down with them. He said to those dining, *"When the Holy Spirit comes upon you, you will be filled with power, and you will be witnesses for me in Jerusalem, in all of Judea and Samaria, and to the ends of the earth."*

Once dinner was over, they left the upper room and headed for the street they had taken so many other times together, leading toward Bethany. When they were on the Mount of Olives, Jesus stopped. He looked into their eyes and hugged each one of them. Then he smiled and raised his eyes toward heaven. *He was taken up to heaven as they watched him, and a cloud hid him from their sight.*

He had accompanied them. He had convinced them of his resurrection. He had allowed them to touch with their hands the fate of every man and woman whom the Lord loves. He had taught them that true power is service, that authentic authority is love, that the greatest power is the weakness of defenseless sacrifice. He had taught them to love God and to serve him in the poor, in the weak, in the humble. He had promised he would never leave them alone, that he would always be there with them at every moment. It was enough that they count on him and not on their own strength, trust in him and not in their own capabilities. For without him, they would do nothing. With him, they would do everything, for everything, in reality, would be done by him.

They embraced one another, continuing to look up toward heaven that day that was incredibly clear and flooded by light. With that small group of friends, in a remote region of the enormous Roman Empire, a new journey began. A small seed that would forever change the history of humanity would blossom from one witness to another, until it would eventually reach us too.

Permissions

Grateful acknowledgment to the following Bible publishers for permission to use their translations in *The Life of Jesus*: Crossway, American Bible Society, and National Council of the Churches of Christ in the United States of America. See below for citations and permissions.

The following Bible citations that appear in Chapters 1–11 are from the ESV® Bible (The Holy Bible, English Standard Version®), copyright © 2001 by Crossway, a publishing ministry of Good News Publishers. Used by Permission. All rights reserved.

1. That Breeze in the House of Nazareth
   Luke 1:26–27, 28–33, 35, 38, 42, 46–48; Matthew 1:19, 20–21
2. During the Night in Bethlehem
   Luke 2:1–5; Matthew 22:21; Luke 2:6, 7, 8–9a, 9b–15, 16–17; John 1:11; Luke 2:18–20, 21, 33–35
3. The Magi, the Flight, and Innocent Blood
   Matthew 2:1–8, 9–10, 11, 12, 13–14, 16–17a
4. Return to Nazareth—Jesus's Hidden Life
   Matthew 2:19–21, Luke 2:40, 41–43, 44, 45, 46–47, 48a, 48b–50, 51–52
5. The Baptism, the Temptations, and the Wine That Ran Out
   Matthew 3:2; Luke 3:1–3, 16–17; John 1:23, 29b–31; Matthew 3:14–15, 17b; 4:3b, 4, 6–7, 9, 10; John 1:35–36, 37, 38–39, 40–42a, 42b, 43b–46a, 46b–51; 2:3, 4, 5–11b; Romans 5:20; John 1:11
6. Return to Jerusalem and a Meeting at the Well
   John 2:15–16, 17, 18–20; 3:2b, 3, 4–8, 9–15; 4:1, 5–6, 7, 9–10, 11–15, 16, 17–24, 25–26, 28–29, 30, 39–42, 34
7. Fishers of Men and Healings in Galilee
   John 4:48, 49, 50; Matthew 4:17b; Luke 4:16b–21, 22, 24b–27, 29–30, 31; 5:3–6, 7, 8–11; 4:33b–34, 35, 36–37, 38b, 39, 43; 5:12b Mark 1:40, 41–42, 44, 45; Luke 5:17–18, 19, 20, 21b, 22b–24, 25–26; Mark 2:14; Luke 5:29–32; 6:13–16
8. "Blessed . . . Blessed. . . ." The Kingdom of God That Raises Up the Lowly
   Matthew 5:3–11, 13a, 14a, 17–19a, 21–22a, 23–24, 27–28, 31–32, 38–48; 6:2–4, 5–6, 7b, 8, 9–13, 14–15, 16–18, 19–21, 25–27; 7:1–3, 7, 11b, 12, 21, 24–27, 28

9. The Centurion, the Widow, and the Sinner

    Luke 7:1, 4–5; Matthew 8:6, 7–9, 10–12, 13; Luke 7:12, 13, 14–15,
    16–17, 36b–38, 39, 40, 41–43, 44–48, 49–50; 8:2b–3; Mark 3:22b,
    23–27, 28–29; Luke 8:19b–21

10. The Parables of the Kingdom, and the Journey by Night

    Matthew 13:2, 3–9, 10–13, 16–17b, 18–23, 24–30, 31b–32, 33, 37–43,
    44–50; Mark 4:35b–36, 37, 38, 38b–39, 39b, 40–41; 5:1, 2b–5, 6–7,
    8b–9, 11–13, 14, 15–17, 18, 19–20

11. Extraordinary Deeds in Galilee, and the First Mission

    Mark 5:22b–23, 24b, 25–27, 28, 29–30, 31, 32, 33, 34, 35, 36b–37, 38,
    39b, 40b, 41–43; Matthew 9:27, 28–30a, 30c, 31, 33c, 34, 35, 36, 37b–38;
    10:1, 6b, 7–10, 16–20, 27–33, 34–37, 38–39, 40–42

∽

**The following Bible citations that appear in Chapters 12–16 are from the
Contemporary English Version Copyright © 1991, 1992, 1995 by American
Bible Society. Used by Permission.**

12. From the Multiplication of the Bread to Life Eternal

    Luke 9:10a, 10b–11a, 11b, 12, 13–14a, 14b–15, 16, 17; Matthew 14:24,
    26–27, 28–29a, 29b, 30–31, 32–33, 35c–36; John 6:26b–27, 33–35, 40,
    42, 43–44, 48–51, 53b–58, 63b–64a, 67b–69; 5:6c; 7–9, 10b, 11–13, 14b,
    16–18; Mark 7:2, 5b, 6–8, 9–13, 14–15, 17–23

13. Crumbs for the Dogs, and the Revelation about the Cross

    Matthew 15:22, 23a, 23b, 24, 25–26, 27, 28a; Mark 7:32, 33–34, 35, 36a,
    36b–37; Matthew 16:1, 2–4, 8–19; Mark 8:22b, 23–24, 25, 26;
    Matthew 16:13b, 14, 15, 16, 17, 20, 21, 22, 23, 24–25; Luke 9:28b,
    29–31, 32, 33, 33c–35, 36, 37, 38–40, 41, 42a, 42b–43a, 43b–44, 45–46,
    47–48; Matthew 18:6–7

14. Forgiveness and Mercy on the Last Day of the Feast of Tabernacles

    Matthew 18:19–20, 12–14, 21, 22, 23–35; John 7:3–5, 6–9, 10; Luke
    9:53–54, 55, 57b, 58b 59–60, 61–62; John 7:11b–13, 14, 15b, 16b–19,
    21–24, 25b–27, 37b–38, 40–44, 45b–49, 51, 52–53; John 8:2c, 4–6, 6b,
    7b–8, 9, 10b, 11, 12, 13–20, 28–29, 31–32, 34–37, 42–44a, 49–51,
    54–56, 58, 59; 9:2–5, 6–7a, 7b, 13–15a, 15b, 16–17a, 18b–19, 20–21,
    24a, 24b, 25, 26, 26–27, 28–29, 30–34, 35b–38, 39–41

15. The Disciples and the Joy of the Mission

    John 10:1–5, 7–9, 11–16, 21; Luke 10:1, 2–12, 16, 17–20, 21–22; 1:52;
    10:23–24

16. "Who Is My Neighbor?"

Luke 10:25b, 26, 27, 28, 29, 30, 31–35, 36–37, 40a, 40b, 41–42; 11:5–13, 14–15, 16–23, 27, 28, 37a, 38, 39–44, 45–46, 47–52, 53–54; 12:1b–2, 4–7, 8–9, 11b–12, 13, 14–15, 16–21, 22–31, 32–40, 47–48, 49–53; 13:11, 12–13, 14, 15–16, 17, 20–21, 22–30, 32–33, 34–35a; John 10:22, 23, 24, 25–30, 31–38, 40

∼

The following Bible citations that appear in Scripture quotations that appear in Chapters 17–19 are from the *Good News Translation in Today's English Version-Second Edition* Copyright © 1992 by American Bible Society. Used by Permission.

17. "I Will Get Up and Return to My Father"

Mark 2:24, 25–26, 27–28; Luke 14:1–2, 3–4a, 4b–6, 8–11, 12–14, 15a, 15b, 16–24, 25–27, 28–33, 34–35; 15:1, 2b, 11–12, 13, 14–20a, 20b, 21–24, 25–32; 16:10, 13, 15–17, 19–31

18. "Unless You Turn and Become Like Children, You Will Never Enter."

Luke 17:5b–6, 7–10; Matthew 19:13b–15; 18:3b–4; Luke 17:12c–13, 14a, 14b, 15–19, 20–21, 22–33; 18:2–8, 10–14; Matthew 19:3b–9, 10–12, 16b–22, 23–28, 30; Matthew 20:1–16

19. Making Yourself Little to Be Truly Great

Matthew 20:17b–19, 20a, 20b–21, 22–23, 24–28; John 11:3b–6, 7–10, 11–15, 16, 17–20, 21–27, 28–31, 32–35, 36–38, 39–41a, 41b–44, 45, 47–48, 49–53, 54; Mark 10:47–48, 49–52; Luke 19:4, 5, 6–7, 8, 9, 11b–27; John 11:55–57; 12:1–8, 9–11

∼

Scripture quotations that appear in Chapter 20–24 are from the *New Revised Standard Version Bible: Catholic Edition*, copyright © 1989, 1993 National Council of the Churches of Christ in the United States of America. Used by Permission. All rights reserved worldwide.

20. "Hosanna to the Son of David!"

Mark 11:2–4a, 4b–5, 6, 7, 8–10; Luke 19:39b, 40, 41–44; John 12:20, 21–22, 23–28a, 28b, 29–33, 34–36a, 36b; Mark 11:11b, 12, 13, 14, 15, 19, 20–21, 22–25, 27–28, 29–30, 31–32, 33; 12:1–11; Matthew 21:28–32; Mark 12:12c, 13–14, 15b–16a, 16b, 17a, 18b–23, 24–27, 28b–31, 32–33, 34, 38–40, 41a, 41b, 42, 43–44; 13:1–2, 3–13, 26–27, 35–37

21. Thirty Pieces of Silver and the Last Supper

    Matthew 25:1–4, 5–13, 31–46; 26:2, 3–5, 15–16; Luke 22:7, 8–12, 14–16;
    John 13:4–5, 6–16; Luke 22:19; John 13:21b–26, 27; Matthew 26: 24–25;
    John 13:27b–30; Matthew 26:27–29; John 6:53b–54; Luke 22:24, 25–30;
    John 13:34–35, 36–38; John 14:1–7, 8–16; 15:1–8, 12–17; John 17:1–9,
    20–23; 18:1, 2

22. Gethsemane

    Mark 14:32b–34, 36; Luke 22:43–44; Mark 14:37–39; Luke 22:45–46;
    Mark 14:41; John 17:9, 20–21; Matthew 26:45b–46; Mark 14:44;
    John 18:4–8; Matthew 26:50, 52–54, 55–56a, 56b; John 18:13–14, 19–23,
    15c, 16–18, 25b–27; Mark 14:56, 58–59; John 2:19; Mark 14:60b–61,
    61b, 62; Luke 22:70; Mark 14:63–64a, 64b–65; Matthew 27:3–4a, 4b–5a,
    6–8

23. Pontius Pilate and the "King of the Jews"

    John 18:28–30; Luke 23:2, 4b–5, 7b, 8, 9, 10–11; John 18:31a, 31b,
    33–38a, 38b, 39, 40; 19:1, 2–3, 4–5, 6b–7, 9–11, 12b–14a, 14b–15;
    Matthew 27:24

24. Sacrifice on Golgotha

    Mark 15:21; Luke 23:27–28; John 19:19b–20, 21b; Mark 15:22;
    Luke 23:34; John 19:23, 24–25; Mark 15:29–30, 31–32; Luke 23:39b,
    40b–41, 42, 43; John 19:25–27a, 28–29a, 29b; Mark 15:34–35, 37, 38,
    39; John 19:31, 32, 33–34, 36–37; Mark 15:42–43; John 19:38c, 39–40,
    41; Luke 23:55; Matthew 27:63–66

∽

25. The Empty Tomb and the Living Jesus

    Mark 16:1–3; John 20:11–13, 15–17; Matthew 28:9–10; Luke 24:11;
    John 20:4–8, 9; Luke 24:12; Matthew 28:12–15a; Luke 24:13–27, 28–29a,
    29b, 31–32, 33, 36–40, 41b–43, 44–48; John 20:21–23, 24, 25, 26–29

26. From Galilee to the World

    John 21:2–3, 4–5, 6–7a, 7b, 8–9, 10–14, 15–17a, 17b–18, 19b;
    Matthew 28:18–20; Acts 1:13b–14, 8, 9

Acknowledgments

I thank Pope Francis for his precious introduction to the book.

I am grateful to Father Primo Soldi, whose suggestion gave origin to this text, and I thank him also for how he accompanied its composition, chapter after chapter.

A huge thanks goes also to fellow countryman Father Angelo Busetto, for sharing suggestions and corrections during the year I worked on this book.

Thanks also to Father Matteo Visioli, Father Filippo Ciampanelli, Father Luigi Epicoco, and Maria Susi D'Alberti, who read portions of the text, encouraging me to continue. I am grateful to Arnoldo Mosca Mondadori, for his support and advice, and to Roberto Cetera, for the final revision and corrections.

Thanks to Father Francesco Patton as well, for the conversation we had regarding the places in Jerusalem where the passion of Jesus took place.

Finally, I want to say thank you to my family, who always left me time and space on weekends and during vacations to pursue this work about which I was very passionate.

About the Author

ANDREA TORNIELLI is a veteran Vatican reporter and the editorial director of the Vatican Dicastery for Communication. He is the author of *Francis: Pope of a New World*, which was translated into sixteen languages, and he collaborated with Pope Francis on the *New York Times* bestseller *The Name of God Is Mercy*.